Praise page for *Leading the Sustainable Organization*

McAteer's most recent book is a must-have resource for business leaders, entrepreneurs, sustainability professionals, policymakers, and educators who are committed to integrating sustainability into their organizational strategy. *Leading the Sustainable Organization* provides a practical framework for navigating the evolving landscape of environmental challenges, regulatory changes, and competitive pressures. With real-world examples and reflection checklists, it serves as an invaluable guide for professionals across industries who want to stay ahead in today's rapidly changing business environment and lead with purpose toward a sustainable future.

Alex Casiano, Professor, Dean of Academic Affairs, Metropolitan Campus,
Inter-American University of Puerto Rico

Navigating the intersection of business success and sustainability has never been more critical. *Leading the Sustainable Organization* equips emerging and established leaders with the knowledge and tools to drive meaningful change. From addressing climate challenges to fostering ethical leadership, McAteer's book is an invaluable guide for those committed to creating long-term value while tackling pressing global issues. This work is essential for leaders looking to future-proof their organizations in today's rapidly evolving business landscape, equipping them with the tools to drive meaningful change and create long-term value for both shareholders and stakeholders.

Manuel Vexler, Faculty, Sustainability and Artificial Intelligence Programs,
Cornell University
Executive Director AKFI Sustainability Association

I highly recommend this timely, practical and solution-oriented book for anyone seeking to create a sustainable enterprise—one that is simultaneously good for people, profits, and the environment. McAteer does a brilliant job of explaining what it takes to build a culture for sustainability—one that's innovative, collaborative, ethical, and values-based while still being competitive. The book is replete with a plethora of helpful tools, including chapter summaries, self-assessments, case examples, and checklists. The Appendices offering "Sixty-six terms worth knowing," "Eleven databases worth using," and "Eight reflection exercises to refine your thinking" are fantastic resources to kick-start your sustainability journey.

Jeana Wirtenberg, Associate Professor, Rutgers Business School
Executive Director, Rutgers Institute for Corporate Social Innovation

Peter McAteer's *Leading the Sustainable Organization* is an ambitious attempt to provide a roadmap for business leaders navigating the sustainability landscape. Positioned as both a strategic guide and a call to action, the book covers the evolving boundary conditions for businesses, the integration of sustainability into competitive differentiation, and the organizational transformation required to embed sustainable innovation. Given my focus on industrial transformation, economic and product complexity, and sustainable manufacturing, I approached this book with a critical eye on how it aligns with real-world industrial competitiveness, particularly in sectors like aerospace and precision machining. Peter's framework and emphasis on tacit knowledge I found particularly useful for the companies that I work with. I would recommend this book to business owners looking to chart their way through these challenging times.

Naquib Mohd Nor, CEO of Strand Aerospace Malaysia and CEO of the
Advanced Manufacturing and Robotics Accelerator Centre of Excellence,
Malaysia

A must-read for businesses and governments that are passionate about a livable planet and are rethinking the role of (ethical) leadership, organizational learning, and change management. Peter provides a clear transition path for organizations committed to purpose and sustainability but struggling to determine where to start or how to maintain a competitive edge. A truly great book that I will use in my work and discussions with governments.

Robin van Kippersluis, Senior Policy Specialist, Institutions Global Practice,
World Bank

If you want to read one book about business this year, make it this one. Peter has a talent for offering clear, insightful explanations of complex issues supported by real-world experience. Everyone wants to see their organization thrive, and with the advice offered in his latest book, ethical leaders will have new actionable strategies to employ.

Carol Liffman, Director, Risk Advisory Services, DNV Energy Systems

The book is a great way for leaders to learn how to navigate market and regulatory uncertainty while maintaining focus on both results and impact. McAteer offers practical frameworks for business growth, leadership development, and sustainable innovation while maintaining an optimistic vision of the role of business in society. I've read all of his books and this may be the best yet. All leaders in both the public and private sectors will benefit from reading his latest work.

William Eimicke, Professor, Columbia University School of International and
Public Affairs, Founding Director, Columbia University Picker Center for
Executive Education

The book examines the impact of changing boundary conditions on both well-established businesses and emerging enterprises. He offers structured models for understanding new knowledge and government regulations and encourages organizations to embrace innovation in sustainability, learn from intelligent failures, and use social rituals to reinforce a sustainability-focused culture. The book is a compelling guide for both business and government leaders.

Kamal Batra, Member, The Advertising Standards Council of India

Leading the Sustainable Organization

Leading the Sustainable Organization

THE QUEST FOR ETHICAL BRANDS AND A CULTURE OF SUSTAINABLE INNOVATION

PETER McATEER

ANTHEM PRESS

Anthem Press
An imprint of Wimbledon Publishing Company
www.anthempress.com

This edition first published in UK and USA 2025
by ANTHEM PRESS
75–76 Blackfriars Road, London SE1 8HA, UK
or PO Box 9779, London SW19 7ZG, UK
and
244 Madison Ave #116, New York, NY 10016, USA

© 2025 Peter McAteer

British Library Cataloguing-in-Publication Data
A catalogue record for this book is available from the British Library.

Library of Congress Cataloging-in-Publication Data: 2025933728
A catalog record for this book has been requested.

ISBN-13: 978-1-83999-558-3 (Hbk)
ISBN-10: 1-83999-558-0 (Hbk)

This title is also available as an e-book.

Dedicated to future leaders with the ambition to make a difference. May the book add to your skill set and be part of your journey to a sustainable future.

The future will be determined by leaders with great ideas,
the passion to inspire others,
and the commitment to make things happen.
May our shared legacy be a more sustainable planet.

CONTENTS

Contents

FIGURES

Figures

Figures

FOREWORD

The air we breathe. The water we drink. The walks in nature we enjoy. The sun that warms us. The wildfires, hurricanes, floods, heat waves, and other natural disasters that alarm us. Each of these, and many others, comprise the general context of our world, too often taken for granted.

It further amazes and mystifies me when I realize that nearly everything we enjoy in our daily lives comes from the earth: the houses we live in, the clothes we wear, the food we eat, the cars we drive, the technology we use.

Sustainability is about both the general context and specific daily actions of our lives. As Peter points out in this masterful work, paying attention to the planet that grants and sustains life is not new. He summarizes the many agreements and countries involved in paying attention to sustainability over the years with hundreds of countries and many treaties. While attention to sustainability has occurred, the challenges to progress are increasing, not decreasing.

He suggests that organizations, and the executives who lead them, play a critical role in managing the boundary conditions in responding to sustainability challenges. The work on boundary conditions reflects decisions that impact sustainability. As business leaders incorporate sustainability assumptions into strategic choices and allocations, purpose (vision and mission), culture, values, and leadership, the many stakeholders to the organization receive value.

Since sustainability affects all stakeholders, the sustainable organization progresses when each of the many stakeholders receives value from their engaging with the organization. So, sustainability matters for organizations and their stakeholders. Check! Stipulate it!

In this book, Peter goes beyond calls for more organizational sustainability and identifies the value of sustainability for all stakeholders to build specific transition and change plans for creating a sustainable organization. His work implies that the noble aspirations in treaties, declarations, and policies can and should be implemented through daily organizational actions. Making sustainability happen will come from choices around

- creating strategic differentiation to compete on sustainability values and business opportunities;
- crafting purpose (vision, mission, values) statements that inspire employees to give their best;
- building and sharing a knowledge model about why, what, and how to do sustainability;
- ensuring that sustainability efforts are woven into values and ethics;
- deploying a transition plan with clear action steps, milestones, metrics, and accountabilities that moves from compliance to alignment;
- making sustainability part of the culture, DNA, or identity of an organization;
- weaving personal commitment to sustainability into team performance and action;
- telling the story, or communicating about the sustainability work, in private and public (e.g., SEC documents) reporting;
- sticking with the sustainability efforts in the face of inevitable derailment factors; and
- future-proofing the organization to stay on the sustainability journey with resources (people, time, attention, budget).

For each of these elements of transition, Peter lays out specific choices, provides a diagnostic to assess your organization, and offers examples of those who have done it.

This work provides a thorough blueprint to move the sustainability movement from science to solutions, from aspiration to action, and from theory to impact.

I am grateful for the insights so that our grandchildren will have air to breathe, water to drink, nature to enjoy, sun that shines, and fewer natural disasters that harm. With care, the Earth can continue to provide for future generations.

Thank you, Peter, and thank you, Earth!

Dave Ulrich
Rensis Likert Professor, Ross School of Business (retired)
Partner, the RBL Group
Alpine, Utah, USA
February 2025

INTRODUCTION

Never before have we been presented with the prospect of redesigning business at scale to create a sustainable future for our planet and the people who inhabit it. Over the past several decades, more and more business leaders have recognized the importance of addressing climate change and the broader issues of sustainability. Jamie Dimon, CEO of J.P. Morgan, has said, "Companies 'have a moral obligation' to do more for society."[1] Jeff Bezos, founder of Amazon, made a similarly supportive statement at COP26 in Glasgow, Scotland: "We must conserve what we still have, we must restore what we've lost, and we must grow what we need to live without degrading the planet for future generations to come."[2] Tim Cook, Apple CEO, adds, "Businesses have a profound opportunity to help build a more sustainable future, one born of our common concern for the planet we share."[3]

There are more voices on this topic, but most people now believe that climate change and sustainability are issues to be addressed. In the aftermath of the Paris Agreement[4] in 2015 and the publication of the United Nations document, "*Transforming our World; the 2030 Agenda for Sustainable Development.*"[5] my consulting and training became focused on helping companies respond to these new challenges. This led to my first book on this topic, *Sustainability Is the New Advantage: Leadership, Change, and the Future of Business* (2019, 2021).[6] My goal then was to help companies think about the nature of sustainability and how a sustainable business might behave differently than a legacy business. That effort proved successful and led to feedback and insights based on the evolution of the market during the next few years. I wrote a second book, *Pathways to Action: How Keystone Organizations Can Lead the Fight for Climate Change* (2022),[7] to address the challenge faced by many early adopter and best-practice companies, which is: *"How do we accelerate action when the marketplace is not yet aligned with our goals?"*

As we pass the midpoint of the Sustainable Development Goal (SDG) targets (2015–2030), the world has certainly changed. *The Guardian* in the United Kingdom surveyed climate experts who had participated in the Intergovernmental Panel on Climate Change assessments as lead author or reviewers since 2018. The consensus of the respondents is that we will not meet our goal of keeping the increase in average global temperatures below 1.5°C.[8] More than three-quarters of those surveyed expect an average temperature rise of at least 2.5°C by the end of this century. According to the survey, "Younger scientists were more pessimistic, with 52% of respondents under 50 expecting a rise of at least 3C, compared with 38% of those over 50. Female scientists were also more downbeat than male scientists, with 49% thinking global temperature would rise at least 3C, compared with 38%. There was little difference between scientists from different continents."[9]

So why all the pessimism? Is sustainability the new "dismal science," to borrow a phrase used by Thomas Carlyle in the nineteenth century? He had made the observation that as business output increases, populations tend to increase even more, so we don't make any real progress. Are we introducing more regulations only to see more resistance and slower progress on the goals that really matter? There are genuine concerns linked to the basic science where we see increases in temperature, resulting in melting ice caps and a continuation of the behavior that created the problems in the first place. There is also a feeling among some that none of us can individually control such a big challenge.

Any sense of inevitability or despair is misplaced. John Kotter, the noted author and change management specialist, describes the first stage of change management as the creation of a sense of urgency. "By far the biggest mistake people make when trying to change organizations is to plunge ahead without establishing a high enough sense of urgency in fellow managers and employees. This error is fatal because transformations always fail to achieve their objectives when complacency levels are high."[10] With Kotter's words in mind, I believe it's fair to say that we are making progress, but just not enough yet to avoid the long-term consequences of a warming climate. Part of this is the result of too many legacy industries moving slowly or resisting the transformation steps needed in order to preserve their legacy revenue streams and profits. Although we are now in a catch-up mode, I don't see the need for pessimism. For urgency, yes! Pessimism, no.

There are reasons for optimism. Major markets are increasing the requirements for ESG reporting and compliance, venture investments in sustainable solutions are growing, and the markets now support hundreds of new sustainability start-ups. Sustainability is now a generally accepted business challenge. Almost all the largest companies have sustainability commitments, and strong public policy is transforming many industries toward a more sustainable future. We are slowly but surely reaching tipping points in several industries, where cost reductions, overall sales, and the service and support infrastructures are catching up with comparable legacy options.

What needs to be done? We must accelerate our business transformations to focus on opportunity and competitive advantage within the new boundary conditions of sustainability. A new generation of business leaders must manage the transition from making legacy companies more carbon and waste efficient to operating new sustainable businesses. If we do, we will be presented with the largest opportunity for business redesign in history. The vast majority of the new infrastructure the world will require by 2050 still needs to be built. That represents a huge opportunity. Hundreds of billions of dollars in new investment will help companies transition away from carbon-intensive fuels and wasteful business practices. There are also new public policies and ESG frameworks that are changing the conditions within which businesses operate (I call these "boundary conditions" throughout the book). Beyond the need for reduced emissions, the global population has increased from 2.5 billion to 8 billion since 1950 and will increase to more than 9.5 billion people by 2050.[11] Creating a more sustainable future with less hunger, better equity, more respect for our shared environment, and more livable communities will require innovations across all industries.

I wrote *Leading the Sustainable Organization* to address many of the key questions asked by my clients and students. My goal is to help thousands of companies struggling with their legacy business transitions to plan better, act with more confidence, and lead us into the future. Those of you reading this book who are already in business leadership positions, you are the best hope for reaching the goals set for 2030. You need to act now. For those who are younger or still in school, you are the future of the sustainability movement and need to build the skills that allow your voices to be heard and also set you up as your generation's change agents.

I hope every reader chooses to be a climate change champion and co-creator of a more sustainable future.

Regards from Thailand,
Peter McAteer

Chapter 1

UNDERSTANDING THE NEW BOUNDARY CONDITIONS

It is not just about inventing new solutions, but about transforming our relationship with the planet.
—JOHAN ROCKSTRÖM, DIRECTOR OF THE POTSDAM INSTITUTE FOR CLIMATE IMPACT RESEARCH[1]

I t's hard to avoid the topic of sustainability these days. Terms like ESG, diversity, equity and inclusion, and global warming are all over the news. In many ways, sustainability and climate change have become the biggest topics in recent memory. But perhaps the phrase "recent memory" is part of the problem. The history of sustainability can easily be traced back to the beginning of the industrial revolution. Any presentation of the origins of climate change will start with a slide showing the stability of atmospheric greenhouse gases that characterized the glacial epoch, which lasted for 12,000 years. That is until the start of the modern industrial revolution in the nineteenth century.

Challenges: What are the new boundary conditions of the sustainable business marketplace? How do they shape corporate behavior towards shared goals for a more livable planet?

An American woman, Eunice Newton Foote, is credited with documenting the properties of carbon dioxide to absorb heat from sunlight in 1856.[2] John Tyndall, an Irish scientist, is credited with independently conducting research on the heat absorption properties of water vapor and carbon dioxide in 1859. He commented in his journal, "Thus the atmosphere admits of the entrance of the solar heat; but checks its exit, and the result is a tendency to accumulate heat at the surface of the planet."[3] Svante Arrhenius, a Swedish scientist and winner of the Nobel Prize in Chemistry in 1903, is often credited with research that characterized the relationship between excess atmospheric gases and a warming planet in 1896. Many others have contributed along the way, but most of the real insights into climate science begin post-World War II. By the 1950s technical innovations and improved measurement techniques for greenhouse gases contributed to better data from the oceans, ice cores, and sediments. The results were data models that offered a more compelling picture of a changing planet and our first predictive models for things like planetary boundaries and tipping points.

I find this contextual information to be both fascinating and relevant to an understanding of our changing world. Examining the sustainability knowledge timeline in parallel with discoveries in human development and the evolution of business tells us how our modern era and the current sustainability challenges developed. But this book is about "leading the sustainable organization," so the important question becomes, "does any of this really matter to today's business executive?" Although it offers some sense of history and context, the answer is probably not!

Every business leader of a large corporation today is aware there are Sustainable Development Goals (SDGs). By itself, this is a huge change from a few decades ago when few executives had internalized the millennium development goals (MDGs) introduced in the year 2000. When I discuss sustainability with many leaders, we can quickly narrow the priority business drivers down to the twin issues of climate change and biodiversity. These issues affect everyone and account for most of the changing business risk. Extreme weather events in particular, cause business interruptions, disrupt supply chains and cause insurance losses. Although the basic climate science may not be fully understood by everyone, most leaders are willing to listen to a trusted authority on potential challenges. Financial losses get everyone's attention!

Despite a generalized understanding of sustainability and climate change, most business leaders I meet don't appreciate that 30 percent of excess greenhouse gases are absorbed by the biosphere. Almost 50 percent of the excess carbon gases we emit are absorbed by terrestrial and marine ecosystems that prevent climate warming from getting worse than it already is. According to the European Union, "Terrestrial ecosystems store about 2,100 Gt of carbon in living organisms, litter and soil organic matter: almost three times as much as is currently present in the atmosphere."[4]

Although the framework conventions on climate change and biodiversity were both created in 1992, climate change has received most of the attention over the past 30 years. The challenge of biodiversity remains poorly understood, mostly because the problem is so big, but additionally because most people don't feel personally responsible. This is likely to change as biodiversity issues become a more prominent part of regulatory changes affecting key industries. Companies will need to become accustomed to discussing biodiversity's impact in the same way we now discuss climate impact. These are large global challenges, they are hard to fix, and they have more impact than most people realize.

These two drivers are threats and disruptive by themselves, but they also create a ripple effect among many of the other SDGs. More extreme weather events, for example, not only create greater insurance losses, but they also damage infrastructure and create political instability. If crops fail because of changing weather patterns, you can expect more hunger, more poverty and more migration of poor people. If you fail to address the loss of biodiversity, then you affect the productivity of the land and the seas that are a source of food for billions of people.

The Environment and Biodiversity: Fast Losses and Slow Recovery

While any business would value market stability and a known set of boundaries, the simple fact is that natural losses often happen fast while recovery happens slowly. The 2022–2023 Alaskan King Crab fishing season was canceled for the first time in history due to the precipitous decline in the species. Some estimates suggest the population declined by 80–90 percent due to changes in water temperature in 2018–2019.[5] The current theory is that the rapid changes in water temperature caused the crabs to migrate to deeper, colder water where there was little food, and as a consequence they starved to death. Regardless of the exact cause, an estimated 10 billion crabs disappeared.[6] Current estimates suggest it may take six to ten years to rebuild the fishery. This example offers some insight into the nature of our sustainability challenges.

The decline in the crab population is a fact and has a corollary to carbon emissions. When we put a gigaton of carbon into the atmosphere, that is not debatable. However, when we say the crab fishery will take six to ten years to rebound, this is an estimate. It is a guess based on a scenario humans have never witnessed. The same is true with emissions credits and carbon sequestration. The emissions are a measurable fact. But sequestering carbon in a growing tree is subject to a dozen conditions that may or may not be true over time. This example plays out in real life over and over again, despite good intentions.

CALIFORNIA WILDFIRES: The recent California wildfires in 2020 had a devastating effect on the coastal redwoods and giant sequoias. According to the California Save the Redwoods League, "Of the acres burned by mid-October, coast redwoods comprised more than 81,000 acres, including more than 11,000 acres of old growth (roughly 9 percent of all old growth left). In the giant sequoia range, roughly 16,000 acres (or 34 percent of the range) had burned, most of which is old growth."[7] These ancient groves include trees several hundred to over one thousand years of age. Recovery of the trees and the surrounding ecosystem takes a very, very long time. Can the recovery happen on such time scales when faced with more frequent and intense fires?

AMAZON RAIN FOREST: The Amazon is considered the lungs of planet earth because of the amount of oxygen generated by the forest. The Amazon Conservation Organization used satellite data to create an estimate of forest cover and carbon sequestration in 2022. They estimated that the forest contains almost 57 billion metric tons of carbon above ground. Today, the Amazon area is in the midst of one of the worst droughts the region has ever experienced. Of course, with drought comes the risk of wildfires. What if the Amazon starts to burn? Is there a point where it releases so much additional carbon or loses so much contiguous forest canopy that it can never fully recover?

FLORIDA CITRUS CROPS: Florida orange production has been devastated in recent years by a series of hurricanes including Irma (2017), Ian (2022), Helene (2024) and now Milton (2024). As recently as 2014, Florida farmers produced over 70% of US oranges each year between 2000 and 2015 according to the American Farm Bureau Federation.[8] Today that production is down to less than 26%. According to the same sources, "Between 2002 and 2017, the number of citrus growers in Florida decreased from 7,389 to 2,775 (a 62% decline) and the number of juice processing facilities decreased from 41 in 2003 to 14 in 2017 (a 66% decline). This is particularly biting in a state where citrus supports over 32,000 direct and indirect jobs, $1.61 billion in labor income and nearly $7 billion in output to the economy as of the 2020-2021 marketing year."[9] According to the Florida Department of Agriculture, "The 2024 Commercial Citrus Inventory for Florida shows total citrus acreage of 274,705 acres, down 17% from the

2023 annual survey."[10] Will those growers return? Will customers turn to other sources? How many more hurricanes before citrus production is no longer viable in Florida?

Although we have been working as a society on some issues like poverty and hunger for centuries, the issues of climate change and biodiversity are different. The time scale within which we need to see change is short. The generally accepted timelines are 2030 and 2050, to mitigate the worst effects of each challenge. Those dates are memorialized as target goals to minimize climate change, but also to stop the loss of biodiversity and begin to restore some of what we have lost. Since most economic activity is driven by business, the solutions to all things sustainable must be led by the business community with support from positive, enabling public policy.

Sustainability and climate change are therefore business drivers, as powerful and influential as any past economic, technology, or political driver of the past. Hundreds of multilateral agreements have been put in place since 1970 and many have generated global goals, compliance frameworks, and business standards. These treaties, conventions, protocols, and amendments (UN language for different types of agreements) have covered a diverse set of issues such as greenhouses gases, desertification, migratory species that transit national borders, hazardous waste and chemicals, and use of the sea.

Intergovernmental Agreements Are the New Standard for Business Behavior

What often seems confusing is the idea that there are signatories and parties to agreements. Some parties are countries and member states of the United Nations, some signatories are non-member states such as the Cook Islands and Niue, some parties have "observer state" status, such as Palestine, and other parties are organizations such as the European Union. When a UN agreement is signed, it then must undergo host nation parliamentary review and approval. In the case of the European Union, that means 27 EU members review it individually before it becomes law within the EU. From the date of signing until enough members approve the agreement within their parliamentary process may take years. Even then, it depends on which country does not approve the agreement, since some countries by virtue of their size, economic output, population, or geographic location can render an agreement ineffective by not agreeing to the terms. Figure 1.1 is from the United Nations Treaty Collection archives for illustration purposes.[11]

Some of the most important new policy guidelines for sustainability have emerged out of international agreements. Carbon credits were first mentioned in the Kyoto Protocol in 1997 and led directly to the first major carbon management program, the European Union Emissions Trading Scheme. However, the program did not start until 2005 because the EU member states voting process on the Kyoto Protocol was not completed until 2002. Following the voting process, the EU invested several more years to solicit feedback on the new carbon trading scheme. The new system was introduced in phases. The first phase was introduced in 2005 and lasted until 2007 as a pilot program. The

Agreement (Treaty, Convention or Protocol)	Date of Agreement	Parties (as of March 2022)
Vienna Convention (Ozone)	1985	198
UN Framework Convention on Climate Change (UNFCCC)	1992	198
Convention on Biological Diversity (CBD)	1992	193
UN Convention to Combat Desertification (UNCDD)	1996	197
Kyoto Protocol (greenhouse gas emissions)	1997	192
World Heritage Convention	1972	184
Cities Convention on International Trade in Endangered Species of Wild Fauna and Flora	1973	184
Stockholm Convention on Persistent Organic Pollutants	2001	186
Cartagena Protocol on Biosafety	2000	173
UN Convention on Law of the Sea (UNCLOS)	1982	170
Rotterdam Convention (Hazardous Chemicals)	1998	166
Convention on the Conservation of Migratory Species of Wild Animals	1979	133

Figure 1.1 List of treaties and agreement dates.

second phase lasted from 2008 until 2012, and the third phase started in 2013 and lasted until 2020. We are now in the fourth phase. Each phase expanded the number of industries and installations covered and changed the emissions allocation system according to feedback. The regulations continue to be updated to reflect the progress needed to meet EU commitments for emissions reductions. During this time, we have seen the growth in both the regulated and voluntary carbon markets (VCMs), but the global impact of the largest carbon regulatory program has taken over two decades to evolve and is still considered a work in progress. In the meantime, global emissions continue to increase.

There are now over thirty mandatory carbon markets around the world according to Bloomberg NEF,[12] covering approximately one-fifth of global emissions. This includes programs in the European Union, Germany, California (United States), South Korea, and China, and now approach 1 trillion USD in annual value of the credits exchanged. VCMs are much smaller and measured in the range of several billion dollars depending on the source you consult. There is no central authoritative source for VCM data. The voluntary market is expected to increase between 10 and 40 billion USD by 2030, although this may be affected by how much expansion we see in the major mandatory markets and changes in the pricing mechanisms.

One recent change that may drive growth is the expansion of trading platforms that deal specifically in carbon credits. According to the World Bank's 2023 *Carbon Report*, "The ability to trade carbon credits on different exchanges is also expanding. The Intercontinental Exchange and the European Energy Exchange, two large commodities trading platforms, both listed new futures contracts for carbon credits. In addition, several new exchanges and platforms focused on carbon trading were launched in different parts of the world, including Abu Dhabi, Hong Kong, Kenya, Malaysia, Saudi Arabia, Singapore, and Thailand."[13] The carbon markets have led to the movement of billions of dollars in capital within industries and between companies. This can influence corporate decision-making since the capital transfers may change the competitive position of more sustainable companies versus their legacy peers.

Intergovernmental and regional policy directives have also led to a host of new legal standards, tax and tariff regulations, as well as government subsidies for emerging industries. These shape market conditions within which the sustainable business must compete and thrive. It is important to note that these new boundary conditions are just a start. The speed with which business practices must change, and the resulting impact on business models and traditions is potentially profound. Our ability to get 198 parties to agree to an international treaty with real goals and guidelines is inherently difficult and subject to significant compromise. Yet the consequences of failure will not yield and our inability to move with urgency will not change the science. The global business market is set for the most turbulent period in history.

Traditional Boundary Conditions

Figure 1.2 offers a summary of some traditional business boundary conditions. The outer circle includes some of the challenges faced by all businesses including competition behavior, consumer trends, and market innovations. The inner circle contains choices that a business leader makes after consideration of the boundary conditions. Traditional business choices like organizational purpose and business models are evolving, so the meaning of these choices changes to fit the new conditions. As sustainability drives more radical change, business leaders must consider new business scenarios outside their historical experience.

Boundary conditions are something a business executive must account for as they make their choices about where their company will go, what customers they will serve, and the type of products they will make. For much of the last 40 years, the key conditions have been market innovations due to technology changes, globalization, and a more integrated global supply chain. As we look forward, we anticipate additional changes in technology in artificial intelligence, wearable

Figure 1.2 Traditional boundary conditions.

technologies, cloud computing, robotics and the like. When market innovations evolve along the same dimension, for example technology and globalization, we tend to forget that additional influences may exist, that is until a problem emerges. Although sustainability seems to have emerged rapidly, it has been slowly brewing for a long time.

Public Policy Becomes Part of the Competitive Landscape

There is an enormous amount of focus on the issues of ESG regulations, investment, and ratings. Some leaders feel there is too much regulation, others too little. Some may agree on a topic like climate change but disagree on other elements of sustainability that they feel are social reengineering. Each major intergovernmental treaty is followed by a regular Conference of the Parties (COP) meeting, where all the signatories meet to discuss progress. As time progresses, the attendees change, the politics evolves, and the execution of the original agreement may speed up or slow down. During the past decade, certainly since the Paris Agreement in 2015, annual COP meetings produce new commitments and an evolution or update to regional policies, industry association, and business guidelines. These expanding layers of boundary conditions are illustrated in Figure 1.3.

Each boundary condition is something that restricts, opens, or redefines business opportunity as well as costs and compliance. Some of these boundary conditions will appear as voluntary or involuntary boundaries depending on the industry and geography. Some boundaries may be legacy choices made decades earlier and may need to be revisited.

The challenge for a business leader is to understand these boundary conditions and their impact on both an existing legacy business as well as opportunities for new businesses, markets, products, and customers. Recent changes by the U.S. administration of President Donald Trump are a useful illustration. They have gained a lot of press coverage and are perceived as a major change in direction for international agreements. But have the boundaries really changed?

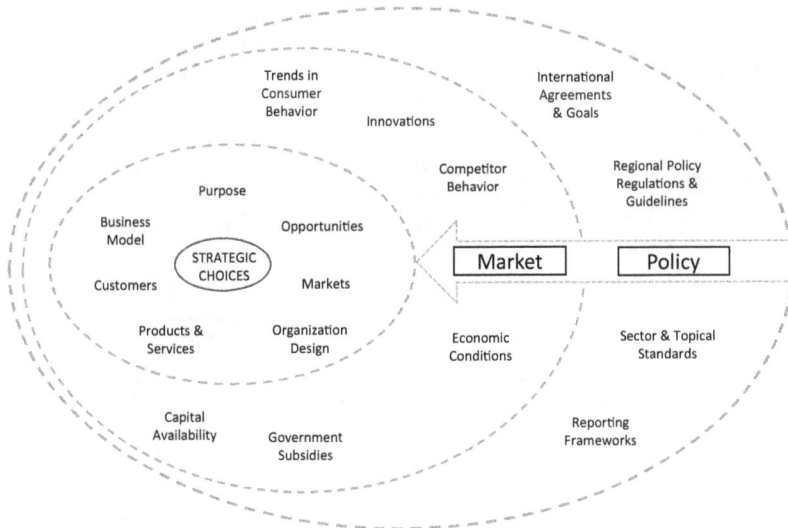

Figure 1.3 Expanding strategic boundary conditions.

During the first term of U.S. president Trump, the United States withdrew from the Paris Agreement on November 20, 2020.[14] The press and social media coverage suggested that United States withdrawal would have devastating consequences. The administration of U.S. president Biden rejoined the Paris Agreement on February 19, 2021.[15] The Paris Agreement has provisions that if a signatory to the agreement submits a notice of withdrawal, it becomes effective one year after the notice. President Trump's withdrawal notices also included ending contributions to the Green Climate Fund and the intent to cease updates to the U.S. NDC. The short duration of the withdrawal and the longer timelines associated with implementation guidelines tended to mitigate the impact. The net effect was also limited because of the swift change in direction by the succeeding administration.

For companies trying to consider these changes as part of their long-term business planning, the situation is more complex. Reelected in 2024, the Trump administration again ended U.S. participation in the Paris Agreement,[16] though an executive order issued in January of 2025. They also eliminated U.S. domestic support for a variety of green business incentives and subsidies. Since the United States is also signatory

Examples of Mandatory Business Boundaries	Examples of Past Boundary Decisions That May Need to be Revisited	Examples of Voluntary Business Boundaries
Intergovernmental treaties, conventions and protocols	Legal/tax status	Strategy & purpose
National & regional government requirements	Organization size	Values & ethical frameworks
Local government requirements	Exchange listing	Competitive response
Reporting frameworks	Partnerships	New product and service choices
Topical standards	Product and service choices	Risk tolerance
Sector standards		Markets where you choose to operate
		Customer segments
		New partnerships & memberships

Figure 1.4 Voluntary and involuntary boundaries.

to a variety of overlapping environmental agreements and is a member of various international organizations, they are still required to submit climate and sustainability data. U.S. multinationals are also committed to submitting data to a variety of international organizations and investors still look for robust climate disclosures. So, what is the appropriate response for a responsible business leader committed to a more sustainable future? Consider the following.

- The United States position on climate change in particular, and more broadly on a range of sustainability issues, has not been universal and consistent as evidenced by its withdrawal from key treaties and obligations under more conservative political administrations. The United States was not a signatory to the Kyoto Treaty in 1997, which did diminish its overall impact, yet that agreement started a variety of important programs like carbon credit markets where U.S. companies participated. As such, large global actions may be a political signal for change that is largely relevant only to the other parties to the treaty. If such U.S. action is accompanied by a withdrawal of funding that last more than one fiscal year, such as U.S. funding for the UN Climate Secretariate, then the issue is more serious.

- Operating guidance, support, and funding are often the important actions that a business must track. The rules and guidance issued by U.S. agencies such as the National Oceanographic and Atmospheric Administration (NOAA), the Department of Commerce (DOC), the Food and Drug Administration (FDA), and the Environmental Protection Agency (EPA), to name just a few, are where commitments influence investments. It takes time for policy to translate into operating practices and delays can change the impact. Policy changes can also be reversed or extended in succeeding administrations. However, if those changes affect multi-year funding, staffing levels, grant approvals or program cancellations, then the changes will have a more lasting effect. Historically, it is not uncommon for policy positions to be modified or reviewed even if the general direction remains the same.

- Government officials in Germany sent a letter[17] to the European Union asking it to change plans for Corporate Sustainability Reporting Directive (CSRD) reporting, citing the increased burden to EU businesses. Similarly, the French government has drafted a letter asking the EU to delay both the Corporate Sustainability Due Diligence Directive (CSDDD) and the rollout schedule of the CSRD.[18] This follows concerning reports on European competitiveness[19] from the European Commissions and industry concerns about the level of regulation on small to medium enterprises. Both countries have seen increased support for conservative political parties that resist aspects of what is seen as social reengineering.

- Recent COP meetings, namely COP28 in the UAE and COP29 in Azerbaijan have been dominated by current and former oil executives with hundreds of oil industry lobbyists invited as registered guests. These meetings have stalled progress on a collective call to phase out fossil fuel production. With two-thirds of the proven oil and gas reserves in the world dominated by National Oil Companies (NOCs), we are seeing increased resistance to formal bans on fossil fuels that will affect national economic growth.

Collectively, these and other examples of political actions at the national and intergovernmental level signal growing resistance to change or the speed of change. Some resistance may be very specific, if for example, NOCs fear their fossil fuel assets may become less valuable. In other instances, resistance may be more general if political parties are concerned about economic conditions, unemployment increases, and if the changes are perceived as a threat to key constituencies. Perhaps most troubling of the Trump era changes are attempts to eliminate climate change references within regulatory agencies such as the U.S. Department of Agriculture (USDA).[20] Eliminating climate references to agriculture, water management, and wildfires specifically hurts agriculture businesses dependent on sound scientific advice.

These changes often reveal patterns that must be viewed in terms of overall market trends and impact and compared with contradictory data. For example, despite global political changes suggesting a pull-back on sustainability priorities, we still see large firms like China's Xuzhou Construction Machinery Group signing major deals for all electric mining equipment with industry leaders like Australia's Fortescue,[21] which is the fourth largest iron ore mining company in the world (2023). Fortescue also signaled a continuing commitment to commercial decarbonization[22] in 2024 as well as its labor relations plan and commitment to eliminating forced labor practices.

Using the last two examples, with the agriculture and mining industries, both are directly influenced by climate science and changing markets, but they also have different investment timelines. Industries will react differently to political boundary changes to seek compliance, but also to preserve business options based less on ideology and more on pragmatic business considerations. An illustration of this can be seen in banking where a number of major Canadian and U.S. banks withdrew commitments to the Net Zero Banking Alliance formed in 2021 to help reduce emissions. Similar withdrawals were seen internationally from the Alliance for Net Zero.[23] However, it is unlikely that the public retreat from commitments by the banking sector will cause them to ignore the threats posed by extreme weather and other events.

Figure 1.5 offers a simple method for categorizing boundary changes. The legend at the left of the chart suggests you can chart a boundary change in terms of the potential for business impact (P1) on an industry-wide or competitive basis, the predicted impact (P2) on your business that may take into account mitigation efforts or your unique market position, and finally the actual impact (P3) that may differ from your original assessment or result from factors that were not considered. The

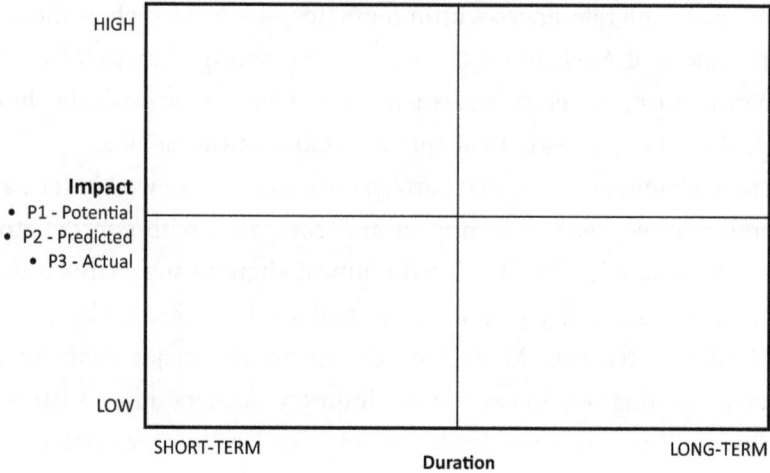

Figure 1.5 Impact and duration of boundary changes.

goal of any risk analysis is learning from the process, so your organization gets better at determining the impact of any boundary changes on business decision-making.

For example:

- Is this a transitory change that will pass in a few years, a temporary pause to allow greater input or investment, or a needed pushback to prevent unnecessary economic harm?
- Are there historical precedents for the changes that offer insights into actual impact?
- Are the public policy positions likely to be of high impact or long duration? Both can be a serious business concern.

- Are the changes to public policy or the regulatory bodies legislative or executive in nature? Executive orders can change with each administration, while broader legislative directives often require a collective decision or amendment from multiple parties.
- Are these changes market specific or broader in nature? What are the keystone companies doing in each market?

- If you have already made long-term investment decisions such as refurbishing a manufacturing plant, locating a new business facility, or changing a product formulation, what options do you have to manage the risk?

It's useful to remember that current or future boundary conditions may alter the decision-making landscape, but they do not diminish the challenges of climate change and biodiversity losses nor the underlying science. Large-scale systemic changes are often accompanied by problems and the rate of change is rarely linear in nature. Change, resistance, redirection, and new beginnings are all part of the process. The goal of a sustainable business is to find opportunity in these challenges and continuously find ways to make positive forward progress.

Science-Based Drivers Are Here to Stay

Behind policy changes and guidelines is a series of global trends and science-based drivers that can be challenging to understand and interpret. Interpreting climate modeling, for example, requires an understanding of differential equations and calculus and a lot of time to take a deep dive into the data. If you lack the time or the calculus skills, you need to trust the source and the interpretation. The business solution is to create an intelligence capability that tracks these drivers and validates the data through multiple perspectives so you can anticipate longer-term trends that influence market opportunities. Added to these considerations are two additional areas of concern, what I describe in Figure 1.6 as "Clouds of Uncertainty" and "Clouds of Misinformation."

Uncertainty includes potentially new boundaries under discussion such as scope 4 emissions (i.e., emissions avoidance) or possible regulations on forever chemicals (PFAS).[24] Will they be implemented? In what form? In what market or industry? Although these are difficult questions to answer, doing so will influence decision-making. The

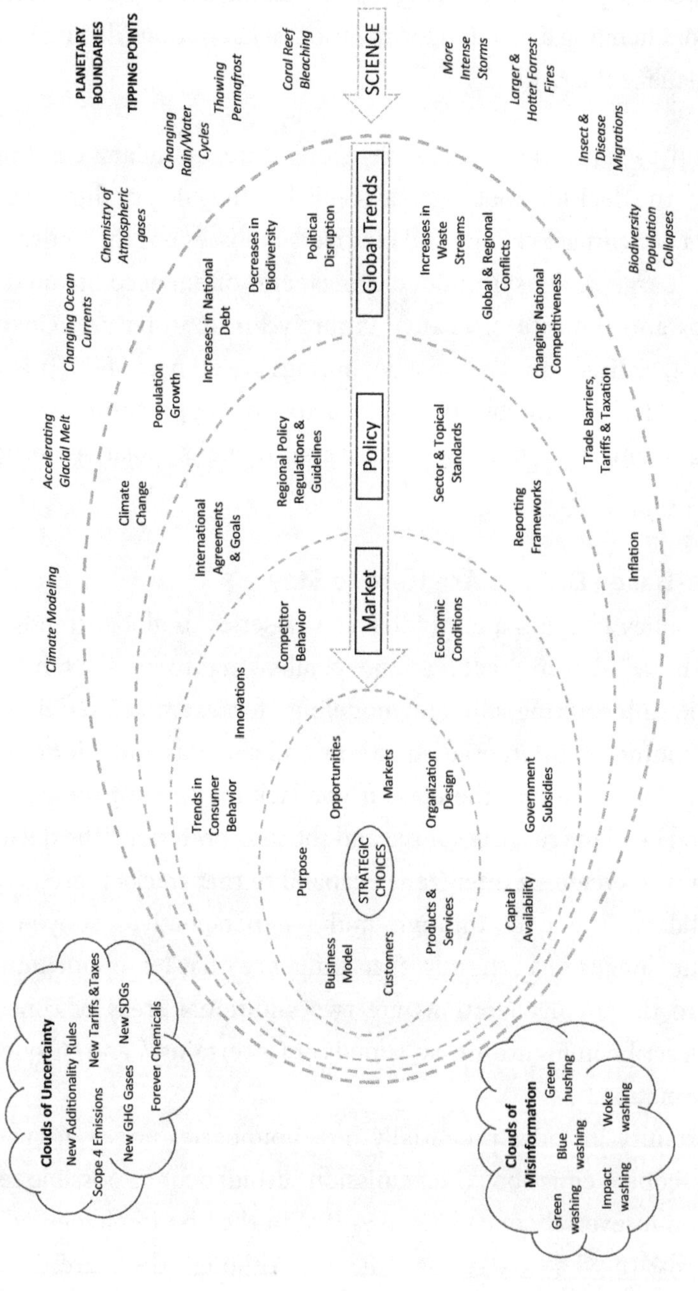

Figure 1.6 Full model of existing and new boundary conditions.

Clouds of Misinformation are all the half-truths, misstatements, and misrepresentations that can affect perceptions. These may be generated by social media or by businesses themselves. In business terms, these may be referred to as greenwashing, blue washing, or green gaslighting. Any such reference to your company is to be avoided. Business leaders need to be aware of the prevalence of this messaging and how it may influence consumers, policy makers, and investors alike.

A significant challenge for any business leader is to consider what new information is important, what information is background noise, and which roles need to develop knowledge in depth? (Note: I have devoted a chapter to "building a model of working knowledge" and another chapter to "creating a culture of sustainable oriented innovation" to help respond to the market opportunities in an evolving marketplace.) The more senior the leader, the less they need to know the details of a knowledge domain in depth, but they always need sufficient awareness and the critical thinking skills to make a business decision.

A Model for Understanding Knowledge

The knowledge we acquire can be divided into different categories depending on their validity and reliability.

1. Knowledge of Enduring Value
   a. Scientific Knowledge—Climate change in particular is based on a range of empirical facts subject to the scientific method. It may be inconvenient and we may not like the truths it tells, but it has been the subject of rigorous testing and verification. Scientific knowledge may also be variable in nature in that some scientific truths are defined in relation to other variables and may be quite complex to understand. However, the fact that it is based on observations and experimental results allows us to create increasingly accurate models and assessments. Since most people may not understand the complexity of the basic science, trust in the organizations that develop the

science becomes almost as important as the facts and insights that evolve from their work.

b. Heuristics—I'll call this a subset of knowledge of enduring value since many heuristics have remained relevant and consistent over time. Heuristics are not empirical knowledge. Instead, they fit the "good enough" standard and serve as a way to problem-solve until a better method evolves. Unlike scientists who test and refine observations over time, businesses need to make decisions on the best available information—today. As such, business practices are filled with heuristics. For example, Michael Porter's five forces framework remains of value in many organizations even if some consultants might disagree with its completeness. For many leaders, it works! Is it less applicable in a sustainable future? Perhaps. Heuristics do not need to remain fixed and can evolve with new conditions.

2. Public Policy Knowledge—I've separated out public policy since it is clearly not a scientific truth, but it is often a set of practices or regulations we need to comply with. In some instances we can refer to this as fixed knowledge in that it applies to a law or public policy requirement that can last for multiple years or even decades. As such, it deserves its own category. It may be subject to lobbying and change, but it will serve as a necessary guide to capital allocation and risk assessment decisions in the meantime. If we need to comply with its directives, someone in the organization must be accountable for understanding the details, managing its requirements, and tracking the evolution of its boundaries.

3. Breakthrough Knowledge—Truly breakthrough ideas are rare, and they tend to emerge during periods of adversity, or from decades of research. Some knowledge may not yet be of enduring value, since the underlying ideas have not had the opportunity to stand the test of time. They may exist as a heuristic or hold the promise of a more elegant, lower cost, or long-term solution. We are likely on the edge of many scientific and business breakthroughs and it

remains to be seen what new models and practices will become generally accepted and valued in years to come. The key issue with breakthrough knowledge is we may not be the source of the innovation, but we need to judge, adapt, and respond to it because of its potential to disrupt markets and industries.

4. Social Knowledge—Social media is so pervasive and the emergence of deep fakes and AI-generated content so compelling, that we need to be aware of the challenges of misinformation. The major energy and other industry transformations underway will undoubtedly close some companies and cause layoffs. Misinformation is often introduced as a way to slow progress, extend the life of stranded assets, or sow confusion among politicians and consumers. The pervasiveness of personal communication devices, and the speed which information can be shared, makes this a challenge for leaders who may need to devote time to dealing with misinformation among customers, employees, shareholders, and community members at large.

5. Personal Knowledge—We all grow up with certain influences, education, role models, and belief systems within the communities where we live and work. These may guide our acceptance or rejection of new ideas and represent biases for certain social beliefs. They may be deeply grounded in religious theology or other ideologies. The more we are exposed to media and feedback that reinforce these belief systems, the more skepticism may exist to accept ideas that lie outside that of our community of knowledge. In general it is very hard to change people's personal beliefs, but I see belief systems as a potential anchor for sustainability practices. No major religion holds that we must ignore the poor, destroy the environment, or make money at the exclusion of all else. At the same time, there is a rise in nationalism and new political camps all over the world. Any cross-border or international business leader needs to be aware of such belief systems and how they may affect sustainable business perceptions and market acceptance.

Do We Need to Rethink Regulation?

If you look at all of the intergovernmental agreements, frameworks, and policies around the world, you might say there is enough or even excessive regulation. That is a valid observation from the seat of someone trying to cope with increased regulations on a small budget or with limited staff. Yet regulations don't become law without one or more antecedent event. The current Global Reporting Initiative (GRI) was a direct result of the Exxon Valdez disaster in 1997. For everyone that thinks there are too many regulations that make it difficult to innovate or compete, consider the following.

- According to the World Shipping Council (WSC), more than 250 million containers are transported across our oceans every year.[25] Based on data from the WSC and as reported by Euro News, "more than 20,000 shipping containers have tumbled overboard in the last decade and a half."[26] However, the data does not cover all shipping or losses, because it is based on data self-reported by WSC members. That leaves an ongoing legacy of unknown toxicity both on the seabed and floating in our oceans. As extreme storms get worse, will the problem?

- Organizations such as Project Tangaroa have created a database of "8,500 wrecks classified as 'potentially polluting wrecks' (PPW), mainly originating from World War I and II, containing oil, chemicals and munitions."[27] Although these wrecks have been out of sight and mind for the past seventy to one hundred years, the cumulative effects of marine corrosion and storms are beginning to release unknown quantities of fuel oil and hazardous chemicals.

- PFAS, a group of almost 15,000 chemicals, often called forever chemicals because they resist degrading, and tend to accumulate in our environment. New studies[28] suggest the chemicals accumulate in our blood over time and are now in our soil, food, and water. They are suspected as a cause or compounding factor in certain cancers and disease conditions.

- Plastics are essentially everywhere. They are part of the products we buy, the clothes we wear, and are found in our food. Studies in recent years have established that microplastics are in our blood[29] with unknown long-term consequences for human health. There is already a new intergovernmental treaty on plastics under consideration at the United Nations. Will it help address the existing problems? Will it go far enough? Or too far?

It would be easy to keep adding examples that illustrate both the cumulative and ongoing impact of human activities on our environment. Since we know that the human population continues to increase and that economic activity will add new production and consumption, we need to address how we think about regulation and what it is meant to achieve.

- Are we better off with more effective regulation that is specifically focused on eliminating environmental and biodiversity negatives and long-term human impact?
- Should we rethink our regulatory frameworks to be more harmonized so they cover our planetary systems rather than national boundaries?
- Would we be better off with a combination of education, incentives, and regulations that allow us to innovate and grow without creating long-term harm to ourselves, the environment, and the communities where we live and work?
- Many small to medium-sized businesses (SMEs) simply don't have the resources to be ESG compliant. Do we need a clear global system of incentives, subsidies, and training to help SMEs become more sustainable and compliant?

Self-Imposed Boundary Conditions

The boundary conditions described above may seem like a lot to worry about. But most are imposed by market drivers or legislative mandates that do not require a leader to ask "if" they should choose a market opportunity or "how" they should act. One of the most important boundary conditions to our behavior is the sense of personal and shared ethical standards. This topic gets additional attention in later chapters on purpose and ethical brands, but it is the ultimate guide to our behavior and decision-making. Will we continue to engage in business behavior that science tells us is fundamentally at odds with preserving our environment or the communities where we live? Should we continue to engage in wasteful or destructive behavior even if it remains legal? Should we lobby for longer transition periods for legacy business, even if the science tells us that such businesses make the problems of sustainability worse?

The SDGs as well as the other major legislative actions are often grounded in ethical concepts. Most people don't read the preambles or concern themselves with the rhetoric of the speeches that surround the legislative meetings. They often respond to the mandates that emerge and the implementation timelines. The ultimate driver of a more sustainable future is a leadership team bound by a business purpose that seeks to generate real social and natural capital in addition to profits. Their priorities tempered by a respect for our shared environment and translated into business practices that ensure the hundreds of thousands of employees act in accordance to such guiding principles.

Summary

- Boundary conditions are factors that frame your decision-making process. Traditionally such factors would include financial and risk assessments as well as competitive analysis. Those issues don't disappear, but we must now add new considerations.
- Any new condition that restricts, opens, or redefines business opportunity as well as costs and compliance may affect your business strategy. This may include global goals and protocols, new laws, compliance frameworks, ethical standards, regional public

policy, or expectations for transparency. Business boundary conditions have become both more numerous and more variable.

- Boundary conditions will continue to evolve as political considerations, resistance, and innovation affect the speed and direction of change. Leadership teams need to balance the short- and long-term impact of these conditions when making longer-term business decisions.

- If you don't have the skills to understand the science, you need to find trusted sources of information or trusted advisors.

- Knowledge management becomes increasingly important during turbulent times, particularly when the science of climate change has the potential to dramatically affect our perception of risks and opportunities. This applies to known conditions as well as issues that remain uncertain.

- Misinformation is important because it spreads so rapidly on social media. Customer perceptions can be influenced, brand value can be diminished, and leadership resources can be affected if misinformation is not managed appropriately.

- The ultimate business boundary condition are the ethical frameworks that shape our business purpose and personal behavior.

Boundary Condition Reflection Checklist

Boundary Condition Checklist		
Is it more or less true that your organization …		**Ranking**
1	Has at least an annual briefing for senior leadership on international treaties, agreements, and goals, and their potential business impact?	1 2 3 4 5 6 7 8 9 10
2	Has a dedicated position that tracks new public policy, market trends, and scientific issues related to sustainability?	1 2 3 4 5 6 7 8 9 10

Boundary Condition Checklist		
Is it more or less true that your organization ...		**Ranking**
3	Subscribes to information sources that track changes in mandatory compliance guidelines and policy regulations?	1 2 3 4 5 6 7 8 9 10
4	Has delegated responsibility for sustainability compliance, data collection, and reporting among key functional organizations and has integrated processes for summarizing the reporting?	1 2 3 4 5 6 7 8 9 10
5	Has briefing or training activities designed to update geographic, business unit, and functional leaders on the impact of new boundary conditions on the business?	1 2 3 4 5 6 7 8 9 10
6	Conducts routine risk assessment activities that incorporate the business impact of boundary conditions as well as the impact the business is having on the environment and the communities where you live and work?	1 2 3 4 5 6 7 8 9 10
7	Participates in global discussions such as community of practice meetings or the regional outreach from such meetings?	1 2 3 4 5 6 7 8 9 10
8	Participates in industry associations where new policy directives, boundary conditions, and possible industry-wide commitments are discussed and developed?	1 2 3 4 5 6 7 8 9 10
9	Has incorporated boundary condition issues in key practices such as business development, organization development, sales planning, product development, and product support to ensure alignment and compliance?	1 2 3 4 5 6 7 8 9 10
10	Has a business intelligence function that looks to future proof the organization by tracking future policy schedules as well as international and regional policy discussions that may yield new boundary conditions?	1 2 3 4 5 6 7 8 9 10
Total Score		

Scoring

- Score less than 50—You need to step up efforts to insure you have the necessary knowledge to understand boundary conditions and their impact on your business.
- Score less than 80—You have both strengths and weaknesses. You need to leverage your positive knowledge and relationships and prioritize capability improvements.
- Score greater than 80—Your organization is strongly positioned to support a sustainable organization. Focus on continued capability development and operational excellence to enhance your value to the organization.

Chapter 2

DISCOVERING COMPETITIVE DIFFERENTIATION IN SUSTAINABILITY

Sustainability and profitability go hand in hand. That's how you build a resilient company, whether you're an incumbent or starting from scratch. —HENRIK HENRIKSSON, CEO OF H2 GREEN STEEL[1]

W e hear a lot about resilience in business. While there are many facets to resilience, one that ranks high on a level of importance is seeking and understanding the knowledge of enduring value that we associate with competitive advantage. Although I do not unpack the long historical context of sustainability and human development in this book, the more recent history is important. It helps explain current market issues and illustrates the danger of focusing only on your immediate business segment, to the exclusion of other industries or to human development, the environment, and biodiversity in general.

An appropriate review of sustainability for most business leaders starts with the date 1950 and moves forward. The post–World War II era marks the beginning of an era of explosive growth in economic development, population growth, and productivity never before seen in human history. Global GDP in 1950 was about 10 trillion USD and today it is over 105 trillion USD (World Bank data).[2] Investment banking firm Goldman Sachs predicts that by 2050 global GDP will come close to 240 trillion USD.[3] That means over 120 trillion USD more in annual production and consumption by the year we expect to reach net-zero emissions. Think about that for a moment. This means we must greatly reduce emissions, pollution, habitat and biodiversity losses while simultaneously restricting any change in average global temperature to less than 2°C, all while doubling the global economy and increasing the global population by 1.5 billion. This is an incredibly difficult assignment under any conditions but is what we need to do.

Three Great Storylines Converge

Understanding a significant challenge often requires stepping back to look at the storyline of how we arrived at this place. During the post–World War II decades, we have three distinct storylines that were supported by different organizations, authors, and advocates. The language and innovations have a historical relationship, but the storylines largely operate independently. Part of this is due to the roles people have, and their training and career choices. Individuals involved in international relations, diplomacy, or intergovernmental organizations, for example, do not often have extensive business experience. Similarly, people who work in the high-technology, manufacturing, pharmaceutical, or aerospace industries have not spent much time at the United Nations. Yet the storylines of business development, human development, and sustainability need to connect for people to see the reality of our common challenge and the shared accountability for solutions.

The business innovation storyline has been one of the great success stories of modern times. Competitive advantage and business strategy have enjoyed a range of innovations from people like Bruce Henderson, founder of the Boston Consulting Group in 1963, who introduced the ideas of the growth share matrix and portfolio management.[4] These were major influences on business strategy in the 1960s and 1970s. In 1973 Bill Bain founded Bain and Company, one of the largest consulting firms working in that era. He differentiated his consulting work by focusing not only on strategy development but strategy implementation and long-term client relationships.[5] Later, the company that bears his name would introduce the Net Promoter Score System,[6] which the company says is highly correlated with long-term value creation. In the 1970s and 1980s, Fred Gluck, the longtime CEO of McKinsey and Company, introduced the idea of "centers of competence" and worked to provide more rigor to the idea of strategic management.[7] In parallel, Professor Michael Porter of Harvard wrote about the five forces of competitive advantage (1979)[8] as well as the influential books *Competitive Strategy* (1980)[9] and *Competitive Advantage* (1985).[10]

Business innovation, strategy, and competitive differentiation have many other significant contributors, and the topic remains very relevant today. Although we didn't envision product ecosystems and networked

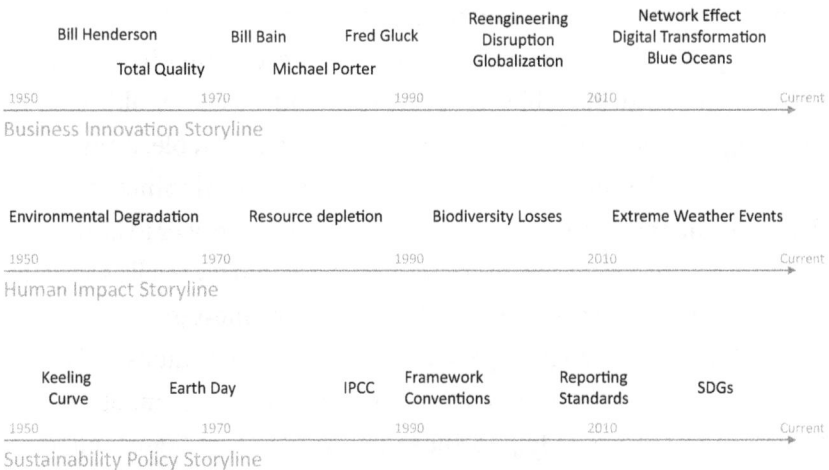

			Reengineering Disruption	Network Effect Digital Transformation
Bill Henderson	Bill Bain	Fred Gluck		Blue Oceans
Total Quality	Michael Porter		Globalization	
1950	1970	1990	2010	Current

Business Innovation Storyline

Environmental Degradation	Resource depletion	Biodiversity Losses	Extreme Weather Events
1950	1970	1990	2010 Current

Human Impact Storyline

Keeling Curve	Earth Day	IPCC	Framework Conventions	Reporting Standards	SDGs
1950	1970	1990	2010		Current

Sustainability Policy Storyline

Figure 2.1 Parallel story lines.

organizations in the 1970s and 1980s, they have become key drivers of companies like Apple, Amazon, and Alibaba, which are preeminent companies today.

The era of post–World War II economic growth also saw the members of the United Nations grow from 51 to 193, largely because of decolonialization. Innovations in areas like health care, education, and communication helped improve people's lives, and growth in the global economy lifted hundreds of millions of people out of poverty. At the same time, we still have ongoing conflicts and wars, human trafficking and forced human labor remain a problem, millions of people now migrate due to extreme weather events, and food security is a growing problem caused by climate change. Our historical economic development came with a cost that is now due. The depletion of our global commons and the need for ever more fossil fuel-based energy leads us down a path that does not end well.

We have been slow to see the storylines of business innovation, human development, and sustainability as connected and intertwined. Long-term success in each storyline is dependent on the other two. As we finally see the bigger picture, we are left to ask, can we continue economic growth while eliminating the type of environmental and social harms that have characterized the last 75 years.

Many governments around the world are responding by expanding investments in sustainable infrastructure and business, although no meaningful alternative to continued growth is on the table. As an example, the United Kingdom's economy has grown slowly since its Brexit decision, and the new government has decided the answer to its need for health care, infrastructure and educational spending, as well as its ambitious climate policies, is to expand trade and business growth.[11] In the United States, the Congress passed some of the largest industrial incentives in history with the United States Innovation and Competition Act (2021),[12] the Creating Helpful Incentives to Produce Semiconductors and Science Act (2022),[13] and the Infrastructure Investment and Jobs Act (2021).[14] This has added tens of billions of dollars in support for new businesses, infrastructure development, and clean industries. Each of the major global markets are doing variations of the same thing to keep their economies on an upward trajectory.

How Does Sustainability Change the Nature of Competition Advantage?

Recently, the European Council called for a "New European Competitiveness Deal"[15] to go with its "Green New Deal." A study by the Kiel Institute[16] in Germany states, "Estimates suggest that China's overall subsidies range between three to nine times that of other OECD countries such as the USA or Germany." Mario Draghi, the former prime minister of Italy, chaired a study of competitiveness (2024) for the European Union and concluded, "Europe must profoundly refocus its collective efforts on closing the innovation gap with the US and China, especially in advanced technologies. Europe is stuck in a static industrial structure with few new companies rising up to disrupt existing industries or develop new growth engines. In fact, there is no EU company with a market capitalization over EUR 100 billion that has been set up from scratch in the last fifty years, while all six US companies with a valuation above EUR 1 trillion have been created in this period. This lack of dynamism is self-fulfilling."[17] Everyone sees the need for business growth to generate the tax revenue and innovation to make the change to a more sustainable future.

Consistent with the idea of knowledge of enduring value discussed in Chapter 1, we don't throw out the practices that are still being used and that have established value. Instead, we adapt them to the new realities of boundary conditions that were not actively considered during the 1950s through the 2000s. As the new EU report on competitiveness highlights, "If Europe cannot become more productive, we will be forced to choose. We will not be able to become, at once, a leader in new technologies, a beacon of climate responsibility and an independent player on the world stage. We will not be able to finance our social model. We will have to scale back some, if not all, of our ambitions."[18]

Emphasizes overall market conditions (external), business structure and positioning as key drivers.

Emphasizes the importance of company level (internal) attributes such as of uniqueness and value.

Market Based View

Resource Based View

Competitive Advantage

Emphasizes the value of knowledge, expertise and intellectual assets.

Knowledge Based View

Relationship Based View

Emphasizes the importance of networks & B2B experience.

Demand Based View

This is a broad category that emphasizes market niches where there is less direct competition or a defensible moat to reduce competition, allowing for greater pricing flexibility.

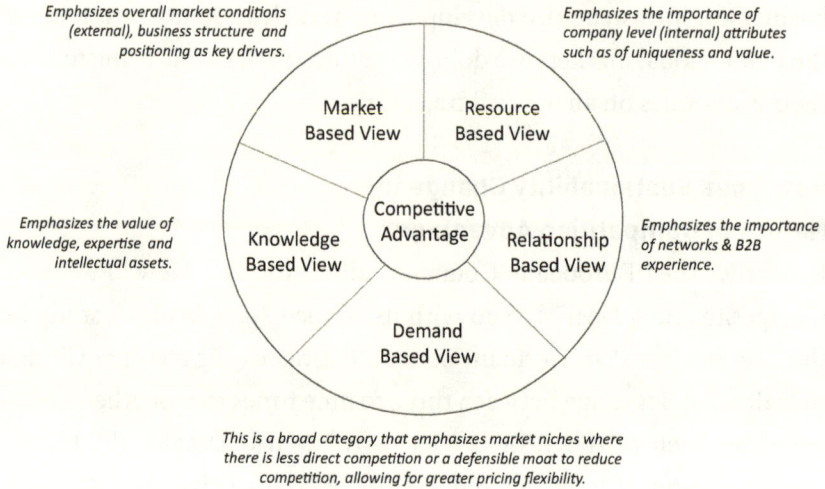

Figure 2.2 Perspectives on competitive differentiation.

There has been some debate on issues like degrowth or decoupled growth for many decades. Unfortunately, no one has developed a practical national model for increasing productivity, while limiting population growth, reducing environmental negatives, and increasing social services. In the meantime, we focus on competitive differentiation in an era of ever more science, regulation, and political discourse, with an aspiration to reduce our negative impact while restoring some of what we have already lost.

Business leaders may be forgiven if a lot of leadership time is spent discussing new regulations and global frameworks instead of long-term global changes. There is a lot to learn, a lot of new risks to consider and major business transitions to plan. Most leaders in business today never studied sustainability during their academic studies and their careers were not defined by achievements in these areas.

Challenges: Where are the new opportunities for sustainable business? How do we combine our existing capability with new boundary conditions to help re-define our legacy businesses and create new sustainable products and services?

New Boundaries Require Everyone to Adjust

Figure 2.3 illustrates just some of the global goals and protocols, regional regulations, reporting frameworks and ratings, and third-party opinion sources that may need to think about. Each of the broad categories is represented in the model of boundary conditions described in the preceding chapters, but it is in the operational details where the work begins. Traditional choices about what markets a company may operate in, particularly for legacy businesses, may be based on outdated market assessments. New boundary conditions may open new windows of opportunity, but they may also impose costs or call into question decisions on where to locate, how to source products, or whether to compete in each market at all.

Beyond the broad issue categories listed in the graphic above, you have industry-specific boundary conditions to follow. For example, if you are in the finance and insurance industries, you may be adding the United Nations Environmental Program (UNEP) Principles for Sustainable Insurance[19] to your global goals and protocols, or you may be committed to the United Nations Principles for Responsible Investing. Similarly, if you are in the textile industry, you may be following the

Global Goals & Protocols

- UN Sustainable Development Goals SDGs
- UN Global Compact
- Greenhouse Gas Protocol – World Resources Institute (WRI) & World Business Council for Sustainable Development (WBCSD)
- Science Based Targets – CDP, The UN Global Compact, WRI and the Worldwide Fund for Nature

Regional Regulations & Guidelines

- CSRD – EU Corporate Sustainability Reporting Directives
- European Union - Taxonomy Regulations
- European Union - Sustainable Finance Regulations
- China Climate Disclosure Regime
- US SEC Climate Disclosure Rules
- Australia Climate Risk Reporting

Reporting Frameworks

- Global Reporting Initiative
- Climate Disclosure Standards Board
- SASB – Sustainability Accounting Standards Board
- TCFD & TNFD
- ISO – International Organization for Standardization

ESG Ratings & Indices

- SP Global ESG Scores
- Thompson Reuters ESG Data
- Corporate Knights Global 100 Index
- Bloomberg Sustainalytics
- EcoVadis Supply Chain Scorecards
- Dow Jones Sustainability indices
- FTSE4Good – Financial Times/Russel group
- MSCI – Morgan Stanley Capital International
- Third Party Opinions

Figure 2.3 Matrix of boundary conditions.

Fashion Industry Charter for Climate Action,[20] or if you are in a functional or supply chain role, you may be a member of the Supplier Ethical Data Exchange[21] (Sedex). All these decisions may show your commitment to doing the right thing, although none of them describe how your products or services are distinguished as unique in the marketplace.

Each of the challenges described above are worthy of leadership time, but identifying, studying, and complying with the new boundary conditions should not take away from the primary mission of the business, which is to find a competitive position that allows the business to profitably provide a sustainable business solution that really makes a difference. The goals, frameworks, and regulations described above are part of the new competitive landscape of boundary conditions within which leaders must identify, build, and scale new capabilities that are critical to success.

Listed in Figure 2.4 are some of the specific attributes of each view on competition. Each "view" or perspective emerged during the last seven decades to match the market shifts and changes underway (i.e., the boundary conditions). None of these views are considered comprehensive by many partitioners. Each represents an evolution in thinking, not that the old view is no longer valid. In some ways, the market-based view is gaining in importance because of changes in the prominence of a specific boundary such as country-level subsidies. As sustainability increases as a driver of business development, it will be important to consider all perspectives to maximize competitive opportunities.

Where Is the Opportunity in Sustainability?

Competitive advantage always relates to business opportunity. If there is an emerging need, and the potential for high returns, then assessing the opportunity makes sense. The traditional approach is expressed in Figure 2.5. Today this means an expanded view of the potential impact, as well as the risks, the required resource commitments, and the complexity of the change. As we'll discuss in later chapters, many companies first look for ways to experiment and develop a proof-of-concept before they commit the resources to scale the idea. The important distinction

Market Based View		Resource Based View		Knowledge Based View	Relationship Based View	Demand Based View
Bain SCP Model (1968)	Michael Porter 5 Forces (1980)	Michael Porter (1990)	Prahalad & Hamel (1990)	Prahalad & Hamel (1994)	Dyer and Singh (1998)	Chan & Mauborgne (2004)
Structure	Barriers to entry	Cost	Resources	Knowledge	Networks	Identifying gaps in existing markets
Conduct	Threat of substitutes	Focus	Capabilities	Intellectual assets	Interfirm cooperation	Identifying new markets (blue oceans)
Performance	Bargaining power of rivals	Qualitative & attribute differentiation	Core Competencies	Competencies	Relationship specific combinations of resources	Creating new demand
	Bargaining power of suppliers					Avoiding rivals
	Competitors					

Figure 2.4 Research perspectives on competitive advantage.

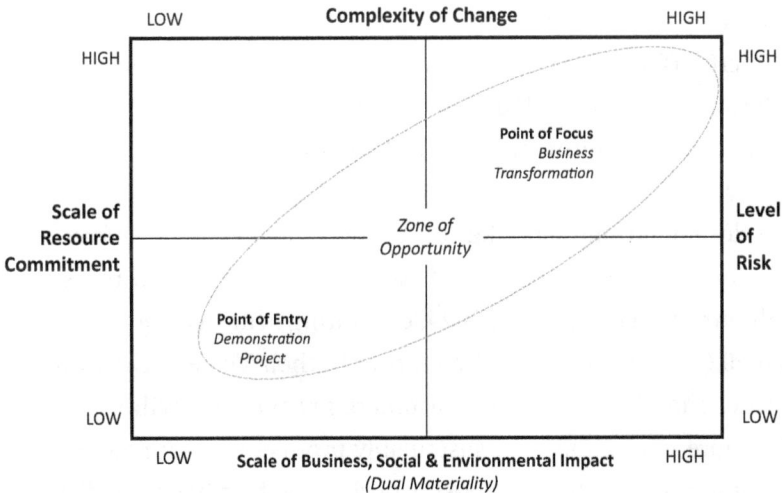

Figure 2.5 Testing new market opportunities with demonstration projects.

made in the graphic is that experiments (your point of entry) are best served if you already have a longer-term vision, (i.e., your North Star). In that way, you can ask the right questions as you design your experiment (demonstration project). Learning from your demonstration project is more that determining if customers like your idea. You can also gain insights on broader trends, use the project to develop internal capability, test features that may be relevant in other applications, and even test partnership opportunities in a low-risk environment.

The figure below differs from traditional opportunity assessments in one very important way. The value dimension, the lower x axis, represents dual materiality. Instead of just looking at the business financial impact, sustainability asks a different question. It asks each business to not only consider the impact on the business but also the society and the environment. Thus, there is a consideration for the new product idea will have on the business (internal focus) and the impact the business will have on the environment and society (external focus). This is the definition of dual materiality.

Under the broad banner of sustainability, there is literally opportunity everywhere you look in both developed and developing markets. Opportunity is often framed around potential market size or what is called the "addressable market." The Glasgow Financial Alliance for Net Zero[22] (GFANZ), which was announced in Scotland as part of the 26th Conference of the Parties (COP26) meeting, resulted in ~150 trillion USD in commitments toward the key climate goal of reaching net zero by 2050.

In developed markets like the United States, the European Union and China in particular, there is substantial commercial investments in all transition markets. In 2024, consulting firm PWC surveyed more than 20,000 consumers in 31 countries in their Voice of the Consumer Survey. They found, "some consumers say they are willing to spend 9.7% more, on average, for sustainably produced or sourced goods, as almost nine-in-ten (85%) report experiencing first-hand the disruptive effects of climate change in their daily lives."[23]

Global companies like Unilever have been increasing growth and profitability by creating sustainable brand portfolios. Under its Sustainable Living Strategy,[24] Unilever makes three commitments: (1) to improve the health and well-being of more than 1 billion people, (2) to reduce its environmental impact by half, and (3) to enhance livelihoods of millions of people. Today, it reports 28 sustainable living product brands with seven of its ten best-selling brands fitting that category. According to Unilever's reporting in 2019, nine years after the strategy was started, "Sustainable Living Brands are growing 69% faster than the rest of the business and delivering 75% of the company's growth."[25] By 2022, Unilever was creating follow-on programs like its Clean Future Strategy[26] that incorporated sustainable design concepts in its product development. "We are investing €1 billion over ten years to change the way our cleaning products are created, manufactured and packaged, the re-engineered capsules contain powerful biodegradable active ingredients, 65% of which are derived from plant sources."

Other major brands like Adidas have incorporated sustainability into their brand strategy by partnering with the organization "Parley for the Oceans,"[27] which allows the company to reuse ocean plastic in its footwear. "Over the last five years, we have steadily decreased the use of virgin polyester from our products and, by the end of 2020, more than half of all the polyester used in our products was recycled polyester."[28] In a separate announcement, Adidas states, "Plastic waste is a problem. Innovation is our solution. These shoes are made in part with re-imagined plastic waste, intercepted on remote islands, beaches, coastal communities and shorelines, preventing it from polluting our oceans."[29]

NVIDIA is one of the most valued companies in the world and a major player in the artificial intelligence (AI) boom. Its products are in high demand from every major AI company and data center operator. Its latest Blackwell Platform product line promises not only big leaps in performance but also significant improvements in energy efficiency. "NVIDIA's Blackwell platform has achieved groundbreaking energy efficiency in AI computing, reducing energy consumption by up to 2,000x over the past decade for training models like GPT-4."[30] When asked a question about the future opportunities for a more sustainable data center, Jensen Huang, CEO of NVIDIA stated, "I am horrible at forecasting, but I am very good at first principal reasoning of the size of the opportunity."[31] His key insight with future computing is that all of today's data is retrieval-based because it is pre-recorded. AI will create a generative future where computers organize the information and create insights that have meaning to the person asking the question. His observation provides a framework within which you can innovate products, because it suggests that "one day all of the computers in the world will be changed, 100% [...] one hundred percent of the trillions of dollars of infrastructure will be completely changed and there will be new infrastructure built on top of that."[32] That vision will require not only new sources of alternative energy, but products designed to be much more efficient, with a substantially reduced waste stream, capable of being recycled, remanufactured, or reused.

Opportunities in Developed Markets

The three major developed markets listed below dominate global economic development with over 60 percent of global GDP (all GDP data from World Bank, 2023 using generative AI query). The United States, China, and the European Union dominate technology innovation, newer green industries, intellectual property registrations, and they sustain the largest venture capital markets. These markets also dominate ESG reporting and disclosure requirements, have the dominant global listing exchanges for public companies, and have the largest subsidy, incentive, and taxation schemes, which influence opportunity, competitive advantage, and foreign direct investment.

The European Union's Cross Border Adjustment Mechanism (CBAM), for example, is one of the most talked about new boundary conditions around the world. Small- and medium-sized businesses in particular are concerned about what the taxes will be and if the impact on pricing will make them less competitive. The goal of the program is to level the playing field for all companies doing businesses in the EU by pricing in all emissions in the products sold in the EU.

Perceived subsidies by the Chinese government have created a wave of tariffs in the US and EU as those markets seek to protect their domestic green industries from lower-priced Chinese company competition.

EUROPEAN UNION	UNITED STATES	CHINA
18.35 T GDP (2023)	27.3 T GDP (2023)	17.8 T GDP (2023)
The European Fund for Sustainable Development Plus (EFSD+) aims to mobilize up to €135 billion in public and private financing for sustainable investments in partner countries.	The US Inflation Reduction Act provides ~$360 billion in financial incentives to companies that make green investments in the US.	Subsidized inputs, preferential access to raw materials, forced technology transfers, use of public procurement, and preferential administrative procedures.
Carbon Border Adjustment Mechanism (CBAM)	**U.S. Clean Tech, Tariffs**	**Kiel Institute - China subsidies are 3 to 9 times higher than other OECD countries.**

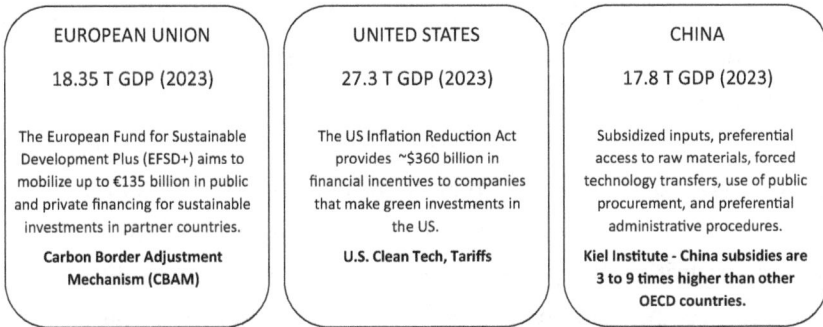

Figure 2.6 Major markets for green opportunities.

The Kiel Institute suggests that their subsidies are three to nine times higher than any other OECD country.[33] The new United States government administration has shown an interest in tariffs to drive manufacturing back to the United States, and the level of financial incentives available to companies investing in high-technology and green industries in the United States have reached historic levels.

The size of these three markets helps describe the level of opportunity available and the desire to accelerate transitions to green industries and newer high-technology industries seen as the future of economic development. The level of taxes, tariffs, and incentives will affect business decisions in many ways, both because of the overall market size and because of the how intertwined the three markets are with global supply chains.

Opportunities in Developing Markets

In developing markets, there remain significant opportunities and large financial commitments to make things happen. The Green Climate Fund, based in South Korea, lists over 15 billion USD in project finance for 270 projects in 130 developing countries on its website.[34] The United States has committed 11.4 billion USD to international climate finance in 2024.[35] The European Investment Bank and the EU Member states provided over 23 billion Euros in public climate finance to developing countries in 2021.[36] This provides new opportunities for companies with strong solutions to market those products and services in developing markets.

The United Nations Conference on Trade and Development (UNCTAD)[37] highlights the investments needs for 48 developing countries by 2030 in a variety of databases, providing a view into the funding opportunities likely to emerge in a range of countries. Figure 2.7 illustrates the percent change in the number of projects initiated with international finance support.[38]

The broad categories listed in Figure 2.8 have been aligned with the related Sustainable Development Goals (SDGs) for easy reference. In each case, there are subcategories requiring innovations to be developed, tested, scaled, and exploited. A great deal of international finance in developing markets requires alignment with the respective SDGs.

The Global Council for the Promotion of International Trade developed a report on both the challenges and opportunities for sustainable growth in emerging markets in 2024. The council highlighted some of the successes of companies like GE Healthcare in Africa, Coco Cola in Brazil, and Alibaba in Southeast Asia,[39] while also noting significant challenges in infrastructure, political instability, and skill gaps. Some of the advantages cited for emerging markets include higher growth rates, large populations, and significant urbanization.

Project Type	2021–2022	2015–2022
Infrastructure: Non-renewable power generation, power distribution and grids, internet, telecommunication and transportation.	26%	16%
Renewable Energy: Power generation	8%	21%
Water & Sanitation: Both commercial and residential	20%	13%
Health and Education: Construction of schools and health care facilities and related infrastructure.	8%	11%
Agriculture: Fertilizers, pest control and chemicals, planting, harvesting, automation and productivity enhancements	6%	–19%

Figure 2.7 Percentage change in international investment projects under development.

Category	Primary SDGs Affected
Climate Change & Biodiversity	6, 13, 14 & 15
Food Systems & Agriculture	2, 14 & 15
Energy System Transformation	7 & 13
Social Safety Reforms	1, 3, 4, 5, 8 & 10
Digital Transformation	9
Gender Equity	1, 2, 3, 5 & 8
Education Access & Transformation	4 & 9

Figure 2.8 Primary SDGs affected by investment category.

Consulting firm BCG produced a research report in 2023 highlighting how certain companies in emerging markets were not only performing well but also developing longer-term competitive advantages. "Companies with strong reputations for meeting ESG challenges in emerging markets are rewarded with major growth opportunities. They enjoy higher customer satisfaction. They gain better access to markets, investment capital, and coveted talent."[40]

Summary
- Our understanding of competitive advantage has evolved considerably since the end of World War II with different perspectives on the allocation of resources, market conditions, knowledge assets, resources, product and service demand, and relationships.
- The prominence of any perspective on competitive advantage changes with the importance of different boundary conditions.
- Market-leading firms are finding both growth and increased profits by transitioning their strategies to include more sustainable brands.
- Sustainability has become an era-defining issue since it is the major driver in defining new business boundary conditions.
- Emerging markets offer new opportunities for growth as long as companies can manage the unique challenges related to talent, political stability, and variable infrastructure.

- Enormous amounts of government subsidies are being spent to ensure that major markets maintain their competitive edge in a green economy. The scale of the investments can shift market dynamics for companies prepared to work with partnerships and make long-termcmitments.

Opportunity Reflection Checklist

Opportunity Checklist		
Is it more or less true that your organization ...		**Answer**
1	Has conducted a thorough assessment of new sustainability market boundary conditions that are shaping the competitive landscape?	☐ Yes ☐ No ☐ N/A
2	Has developed a North Star Statement that captures its long-term ambitions as a sustainable business?	☐ Yes ☐ No ☐ N/A
3	Has assessed developed and emerging market trends to understand potential opportunities?	☐ Yes ☐ No ☐ N/A
4	Has identified a series of product opportunities aligned with its sustainability ambitions?	☐ Yes ☐ No ☐ N/A
5	Has considered the availability of incentives in assessing potential opportunities?	☐ Yes ☐ No ☐ N/A
6	Has assessed the complexity of change, level of risk, resource commitment, and scale of dual impact for each new opportunity?	☐ Yes ☐ No ☐ N/A
7	Has designed several demonstration projects or experiments to test proof of concept in areas of perceived opportunity?	☐ Yes ☐ No ☐ N/A
8	Has considered the issues of scale when designing demonstration projects so the organization understands the type of capital and resource commitments required to achieve market leadership?	☐ Yes ☐ No ☐ N/A

Opportunity Checklist	
Is it more or less true that your organization ...	**Answer**
9	Has used demonstration projects as an opportunity to build and expand resource capability?	☐ Yes ☐ No ☐ N/A
10	Has used partnerships where appropriate to reduce risk, expand experimentation, and fill knowledge gaps?	☐ Yes ☐ No ☐ N/A

Scoring:

- If you answer no to many questions, you need to reflect on why. If you are not using partnerships to gain insights, ask why. If you have not assessed market subsidies, started more than one demonstration project, or considered the challenges of scale at the beginning of a project, you are likely ill-prepared to mitigate risks and meet competitive challenges.

Chapter 3

CREATING A PURPOSE-DRIVEN ORGANIZATION

The brands that will thrive in the coming years—both financially and in terms of their impact on the globe—are the ones that have a purpose beyond profit. RICHARD BRANSON, FOUNDER VIRGIN GROUP[1]

A t the dawn of the modern industrial revolution, Adam Smith wrote *The Wealth of Nations*,[2] in which he described the new era of capitalism. Since the beginning of the nineteenth century, we have seen global gross domestic product rise over 100x by 2023.[3] The global population has risen over 8x in that same extent of time.[4] In parallel with the enormous economic growth, we have also degraded our shared environment, participated in the greatest loss of biodiversity since the Cretaceous period,[5] and set in motion fundamental changes to our climate with unknown consequences. In the 2020 Annual Trust Barometer Survey conducted by the marketing firm Edelman, 56 percent of respondents said that "capitalism as it exists today does more harm than good."[6]

Challenges: Can we still have high growth and profitability and comply with sustainability standards? How do we translate the huge global challenges into businesses with impact?

What Is Purpose?

Purpose is an interesting word and has different meanings depending on the context. Traditionally, business purpose was defined as economic value creation for the owners of the business. As Milton Friedman observed in 1970, "The Social Responsibility of Business Is to Increase Its Profits."[7] Friedman was not the only proponent of this line of thinking but was highly influential in monetary policy and consumption analysis, work that led to his receiving the Nobel Prize in economics in 1976.

The American Business Roundtable, an organization of Chief Executive Officers, published a letter on Corporate Governance in 1997 that stated, "The Business Roundtable wishes to emphasize that the principal objective of a business enterprise is to generate economic returns to its owners."[8] Notably, the American Business Roundtable changed that statement in 2019 to say, "The purpose of a corporation [is] to promote an economy that serves all Americans." The roundtable further explained, "companies should serve not only their shareholders, but also deliver value to their customers, invest in employees, deal fairly with suppliers and support the communities in which they operate."[9] The statement was met with praise from advocates for sustainability but also considerable criticism by those that wish to maintain the standard of maximizing shareholder returns with minimum government interference.

Larry Fink, chairperson of Blackrock Investment, made waves in his 2018 letter to shareholders when he called for a new model for corporate governance:

The board is essential to helping a company articulate and pursue its purpose, as well as respond to the questions that are increasingly important to its investors, its consumers, and the communities in which it operates. In the current environment, these stakeholders are demanding that companies exercise

leadership on a broader range of issues. A company's ability to manage environmental, social, and governance matters demonstrates the leadership and good governance that is so essential to sustainable growth, which is why we are increasingly integrating these issues into our investment process.[10]

Larry Fink followed up his 2018 letter to shareholders with an even stronger letter in 2019 titled "Purpose and Profit." He stated, "Purpose is not a mere tagline or marketing campaign; it is a company's fundamental reason for being—what it does every day to create value for its stakeholders. Purpose is not the sole pursuit of profits but the animating force for achieving them."[11]

The sentiment that we must reinvent capitalism to meet the challenges of sustainability has attracted many new voices. Management theorist Garry Hamel, professor at London Business School, has asked leaders "to rethink the fundamental assumptions we have about capitalism, organizational life, and the meaning of work."[12] Strategy expert Michael Porter at Harvard Business School suggests, "The purpose of the corporation must be redefined as creating shared value, not just profit per se. This will drive the next wave of innovation and productivity growth in the global economy."[13] CEOs of major corporations such as Apple's Tim Cook are also on board, "At Apple, we believe that climate change is one of the world's most urgent priorities and we are deeply committed to doing our part."[14] Former Unilever CEO Paul Polman went further by describing his idea for a new type of leadership, "Net positive leaders take responsibility for their total impact on the world, lead with transparency, and focus on the long term. They aim for cooperative leadership, not just competitive leadership, because the world's problems are so immense that it is beyond the scope and ability of a single company to fix them."[15]

For this book, I define purpose as a statement of sustainable business value focused on providing solutions to critical societal challenges.

How Do We Connect Purpose to Sustainability?

Sustainability and climate change are not passing fads or social reengineering. They are based on the facts of a warming climate, growing populations, major declines in biodiversity, and growing challenges with pollution and food security. All corporations will face increased regulations and scrutiny because the status quo only yields bigger problems with less time to solve them. As such, a sustainable, purpose-based business will need to operate under a range of new boundary conditions that will evolve as the global challenges get better or worse. We'll explore these changing boundary conditions further in the following chapters, but I find it useful to also provide a simplified vision with four primary accountabilities:

1. Discover competitive differentiation in sustainability
2. Create recurring multi-capital value
3. Avoid social and environmental negatives
4. Help regenerate natural systems

Business leaders don't have to be altruistic in the search for an inspiring business. There is a huge opportunity in creating a business aligned with our shared societal challenges. For example, more than 325 asset management companies with almost 60 trillion USD under management signed on to the Net Zero Asset Managers Initiative in 2020.[16] According to the Climate Bonds Initiative, various green funding instruments (green, social, sustainability bonds and SLBs) exceeded 4 Trillion USD in 2023.[17] Venture investors have continued to put money into new sustainability companies with organizations like Redwood Materials, a U.S.-based battery recycling company receiving 1.2 billion USD in new funding in 2023.[18]

The Nordic countries of Sweden, Norway, Finland, and Denmark have established themselves as a new base for sustainable entrepreneurship. With ambitious country goals for climate action and consistent public policy, they spawned new companies like Volta trucks (electric

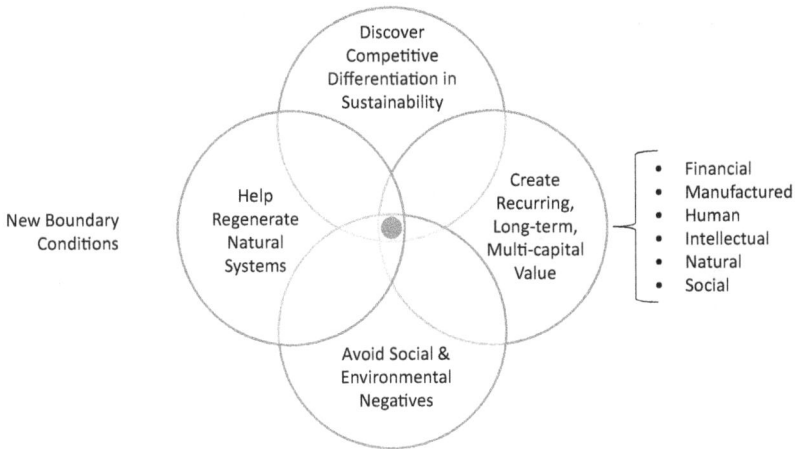

Figure 3.1 Graphic of leadership responsibility.

trucks), Zero North (shipping emissions), LUN (renewable energy), Greenely (energy management), and Infotiles (water management) to name just a few.[19] Regardless of whether there are temporary ups and downs in funding due to changing economic conditions, the drivers behind climate change and biodiversity loss will not go away. The future belongs to companies who can manage the risks and opportunities.

The goal of the leader is to frame sustainable opportunity as a purpose that is both aspirational and actionable. The sustainable purpose-based culture tends to be more collaborative simply because of the low maturity of many of the newer markets and technologies. Collaborative decision-making in such environments achieves better results. Collaboration also taps into that sense of "shared goals, shared actions and shared impact" that helps with motivation, high performance, and continuous innovation.

What Does a Statement of Purpose Look Like?

Finding a new sustainable business purpose may require exploring new business models and innovation techniques as well as educational practices for customers, partners, employees, and investors alike. All of that exploration is part of the journey of problem-solving and innovation, where the company purpose is framed around a "north star" that is a shared pursuit.

Examples of purpose statements

Rooted in Chinese civilization and embracing global culture, striving to be a world-class technology innovator, delivering superior contributions to green energy for the world, and providing a platform of pursuing spiritual and material well-being for employees!

CATL—EV Battery Company (China)[20]

Our vision is to become the Global Leader in Sustainable Energy Solutions. We believe in the power of renewables to ensure long-term energy security, and in building a more sustainable planet for future generations.

Vestas Wind Systems (Denmark)[21]

Our 2025 sustainability vision is to Pioneer Regenerative Supply Chains. At Brambles, we are working to help create a nature positive economy with re-use, resilience and regeneration at its core. It's how we can create more natural and social value than we take, while bringing emissions down to zero as soon as possible.

Brambles—Supply Chain and Logistics (Australia)[22]

Some companies take the idea of a purpose statement further by detailing the alignment of leadership and stakeholders behind the documents. The following is from the Spanish firm Iberdrola Group's Integrated and Corporate Governance Reports for 2024.

The Board of Directors reaffirms that the purpose of the companies making up the Company's group (the "Group"), and thus

their raison d'être, is "to continue building together each day a healthier, more accessible energy model, based on electricity". This purpose, focused on the well-being of people and on the preservation of the planet, reflects the strategy that the Group's companies have been sustainably implementing for years and their commitment to continue fighting along with all their Stakeholders for:

a. A real and global energy transition, based on decarbonization and on the electrification of the energy sector, and generally of the economy as a whole, that contributes to the achievement of the SDGs, particularly with respect to the reaction against climate change, and the generation of new opportunities for environmental, social and economic development.

b. An energy model that is more electric, one that abandons the use of fossil fuels and generalizes renewable energy sources, the efficient storage of energy, smart grids and digitalization.

c. An energy model that is healthier for people, whose short-term health and well-being depend on the environmental quality of their environment.

d. The drive towards more accessible conditions of well-being for all, and the creation of a society that favors inclusion, equality, equity and development.

e. An energy model that is built in collaboration withal players involved and with society as a whole, based on best governance practices that contribute to sustainability.

Does Sustainable Purpose Align with Strategy and Competitive Differentiation?

C. K. Prahalad and Gary Hamel co-authored an influential article in 1990 about the important of core competencies, "The Core Competence of the Corporation."[23] In this article, they describe the conditions of a core competence and why it is the basis for competitive differentiation. As we enter the age of sustainability, our business challenge is to align these insights, what we view as products with rarity, unique designs that are difficult to duplicate, and a superior value to the customer, as ones that also meet standards for sustainability. The greater the value to society, the greater the pressure will be to share the insights and reduce the barriers to competitors.

This issue of "sharing" innovations is a major challenge for corporations which try to protect their advantages. Legendary investor Warren Buffett stated in his 1995 annual meeting of shareholders, "What we're trying to do is find a business with a wide and long-lasting moat around it, surrounded—protecting a terrific economic castle with an honest lord in charge of the castle."[24] Although these techniques for identifying advantage and strength of capability are important for economic value creation, do they meet the conditions of sustainability and greater value to society?

Creating a purpose-based business that is governed by the principles of sustainability must satisfy several conditions.

1. Purpose must be framed in terms of sustainability challenges. It must solve a significant sustainability problem or challenge. Purpose must associate with something that really makes a difference. It must also align long-term with practices that do not harm our environment or biodiversity. The clearer the purpose, the more it can serve as a source of attraction for employees, customers, partners, and investors.

2. Purpose must go beyond what is legally viable and be subject to an ethical framework. Is this business good for society and does it preserve the rights and opportunity of future generations? It must be future-focused and long-term in nature.

3. Purpose must deliver a business that is economically viable: It must allow the business to create value in ways that support the business. Sustainability will not be solved by charity and public

grants, so any business must generate economic value in addition to other value streams.

4. Purpose must deliver multi-value impact that people can experience: It must create value for multiple groups including investors, partners, employees, and the communities where they live and work. Sustainability is a global problem and requires us to work collaboratively. Keeping all constituencies on board and aligned with your purpose requires visible gains along the way to maintain momentum and motivation.

5. Purpose must be aspirational and serve as a source of attraction: The purpose must be compelling enough to attract people who want to work on achieving it. This may be the easiest one to achieve since more and more people report that they want to work for a mission-based business that they believe in.

6. Purpose must enable business design that is actionable, scalable, and adaptable: The business underlying the purpose must be designed to scale capability in ways that are net-positive without excessive investor risks. Solutions that require massive cash infusions or that take a long time to mature are inherently risky and may extend beyond the horizons of employees and investors to participate. New sustainable businesses must be able to prototype ideas and make decisions on scale that can be managed in ways that are both economical and adaptable to changing market requirements.

Creating Your North Star Statement

A "North Star Statement," as the name implies, serves as the guiding light for your business. Ancient mariners used the north star as their fixed point of reference from which all navigation decisions were made. Without it they would be lost. The business intention of a "North Star Statement" is similar. A simple statement, easy to understand, but bold enough to capture the idea that your organization is focused on something important and meaningful to society. A small New Hampshire company in the United States, W.S. Badger Company proclaims, "We are on a journey to create a healthier world. We are inspired to make healing products and run a business where money is the fuel and not the goal, where fun is encouraged and where we cultivate good through our actions and advocacy."[25]

Other organizations such as consulting firm Accenture have developed a product design process that highlights "North Stars" as guides in the development of sustainable products.[26] In 2007, footwear and apparel company Nike partnered with Natural Step to develop a series of North Star goals to align its business with sustainability goals. "These goals address issues such as closing the materials loop, using only sustainable materials, achieving climate stability, water stewardship, thriving communities in its supply chain, and athletes acting as change agents. The intent is to have these goals inform the tools and processes that Nike designers use to design products."[27]

As Figure 3.2 illustrates, the challenge is to balance the traditional issues of complexity, risk, and scale with new opportunities for economic, social, and environmental impact. Although the North Star Statement is a company's guiding vision, transitions often start with

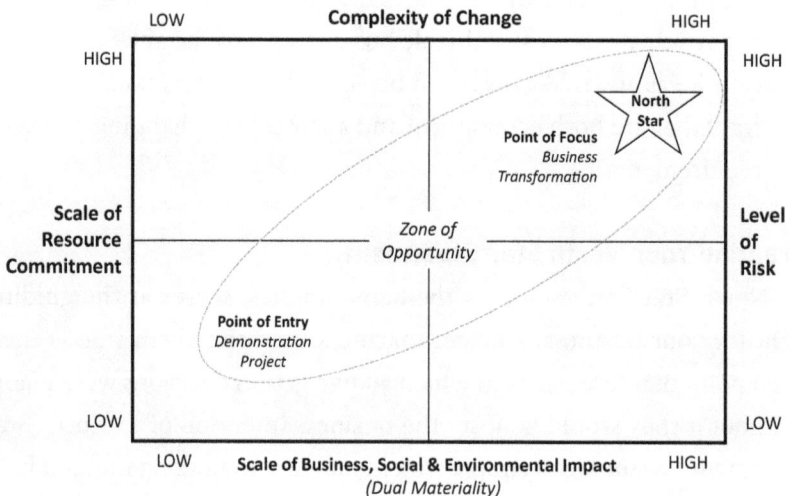

Figure 3.2 Defining your zone of opportunity.

demonstration projects that the company uses to reduce overall risk and complexity while building engagement and support for more ambitious changes.

Traditionally the North Star Statement may have been called a "mission" or "vision" statement because the goal is similar, to describe who you are as an organization, what you do, and where you are going. The difference between a traditional mission statement and a North Star Statement is that you are committing your organization to generating value as a sustainable business that has a positive impact on our shared Sustainable Development Goals (SDGs). Reducing your environmental or biodiversity impact and helping sustain the communities where you live and work must align with your capacity for revenue growth and profitability. The North Star Statement remains a reference point while events on the ground may change and people in the organization may come and go. The aspirational direction of your business, to do well by doing good, becomes core to how your business operates.

Defining Your Business Model in Ways That Reflect Your Purpose

Terms such as conscious capitalism, green capitalism, or inclusive capitalism, have come into more common usage and are generalized terms or philosophies that have value because they blend the idea of economic capitalism with a set of sustainable values. This allows them to be used as a higher-order business statement intended to guide decision-making. Sharing your business model or a philosophy of doing business is one more communication device that provides your organization guidance about how you do business. Collectively these communication practices, when done well, help shape both mental models and day-to-day behavior. A few examples of sustainable business models are listed in the world cloud as shown in Figure 3.3.

There are many new terms such as regenerative agriculture or circular economy and it is reasonable to expect that there will be new models emerging in the years and decades to come. All the business

Green Capitalism	Net Benefit	Decoupled Growth

Conscious Capitalism	Offset Strategy	Regenerative Economics	Nature-based Solutions

Ethical Brands	Inclusive Capitalism	De-growth	Multi-capital Value Creation

Green Growth	Benefit Corporations	Circular Economy	Doughnut Economics

Clean Capitalism	Shared Value Creation	Regenerative Agriculture	Integrated Thinking

Figure 3.3 Searching for a sustainable alternative to capitalism.

model labels shown above are defined in the "Sixty-Six Terms Worth Knowing" section at the end of this book.

When considering different business models, a leader might reflect on the following:

- Which business model aligns with your purpose and long-term aspirations?
- Which business model helps your organization align your North Star Statement with sustainable business practices?
- Which business model is actionable and scalable in your industry or business market?
- Which business model contributes to competitive differentiation?

A sustainable, purpose-based organization must be organized to align with the intent of global sustainability goals. Meeting the letter of current regulations should not be the guide if your goal is to do the right thing. The framing of corporate purpose must also be done in ways that align with the personal values of the people you recruit to join the organization and their ability to act and make a difference. The wording of your North Star Statement is important, as is the leadership behavior that brings the pursuit of your North Star Statement to life on a day-to-day basis.

Figure 3.4 The purpose-based organization.

Certifications and Affinity Groups—You Are Known by the Company You Keep!

One way to communicate your purpose is to participate in affinity groups that have good sustainability credentials or engage with certification organizations to establish the validity of your purpose with third-party verification. As a market matures, certifications appear in all phases of the market to enhance trust and transparency for customer decision-making. The certifications listed below are illustrations of the concept.

- Circularity
    - C2C Certified Circularity[28]—This certification was developed by the Cradle-to-Cradle Products Innovation Institute.

The organization offers a model with goals and metrics that address key stages of circularity from sourcing to product design, systems, packaging, and reuse and recycling paths.

- Operating Practices
  - ISO Standards: The ISO organization has long been the standard for role-based certification. The ISO 14064 series (-1, -2, -3)[29] offer a detailed pathway for the activities in designing, developing, and managing GHG inventories for reporting, projects, and validation.
  - There are numerous certifications for sustainable business practices like environmental management (14001), water (46001), and waste management (24161), that companies can use to demonstrate they have invested in best-in-class practices.
- Natural and Biodiversity
  - Rainforest Alliance—An NGO founded in 1987 operating in over 70 countries. The Certification Program[30] is based on their Rainforest Sustainable Agricultural Standard which has separate frameworks for companies and farmers. The goal is to promote responsible land management, preserve trees, respect human rights, and increase the livelihoods of farmers.
  - Forest Stewardship Council Forest Management Certification[31] is designed for forestry businesses to ensure they are economically viable while being environmentally friendly and socially beneficial. The certification program is based on 10 principles.
- Human Rights
  - Social Accountability International (SAI) SA8000 Accreditation program[32] is managed by the SAI organization and implemented by trained third-party organizations. It includes a review of policies and practices, risk assessments, external verification and monitoring practices, staff training programs, and issue resolution.

There are many other certifications such as the B Corp Certification[33] that assesses an organization's overall ESG performance, ETHY Certification[34] that assesses an organization's claims and alignment with the UN SDGs, and animal welfare certifications such as Leaping Bunny Program[35] provided by the Coalition for Consumer Information on Cosmetics (CCIC), to name just a few. The key questions are as follows: (1) what type of brand do you want to create, and (2) what certification or affiliation helps promote those brand values?

Summary

- A purpose-based organization establishes a clear mandate for the organization to pursue products, services, and business development that has a net-positive impact on society aligned with global sustainability principals and goals.

- A North Star Statement is an aspirational statement of the change you want to create in the world, and it serves as the source of attraction for people who are committed to making a difference.

- Newer business models are an attempt to reframe what it means to be a corporation and the value that such entities bring to their shareholders and society at large. They serve as enabling models that allow the development of capabilities needed to service the new corporate purpose.

- Aligning with global intent is different than saying we can meet one or more of the 169 sub-measures of the SDGs. The goals themselves are our latest and best attempt to describe a way of living more harmoniously with our environment from generation to generation. Leaders must recognize that sustainability practices will evolve and so will the goals. Our purpose must accommodate new learning and experience and always be future-focused on doing what is right.

- Certifications are a way of affiliating your brand with standards of trust and transparency. The certification process can also offer a roadmap for staff in operating functions or a gap analysis. Both are useful for helping your organization make positive progress.

Purpose Reflection Checklist

Purpose Checklist		
Is it more or less true that your organization ...		**Ranking**
1	Has a clear Statement of Purpose that describes how your business adds value to the communities where you live and work?	1 2 3 4 5 6 7 8 9 10
2	Developed the Purpose Statement in collaboration with key stakeholders?	1 2 3 4 5 6 7 8 9 10
3	Takes action to make the Purpose Statement visible both internally and externally and ensures that it is communicated as core to everything you do?	1 2 3 4 5 6 7 8 9 10
4	Has established links between the idea of purpose, behavior, and impact in company incentive and performance management programs to insure alignment?	1 2 3 4 5 6 7 8 9 10
5	Has incorporated the intent of the Purpose Statement into company rituals, such as new employee orientation programs and transition programs when leaders are promoted to positions of greater authority?	1 2 3 4 5 6 7 8 9 10
Total Score		

Scoring:

- Score less than 25—Something is wrong, or you have just started. A low score may suggest you have a statement of purpose but have not implemented it. If your Purpose Statement has been in place for more than one year and you have a low score, it is evidence of a lack of leadership support that needs to be addressed immediately.

- Score less than 40—You are on the right track and likely need to work ensuring the Purpose Statement is anchored in company practices.
- Score greater than 40—Keep working to keep the purpose alive in your daily decision-making and all business planning. It is an important reference point for building an ethical brand and developing ethical leadership capability.

Chapter 4

BUILDING A MODEL OF WORKING KNOWLEDGE

Three rules of work: out of clutter find simplicity. From discord find harmony. In the middle of difficulty lies opportunity. —ALBERT EINSTEIN, NOBEL PRIZE–WINNING PHYSICIST[1]

Developing a working knowledge model is an essential leadership exercise in determining what knowledge is useful to the organization and key individuals. At a high level, there are four components:

1. What does the organization need to know about sustainability?
   a. What knowledge is needed to remain in compliance with regulations?
   b. What knowledge is needed to create competitive differentiation?
2. Who needs to know what?
3. How do we learn the knowledge we need to know?
4. How do we use that knowledge to adapt and succeed in a sustainable future?

The first three components (the model) are addressed in this chapter, and the fourth part (the application) is addressed in the chapters on identifying a competitive advantage and enabling a culture of sustainable-oriented innovation.

Start with a Big Picture Perspective

The simple fact is that we are collectively at the beginning of a journey to create a new form of capitalism that combines the benefits of market-driven economic growth with a more balanced view of respect for life on Earth and our shared environment. To participate in this journey, we need to reflect on the knowledge and skills that will enable success. What remains the same and what is different? What do you need to know to lead a sustainable organization?

> **Challenges: What does a leader need to know to lead a sustainable business? What knowledge from the past is still good, and what new areas of knowledge become necessary? What models can we use to clarify which information is relevant to our specific businesses?**

Our goal should not be to throw out what we've learned about business development and innovation. That accumulated knowledge has led to huge changes in our standard of living and lifted billions of people out of poverty. Since the beginning of the industrial revolution, per capita global income has increased over 800 percent.[2] At the start of the nineteenth century, poverty stood at 60 percent of the world's population. By 2005, that had dropped to 20 percent.[3] Two hundred years ago, only one in five adults had experienced some formal education. Now that ratio is reversed.[4] A lot of good has happened. Instead of throwing out what we have learned, we must rethink our collective goals and channel our innovative energy within new boundary conditions that include reducing the negative impacts of our behavior on our environment, helping to regenerate natural systems, while generating new types of capital. The general concept of what leaders are asked to do is illustrated in Figure 4.1, although this is rarely the starting point that a business uses for mapping knowledge needs. Consider the figure as a simple description of expectations, but lacking the specificity needed to identify requirements.

I have added to the chart the three Sustainable Development Goals (SDGs) most closely associated with the twin challenges of climate change and biodiversity loss. These goals drive a significant number of the compliance reporting requirements for businesses. The intersecting circles illustrate your basic boundary conditions. Every business must seek out competitive differentiation in order to satisfy customers in some market segments. The difference here is that you are pursuing those opportunities within the specific sustainability challenges of SDGs 13, 14, and 15. The need to create multi-capital value is part of the idea of dual materiality, which can include broader value creation outcomes including financial, manufactured, intellectual, human, social and relationship, and natural capital. Avoiding environmental harm and helping to restore natural systems are entirely new considerations for most businesses. Leading a sustainable business will require the

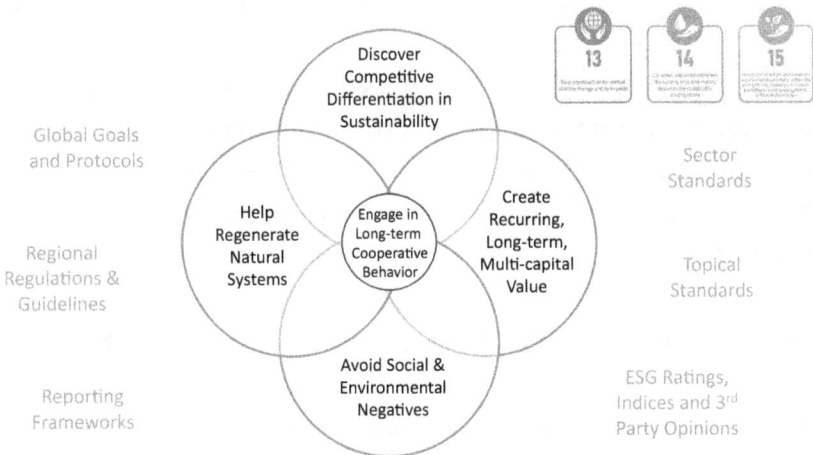

Figure 4.1 Emerging boundaries and leadership accountability.

creation of business practices that embed these boundary conditions in all decision-making.

These broad boundary conditions may be useful for an extended time because they are general categories. However, since we lack progress in some goal areas and there is uncertainty with predicting changes on a global scale, it is likely there will be ongoing detailed changes in policy as well as increased pressure on business leaders and politicians.

Starting with a big picture perspective presents us with a challenge. There are more than 250 global, multilateral environmental treaties, conventions, protocols, agreements, and amendments still in force since 1970. Which ones are important to your business or your policymakers? There are many more agreements related to key areas like human rights and biodiversity, and individual countries add regional and local requirements that add complexity to any cross-border or multinational business.

As an illustration, the current Intergovernmental Panel on Climate Change (IPCC) climate assessment summary for policymakers is 34 pages in length.[5] The full summary report is 115 pages.[6] Each assessment adds three additional sub-reports on (a) the physical science, (b) impacts, adaptation and vulnerability, and (c) mitigation of climate change. If you have more specific interests, you can do a deeper dive into subsections on poverty, health, food, and water, or ocean ecosystems, or take a geographic view in areas like Asia, Australasia, or North America. If you want a comprehensive view of all of the data, you can read more than one thousand pages. By the time you have consumed all of that information, you have not read one of the treaty documents, regional laws, or policy guidelines that try to put that information into action.

Since 1990 when the first IPCC report was published, there have been six full climate assessments, each with four reports and fourteen special reports. The sixth assessment published in 2022–2023 runs to 8,000 pages. There have also been Human Development Reports published most years since 1990[7] and dozens of Conference of the Party (COP)

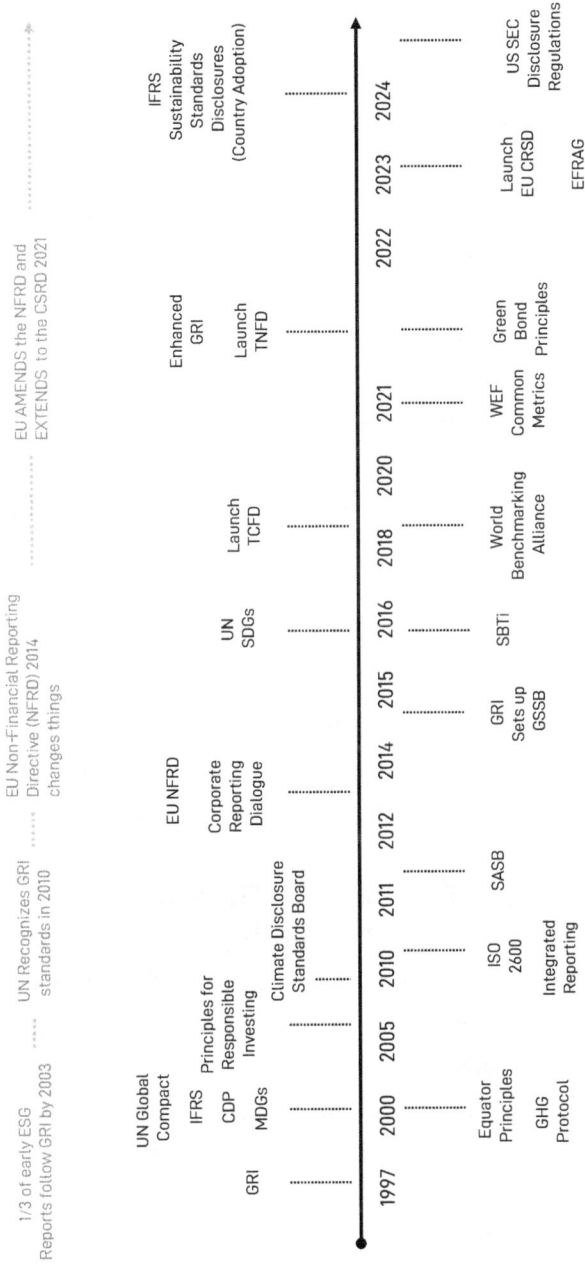

Figure 4.2 Historical timeline of sustainability policy and guidelines.

Reports published for both the Framework Convention on Climate Change[8] (1992) and the Framework Convention on Biodiversity[9] (1992), to name just two of the many important intergovernmental treaties that may affect your organization. This information as well as the reports, policy standards, and guidance frameworks for organizations such as the Sustainability Accounting Standards Board[10] (SASB) would amount to tens of thousands of pages of information. To consume and study this amount of information is an unreasonable task. As we develop leaders for a more sustainable future, we need to provide a knowledge model that allows them to make sense of what is important.

Everything Connects to the Science

We don't usually expect most business leaders to be well versed in science, but sustainability and climate change are not like any other business driver in memory. The science does not depend on market acceptance of products, on relative profitability, or delays desired by consumers or politicians. The science is based on empirical evidence and will be relentless in driving change. The issue for business leaders is to understand the basic conclusions, accommodate the risks and trends in planning, and learn to adapt to achieve competitive advantage.

The basic science of climate change is not difficult to understand. We learned in the nineteenth and twentieth centuries that certain gases can create a "greenhouse effect," a term first coined by Swedish chemist Svante Arrhenius in 1896. The discovery of the phenomenon predates the term and is credited to the work of American Eunice Newton Foote in 1856[11] and Irish physicist John Tyndall in 1859.[12] Although the historical figures involved in these discoveries are interesting, it is not really relevant to most business leaders. The core idea is that changes to atmospheric gases causes warming. This is a scientific fact.

It is equally relevant for most business leaders to understand that the atmospheric gases that cause the greenhouse effect include more than carbon dioxide. The Greenhouse Gas (GHG) Protocol[13] is the current standard for emissions and recommends the measurement of seven gases including carbon dioxide, methane, nitrous oxide, hydro-fluorocarbons, perfluorocarbons, sulfur hexafluoride, and nitrogen trifluoride. All of these gases come from industrial and agricultural processes and the burning of fossil fuels. To improve emissions accounting, these gases are translated into carbon dioxide equivalents through formulas that normalize each gas for its capacity to trap the sun's energy. This is referred to as CO_2eq.

Again, there is interesting historical context for the GHG protocol which starts with a collaboration between the World Resources Institute and several major corporate partners including General Motors and British Petroleum, but the key issue for leaders is the concept of controlling GHG emissions. This is embedded in the Paris Agreement (2015), which is itself linked to the UN Framework Convention on Climate Change, UNFCC (1992).

Finally, the excess energy that is trapped by the Greenhouse Effect is largely stored in the worlds' oceans. Research from the Global Climate Observing System (GCOS)[14] indicates that 89 percent of the energy is stored in the oceans, 6 percent is stored in the land mass, 1 percent is stored in the atmosphere, and the balance is absorbed by the cryosphere (ice). Rising seawater temperatures and the absorption of excess energy by the major ice fields and glaciers contributes significantly to melting and potential sea-level increases. The excess ocean energy is also the engine for many extreme weather events including hurricanes and cyclones.

The reliability of climate change research changes as you move from empirical data focused on discrete questions like, "Does CO_2 cause atmospheric warming," to systemic questions like, "Will there be more hurricanes this year in Florida?" Systemic predictions often involve a large number of variables that make precise predictions challenging. Using hurricanes for example, the United States National Oceanographic and Atmospheric Administration (NOAA) makes annual predictions for different regions.[15] For the Caribbean area this is based in part on ocean temperatures off the west coast of Africa, which for 2024 are above normal. However, other factors are at play such as the presence of a El Nino or La Nina weather system in the Pacific Ocean and the amount of sand blown westward from the Sahara desert. It's important to remember that the probabilities cited in scientific research reports are generally based on average scenarios. When business leaders consider risk assessments, the conclusions often reflect what can go wrong. The good news is that the global and regional predictive climate models are getting much better, as are the satellite systems for measuring things like forest losses or regional changes in temperature. Artificial Intelligence will likely have an enormous impact in this area and both modeling and risk assessments will improve.

One of the key challenges for most business leaders will be the capital allocation decisions associated with new sustainable innovations. In the area of solar panels, as an example, the global manufacturing capacity has grown from approximately 5 gigawatts in 2005 to over 1.2 terawatts in 2022, according to the International Energy Agency.[16] Projections are for the market to double by 2028.[17] At the same time, solar cell conversion efficiency has increased from about 14–15 percent in the year 2000 to 20–22 percent today.[18] What happens with all of the old panels? Is there a waste problem? Is the best market opportunity in panel manufacturing or for subcontracting key components like solar panel power inverters?

A key consideration for any leader is risk assessment. Where scientific principles and trends focus on average scenarios, good business planning often considers scenarios that exceed the average by >25 percent. As such, good risk assessment of a business portfolio will consider how many assets or facilities you have in each geographic area that may be at increased risk for hurricanes, tornadoes, sea-level rise, and extreme heat stress. Risk from one-time events is one thing; risk from continual events is another. A good business leader is not tasked with considering how an average year of storms will affect their business, but rather, can they survive a bad year or remain profitable if the negative trend continues.

The core business questions always start with opportunity and competitive advantage. Is there opportunity for you to drive sustainable growth? How will new public policy affect opportunity? How do you need to evolve your business capability to capitalize on these opportunities? How are boundary conditions likely to evolve with the growing market? How do you balance perceived risks with opportunities?

For a business leader at the level of a general manager or a non-scientific functional manager, it is enough to know the general scientific principles. Predicting changes in weather patterns, potential changes in agricultural or fishing productivity, or the movement of insects or diseases is hard to do. It is also hard to remain scientifically current as a general manager even if you previously held positions in functional specialties. Remaining current on changes in battery technologies, new solar films, or energy storage solutions requires a commitment to consuming a substantial amount of new information on a regular basis.

Sustainability knowledge will continue to be a rapidly changing field. Artificial intelligence should provide a boost to predictive modeling. Changes to earth system modeling, for example, have made enormous strides since the 1980s with faster computer speeds, advances in machine learning, and new insight engines promising to accelerate the number of variables that interact with the partial differential equations used in such models to integrate them forward in time. That will greatly improve weather forecasting and help industries in agriculture, infrastructure, building trades, among many others. In the meantime, anything with the potential for significant economic, environmental, and social benefit or disruption should be based on input from current specialists and third-party opinions. Here are seven scientific issues for all business leaders to understand (general knowledge):

- The Greenhouse Effect exists and it contributes to global warming.
- Nine gases are recognized as creating a greenhouse effect and seven are regulated under the Greenhouse Gas (GHG) Protocol

- All greenhouse gases are normalized and measured as carbon dioxide equivalents or CO_2eq.
- Most of the excess energy from the sun that is reflected back to earth by the Greenhouse Effect is absorbed by the oceans.
- There is a higher probability of extreme weather events with continued increases in greenhouse gases.
- Improvements in artificial intelligence and machine learning are likely to make predictive climate models and risk assessments more accurate in coming years.
- Almost all new sustainability technologies will likely improve in efficiency while reducing in unit costs since we are still in the early stages of large-scale adoption.
- Additional sector-specific knowledge may be warranted as new scientific knowledge evolves.

Think About Boundaries with an Outside-In Perspective

As discussed in Chapter 1, boundary conditions are the set of characteristics, limits, and opportunities within which companies operate. The information model listed in earlier chapters is an outside-in model of boundaries as illustrated in Figure 4.3. Although everything starts with an understanding of the importance of the basic science, the real work starts when we translate those drivers into market changes, new public policy, and longer-term trends.

I see outside-in assessments used more by entrepreneurs than large legacy companies. The entrepreneur is often looking for insights, market gaps or new customer needs, and doesn't bear the burden of worrying

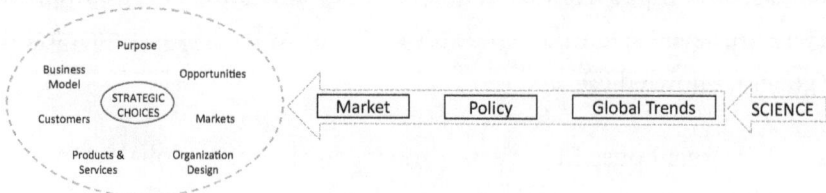

Figure 4.3 Boundary condition outside-in model.

about an existing organization or customer base to support. They may be inspired to action by the science of atmospheric gases, the promise of artificial intelligence, or the radical goal of transforming the energy sector. They can choose to jump right into issues of plastic pollution in the oceans, carbon neutrality, waste recycling, circular resource consumption or biodiversity enhancements, as they imagine new business opportunities. Eventually they will need to consider the same strategic choices that a more mature business faces, but the mental model of an entrepreneur and the perception of risk are often quite different.

Although this can be a useful perspective, many legacy businesses prefer an inside-out perspective because they are always reflecting on the impact of any changes on legacy revenue streams. The starting point tends to be the existing products, customers, and markets with scenarios developed that show the risks of climate change and greater compliance, but also the relative impact on the business of possible changes from competitive behavior. Large-scale business transformations are change resistant for many reasons to resist change. The fact that climate change poses an existential threat and is different than any other historical business driver, does not seem to affect the human tendency to prefer the status quo when it comes to embracing change.

Think About Boundaries with an Inside-Out Perspective

Most legacy businesses always consider how boundary conditions affect existing operations as well as how they open new doors. In each case, any discussion of change leads to the issue of competitive differentiation. Are you an early innovator or a late adopter? Are there large incumbents dominating the business space or is it dominated by smaller firms and new businesses?

Figure 4.4 shows a more traditional hierarchy with the drivers at the top, leading to the legacy strategy and any new strategic choices. Then come organizational decisions that are often long lasting such as tax and legal status, an exchange listing, the basic design of the organization, as well as the markets and customers a business chooses to pursue. Since

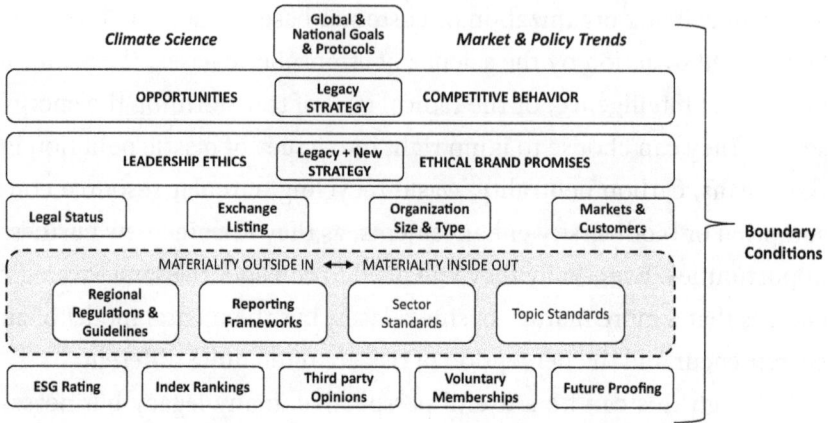

Figure 4.4 Overall boundary model.

guidelines, frameworks, and standards are often delegated to functional, geographic, or business line leaders to sort through, they come next followed by various operational decisions and voluntary choices.

Regardless of the approach you choose, all decisions must eventually be filtered through a number of regulations and frameworks to determine your costs and opportunities. Understanding how each of those considerations is evolving over time tells you something about the risks involved in both short- and long-term capital allocation decisions.

Legal status

Legal status comprises both the location and design of the organization and the tax implications of those choices. Companies have long made decisions on locating their headquarters in a country with lower corporate tax rates. That is the attraction of basing your business in the Cayman Islands, Barbados, or the Isle of Jersey. Other countries like Ireland have attracted big tech companies because of favorable tax treatments and access to the European Union (EU) markets. In that example, location is not just about tax rates, but the tariffs associated with the wider EU market. Specific industries like textiles have often made decisions on where to manufacture and assemble based on domestic content legislation in their customer markets.

Recent consolidation in the UK steel industry gives us a good example. The United Kingdom decided to leave the EU in a decision widely called Brexit, based on a national referendum in 2016 that became effective in 2020. While the UK was within the EU, its exports to mainland Europe were regulated as a member state. Now it is viewed as an importer that needs to be regulated like any other country. This had some immediate impact on where companies with operations in both the UK and the EU chose to expand, but the impact will become more significant in 2026 with the expansion of new EU import regulations. "The carbon tax, known as the carbon border adjustment mechanism (CBAM), is key to the EU's net-zero strategy, and will tax imports where the goods are linked to significant carbon emissions in their country of origin. That means it is likely to affect the most carbon-intensive U.K. exports like steel, aluminum, and electricity, because the levy is applied when taxes on polluting outside the EU—the carbon price—are lower than inside the bloc."[19] This becomes particularly significant for the UK steel industry that exports almost three-quarters of its production to continental Europe.

Tata Steel offers a useful example of how boundary issues often combine. The Tata Steel Port Talbot plant in Wales is one of the company's older steel plants. It has been making steel in the same location for generations, so the closure of the blast furnaces and the installation of electric arc equipment was big news. The immediate impact is the loss of thousands of jobs and the importation of steel supplies from Europe, at least until 2027 when improvements may change the plant output, in theory. The fear is that the closures are a fact and any commitments to future production are just words in a plan.

Some British politicians claimed "net zero hysteria"[20] when the announcement of job reductions was made, the implication was that emissions were the main driver. The big reduction in jobs made this a significant news story. Policy changes may be involved since emissions targets in difficult-to-decarbonize industries like steel are always a consideration. But the changes to Port Talbot were undoubtedly also due to the plant's legal status because the location of a facility after Brexit was a factor. Global trends were likely also relevant since disruptions to global supply chains with the COVID pandemic affected the steel markets.

If you look at similar Tata Steel plants, such as the older IJmuiden plant in the Netherlands, were they subject to the same reductions and changes? Apparently not! The changes at Port Talbot will absolutely reduce emissions, but it will also give Tata more flexibility in the nature of the products produced. Businesses make decision that reduce risk and improve their prospects for future growth. Although sustainability targets were undoubtedly part of the picture, so were a realignment of Tata's European production, the location of non-EU facilities, and of course the new cross-border carbon adjustment mechanism. Legal status and tax issues are always part of longer-term strategic planning.

Global goals and protocols

There are more than 250 international multilateral environmental agreements in effect since 1970. Although there are others that predate this period, the vast majority of such agreements follow the 1972 Stockholm Intergovernmental Conference, also called the United Nations Conference on the Human Environment.[21] This is the starting point for many corporate sustainability experts. One of the outcomes of this 1972 conference was the creation of the United Nations Environmental Programme, which is the co-facilitator (with the World Meteorological Organization) of the IPCC.

With some agreements, there is a cascading relationship of amendments, such as between the Vienna Convention for the Protection of the Ozone Layer[22] (1987) and the Montreal Protocol on Substances that Deplete the Ozone Layer[23] (1985). The Montreal Protocol was subsequently amended on five separate occasions with the latest changes happening in 2016 with the Kigali Amendment.[24] The general flow is from convention to protocol to amendment if you are following UN treaty classification system, so the 250 international agreements generally break down into smaller subsets based on purpose and evolve over time. There are several that every leader should be familiar with since they are the foundation of our current definition of sustainability.

- The Big Three Multilateral International Agreements on Sustainability:
  - The UN Framework Convention on Climate Change 1992 (UNFCCC)—This is the basic reference point for all international negotiations on climate change. It follows the creation of the IPCC in 1987, which was intended to settle the scientific issues. It recognizes the problem of GHG emissions, establishes a general goal of reducing their impact, and establishes some broad mechanisms for follow-up. It was drafted at the UN Conference on Environment and Development (1992), which is frequently called the Rio Convention. That same event also saw the development of the UN Framework Convention on Biodiversity (UNCBD) and the United Nations Convention to Combat Desertification (UNCCD). Collectively, they are designed to work together to address what was then seen as the major global adaptation issues associated with climate change.
  - The UNFCC evolves over time with COP meetings and leads us to the Kyoto Protocol (1997) which is notable for its focus on carbon credits, the Cancun Agreements notable for REDD+ (reducing emissions from deforestation and degradation plus), more formal reduction pledges, and the Durban conference which set up the Green Climate Fund.The UN Framework Convention on Biodiversity (UNCBD)—This convention had three main goals. "The conservation of biological diversity; the sustainable use of the components of biological diversity; and the fair and equitable sharing of the benefits

arising out of the utilization of genetic resources."[25] The most recent change to this Convention is the Kunming-Montreal Global Biodiversity framework.[26] This framework lays out four primary goals for 2050 with 23 targets to be achieved by 2030. These include, "Four overarching goals to be achieved by 2050 focus on ecosystem and species health including to halt human-induced species extinction, the sustainable use of biodiversity, equitable sharing of benefits, and on implementation and finance to include closing the biodiversity finance gap of $700 billion per year.

- Among the twenty-three targets to be achieved by 2030 include a 30 per cent conservation of all land, sea and inland waters, 30 per cent restoration of degraded ecosystems, halving the introduction of invasive species, and $500 billion/year reduction in harmful subsidies."[27]The United National Convention to Combat Desertification (UNCCD)—although this Convention is less well known than the Conventions on biodiversity and climate change, it has also been signed by 197 parties and has an impact beyond the issue of desertification. It is the only legally binding agreement to cover the issue of land degradation, which becomes a larger global issue as variable weather patterns, prolonged drought, and temperature changes affect agricultural production, water conservation, and overall land productivity.

- The Paris Agreement (2015) stands alone as the most referenced agreement. It established the Nationally Determined Contributions (NDCs), a five-year review cycle, and several long-term strategies such as the Enhanced Transparency Framework (ETF) which started in 2024. The Paris Agreement is unique in that it has been signed and ratified by 193 countries plus the EU (as of 2023) in a legally binding agreement. This represents an estimated 98 percent of all global GHG emissions (according to the EDGAR[28] database).

- Transforming Our World: The 2030 Agenda for Sustainable Development[29] happened in parallel to the Paris Agreement but is useful to discuss separately because it gives us the SDGs, the general vision of a sustainable future, the 2030 target date, and the often referenced targets of 2°C change in average global temperature, and 1.5°C if possible. This was agreed at the Sustainable Development Summit held at UN Headquarters in New York in September 2015.

  It is often presumed that the Paris Agreement also gave us the target of Net Zero by 2050. This is partly true in the sense that the parties to the Paris Agreement asked the IPCC to define the impact of limiting average global temperature and the possible pathways of achieving this. The IPCC responded with a special report in 2018, which outlined various pathways for reducing emissions, keeping average global temperature change to 1.5°C by 2030 and achieving net zero by 2050.

- The Big Four Agreements from the United Nations Global Compact:

  The United Nations Global Compact[30] was originally established in the year 2000, the same year that the UN established the Millennium Development Goals (MDGs). The Compact has 10 principles aligned to labor and human rights, the environment, and anti-corruption. The purpose of the Compact was to add a focus on ethics in corporate governance not directly covered in the goals. Although the MDGs have evolved into the SDGs, the Compact remains a voluntary membership programs for organizations to align themselves with both the current SDGs as well as the ethical standards that emerge from the 10 principles aligned to one of the international agreements listed below.

  - The Universal Declaration of Human Rights[31]—This was an important post–World War II document passed by the United Nations in 1948 that establishes the rights of all people to equality, freedom, and dignity, and specifically prohibited slavery and indentured servitude in all forms. The document which has 30 articles also provides for the rights to education, to marry, work, and join a union. The declaration is quite broad in defining rights and is a worthwhile read since many of these rights are still restricted in different parts of the world. Many of the SDGs dealing with gender, equality, poverty, and sustainable production can trace their history to the wording of this document.

- The International Labour Organization 's (ILO) Declaration on Fundamental Principles and Rights at Work[32]—The Declaration on Fundamental Principles and Rights at Work was originally passed in 1998 and recently updated in 2022. The key provisions update some issues already covered in the Universal Declaration of Human Rights, such as slavery, by specifically calling for bans on compulsory labor and child labor. It also reinforces other topics like collective bargaining and the need to eliminate employment discrimination, and adds in new issues such as worker safety and the provision for a safe and healthy work environment.

- The Rio Declaration on Environment and Development[33]— This was a declaration presented at the Rio Summit in 1992 and established 27 principles that cover everything from transboundary activities to support for common environmental legislation, the equitable right to development for all people's as well as issues of poverty reduction and the need to prioritize least development country activities in world affairs.

- The United Nations Convention Against Corruption[34]— Established in 2004, the Convention is a broad-based document of 70 articles that addresses issues of corruption prevention, training, and technical assistance. Unlike many other intergovernmental agreement that lack enforcement mechanisms, this Convention addresses key issues such as law enforcement cooperation, extradition, sovereignty, and asset forfeiture. This convention is a key foundation provision for any anti-corruption policy of a multinational corporation or any corporation handling large amount of cash assets or foreign deposits.

- There are many other international agreements that may apply depending on what part of the world in which your business operates. There are also non-treaty guidelines such as the United Nations Guiding Principles on Business and Human Rights (UNGPs),[35] which was endorsed by the UN Human Rights Council in 2011. The principles align well with the OECD Due Diligence Guidelines or Multinational Enterprises on Responsible Conduct referenced below that many large corporate organizations have used as a methodology for managing cross-border and multi-country business behavior.

Exchange listing

One of the rarely understood international organizations is the Sustainable Stock Exchange Initiative (SSE) developed with the support of the United Nations Partnership Programme. The SSE was co-developed by the United Nations Conference on Trade and Development (UNCTAD), United Nations Environment Programme Finance Initiative (UNEP FI), and the group that coordinates the Principles for Responsible Investing (PRI). According to the SSE, "In September 2015 when the SSE launched its Model Guidance for exchanges, less than 10% of stock exchanges around the world were providing guidance on reporting environmental, social and governance (ESG) information for their market. This gap in guidance on ESG reporting leads to incomplete corporate information, creating a challenge for investors seeking a comprehensive view of a company's material issues."[36]

The goal of harmonizing reporting disclosures for listed companies directly relates to SDG Goal 12 on responsible Production and Consumption. "Target 12.6: Encourage companies, especially large and trans-national companies, to adopt sustainable practices and to integrate sustainability information into their reporting cycle."[37] As of today, the SSE collects data from 122 global stock exchanges and reports that only 59 percent have written ESG reporting standards for their listed companies. Ninety six percent of the companies with reporting guidance align with the GRI standards, while only 71 percent of those with guidance align with the Carbon Disclosures Project and even fewer (67 percent) ailing with the TCFD recommendations.[38] The SSE Exchange database includes over 64,000 listed companies (as of June 2024).

Each of the major standard organizations have committed to increased harmonization, although this process is only several years old. Many stock exchanges and governments have made statements about mandatory disclosures and improved disclosure alignment, although many still maintain voluntary programs. If you are a Malaysian listed company, for example, you would need to review the Bursa Malaysia Sustainability Reporting Guide.[39] The Malaysia Exchange has mandatory reporting, and also made efforts to align its policies with the ISSB. Despite similarities, it becomes important to understand their definitions for who qualifies as a "large listed issuer," their implementation timeline, and other factors. In countries such as Singapore, "Climate reporting is mandatory for all issuers on a comply-or-explain basis."[40] For a Singapore listed company (SGX), "comply and explain" has been the standard since 2016 and continues through FY 2024. Reporting on scope 1 and scope 2 emissions becomes a requirement in FY 2025, and scope 3 emissions reporting will be required in FY 2026.

According to the SSE, mandatory rules were in effect in 27 markets[41] in 2023, including the European Union, the United States, and the United Kingdom. China is the largest market still operating with a comply-or-explain ESG reporting framework, but they introduced new standards for feedback in May of 2024, with implementation scheduled for 2027–2030[42].

Organization size and type

Organizations structure themselves primarily as business units, geographic units, and functional groups within a parent organization and then through ownership structures such as joint ventures when they have less than a full stake in a company. Regulations may specify compliance for organizations by size and type by indicating that rules apply to a specific industry (e.g., automobiles), by their capital structure (e.g., a listed company), their size as measured by annual turnover (e.g., revenue), by their physical presence (e.g., geographic location of operations and employees), or other characteristic.

The new EU Corporate Sustainability Reporting Directive (CSRD) will apply to approximately 50,000 companies. The basic requirements apply to companies with more than 500 employees beginning in 2024. Companies with >250 employees, >50 million Euros in turnover, or >25 million Euros in assets are covered in 2026, and smaller companies with >10 employees, >900,000 Euros in turnover, or >450,000 Euros in assets are covered in 2027. According to the European Parliament, "For nearly 50 000 companies in the EU, collecting and sharing sustainability information will become the norm, compared to about 11,700 companies covered by the current rules."[43]

Analysis by the London Stock Exchange Group (LSEG) suggests substantial number of non-EU companies will also be affected by the new regulations. "Our analysis showed that at least 10,300 non-EU companies will be subject to the CSRD. From a geographical perspective, 31% of the non-EU companies affected are American, followed by 13% Canadian and 11% from the UK. Rather less are from other countries: 8% are Japanese, 6% Australian, 5% from the Cayman Islands, 3% from Bermuda and 2% from Mainland China. In total, companies from more than 60 countries will have to report, including a few from tiny economies like Bahrain and Zimbabwe."[44]

Although many smaller companies are not included in disclosure agreements, they may be affected. Small- to medium-sized companies around the world are part of the global supply chain and need to supply large customers with emissions and other data for compliance reporting. Governments like Malaysia have been proactive in creating support documents to help local companies. The Securities Commission of Malaysia in partnership with Capital Markets Malaysia created the Simplified ESG Disclosure Guide (SEDG) for SMEs in Supply Chains released in October of 2023.[45] This is supplemented with sector guides for agriculture, construction and real estate, energy, manufacturing, transport, and logistics. The commission also provide an SEDG Human Rights and Labour Practices Guide[46] as well as disclosure templates. Although a variety of government agencies around the world have called for incentives and subsidies to help SMEs, the practices are not widespread. Of those that do, the government of Malta offers a good example.[47] The government reimburses 75 percent of the cost of an initial ESG report for SMEs that meet certain criteria, up to 3,000 Euros, as long as the work is done through an approved ESG advisor.

Markets and customers

The world has three major economic powerhouses in the United States, the European Union, and China. Using World Bank Group data for 2023, global gross domestic product is approximately 106 trillion USD. China's GDP is 17.79 trillion USD, or 16.8 percent of the total, the EU's GDP is 18.35 trillion USD, or 17.3 percent of the total, and the United States has a GDP of 27.36 Trillion USD, or 26 percent of the global total. Collectively that equals 60 percent of all global production and consumption.[48] Forward-looking forecasts suggest these three trading blocs will continue to dominate, although emerging economies will tend to grow faster. The big change in the forecast is that India may grow into the top ranks and Europe will drop in comparative rank by 2050. From a sustainability perspective, this means that guidelines and best practices will remain dominated by these players.

For many companies that sell on a business-to-business basis, your largest customers tend to drive your sustainability data collection and reporting concerns. Yes, you are concerned about your general reporting and compliance, but a failure to provide your major customer with scope 2 or scope 3 data may mean the loss of business. As such, customer requirements are increasingly driving transformation in small- to medium-sized businesses and in countries that are export oriented, regardless of domestic sustainability policies.

Several southeast Asian countries which have been key suppliers in the automotive supply chain are all vying for a leadership position in the new EV supply chain. If you are working in Malaysia as an example, then paying attention to the National Sustainability Reporting framework (NSRF)[49] makes sense. The Malaysian government has made green growth central to its economic plans and has several efforts underway to insure harmonization and alignment with their larger export markets. According to a report from Reuters and the Malaysia Investment Development Authority (MIDA), "The nation's New Investment Policy is designed to promote support across green economy growth sectors and shift industries towards enhanced ESG adoption. The measures available include support for companies through workforce training, the development of sustainable financing models, including incentives for adopting green technologies and grants to fund R&D in new green technologies, as well as the introduction of new standards and regulations for ESG disclosures."[50]

Transfertech is a leading printer with production sites in Thailand, Germany, and Vietnam. They use various printing technologies to produce customer-specific products in sportswear, team sports, active wear, fashion, home, and footwear for customers such as Adidas, Puma, Tesco, Champion, Hanes, Reebok, and Nike. They fit into a scope 2 or scope 3 category for emissions for most customers, but also contribute to reporting on waste, water usage, labor practices, and many other categories depending on customer requirements. For companies such as Transfertech, maintaining a competitive position in the marketplace means meeting or exceeding all of the sustainability standards where your customers operate. The company has been proactive in building solar panels on its factory and parking lot roofs, invested in waterless printing systems, use environmentally friendly dyes, and developed comprehensive recycling programs. Transfertech is also a Bluesign Systems Partner since 2015,[51] which validates its commitment to industry best standards for reducing environmental impact.

Regional regulations and guidelines

Regional regulations are the key interpretations of international agreements by regional or national legislative bodies. Individual countries may have additional interpretations and regulations designed to support local businesses or protect local markets so it's important to be respectful of changes in any market where your business decides to operate.

Many smaller economies are developing regulations that mimic the larger economies, although the most stringent policies may be voluntary. This allows local businesses to design their services to be compliant with their primary customer markets while still adhering to the less rigorous demands of the local market.

- *Europe* —The 27 member countries of EU are each signatories to the Paris Agreement (2015). Unlike many other areas of the world, the EU is also signatory to the Paris Agreement as well as many other international treaties and conventions. This provides Europe with a two-level framework of accountability, both country and EU level, that is unique and is one of the reasons it leads the world in sustainability policy and transition.
  - European Green Deal[52] is a policy directive established 2019 that outlines the EU's commitment to build a sustainable future and a goal to make Europe the first net-zero carbon-emitting continent. It sets out objectives for a circular economy plan, a carbon taxation system (Cross Border Adjustment Mechanism—CBAM), a review of energy fuel subsidies, a "farm to fork" agriculture strategy, and a EU forestry strategy, among other objectives.

- The EU Climate Law entered into effect in 2021 effectively writes into law the many of the policy objectives of the EU Green Deal. It is globally significant since it sets legally binding targets for members states to achieve 55 percent net reductions in greenhouse gases by 2030 and net-zero greenhouse gases by 2050.

- EU Sustainable Finance Framework has several important provisions. The first is the Sustainable Finance Disclosure Regulations (SFDR)[53] that went into effect in 2021 and specifically applies to the financial services industry and empowers the European Commissions to determine how participating companies must comply with the various directives. The core issue of the directive is to improve transparency for ESG disclosures that relate to investment impact. It introduces the idea of level 1 (entity) disclosures, which have been in effect since 2021, and level 2 (product) disclosures, which went into effect in 2022. There are updates annually. The second provision is the CSRD,[54] approved in 2022, that mandates how large corporations and listed SMEs report on ESG issues. This mandate replaced the Non-financial Reporting Directive (NFRD),[55] originally implemented in 2014, because, "reports often omit information that investors and other stakeholders think is important. Reported information can be hard to compare from company to company, and users of the information are often unsure whether they can trust it."[56]

- The EU Taxonomy for sustainable activities,[57] passed in 2023, is an update to the original taxonomy developed in 2020. The goal is to help define what activities within the EU are considered environmentally sustainable. The latest updates to the taxonomy are specifically designed to address emerging concerns of greenwashing. The taxonomy covers the six major policy areas developed in the Green New Deal including, biodiversity, the circular economy, climate change mitigation and adaptation, pollution, and water and marine resources, and is connected to the SFDR disclosures to create greater transparency on how products are designed.

- The upcoming Corporate Sustainability Due Diligence Directive (CSDDD)[58] has been approved by the council of the EU but is not yet law and may not be in effect for several years. This will, however, require companies to not just disclose material issues, but have a working process to limit emissions in line with the 1.5°C Paris targets.

- *China*—The Chinese market is one of the largest markets in the world and has also committed itself to ambitious targets. China launched its "Made in China 2025" policy in 2015 and committed itself to green innovation in manufacturing. Although China is a world leader in solar cell production, electric and electric hybrid vehicles and related industries, its manufacturing remains among the world largest polluters.[59] It has lagged in mandatory disclosure rules as well as in offsetting mechanisms, but has recently implemented a series of more ambitious program including a mandatory national carbon trading scheme (2021).[60] On a voluntary basis, 86 percent of the top companies listed on the Shanghai and Shenzhen stock exchange comply with voluntary ESG reporting according to J.P. Morgan (2020). However, the ESG compliance landscape is more fragmented and less rigorous than in other markets. Given China's government policy to be a major player in sustainable development, it is reasonable to expect changes to mandatory behavior in years to come.

  - Guiding Opinions on Building a Green Finance System,[61] introduced in 2016, laid out the information disclosures required in China, primarily for listed companies.
  - Clean Production Audit Measures,[62] adopted in 2016, is a policy intended to put some regulatory teeth in pollution control. It requires companies that use toxic materials and use energy in excess of national consumption targets, and companies

that emit pollutants into the air or water in excess of national targets to conduct an audit. The goal of the audit process is to identify areas for improvement.

- Listed Company Governance Code, updated in 2018,[63] is a general outline of corporate governance requirements. Although this is not a sustainability document, it is reasonable that any changes in board committee requirements or sustainability reporting would also be updated here.
- Measures for the Administration of Information Disclosure of Regulated Companies,[64] released in 2021, updates corporate governance mechanisms. This does not specifically address sustainability but tightens up general corporate reporting and addresses a range of topics from stock issuance to corporate reporting.
- The Measures for the Administration of Legal Disclosures for Enterprise Environmental Information passed in 2022 defines the annual disclosure reporting requirements.
- *The United States*—The United States market is less consistent than the European Union and has both state, regional, and national guidelines. The state of California, for example, has the most rigorous requirements and has recently enacted the "Climate Corporate Data Accountability Act," and the "Greenhouse Gases: Climate-related Financial Risk Act."[65] These have specific disclosure requirements for what are referred to as "reporting entities" and "covered entities" with revenue thresholds and some industry exclusions.
  - United States Securities and Exchange Commission— The latest rules are included in the "The Enhancement and Standardization of Climate-Related Disclosures for Investors,"[66] which became effective on March 28, 2024.

There are significant differences between the US SEC climate reporting rules and EU CSRD, notably around the type of reporting needed for scope 3 emissions and the nature of impact reporting. There are also differences within the United States between the SEC rules and the California rules.

Overall, there is more alignment between the EU and other large economic jurisdictions such as Australia, Singapore, and Hong Kong that are each planning to adopt standards developed by the International Sustainability Standard Board (ISSB). At the moment, the ISSB standards appear to be the preferred practice model of companies that do more voluntary reporting.

There are other important regional networks such as the Organization for Economic Cooperation and Development (OECD). This entity was formed in 1961 and was originally an organization mostly of western European countries plus the United States and Canada. It later expanded to include Japan, Korea, Australia, New Zealand, as well as countries in Latin America South America and Eastern Europe. The OECD has 38 member countries as of 2024. The OECD Due Diligence Guidelines for Multinational Enterprises on Responsible Conduct[67] is an important framework document introduced in 1976 with the idea of providing guidance on maintaining standards on the environment and human rights in supply chains and business relationships. There have been six updates since it was first published with the most recent in 2023.

There are emerging markets worth watching such as India, that are expected to significantly grow their economy by 2050 to become more of a force in the global economy. India has not had a tradition of robust ESG reporting programs, but has required a level of voluntary reporting since 2009. It introduced its framework expectations in the Business Responsibility Report (BRR) of 2012.[68] The new and improved Business Responsibility and Sustainability Report (BRSR) introduced in May 2021, will require a range of ESG disclosures.[69] It includes 140 questions on 98 mandatory indicators and 42 voluntary questions on leadership indicators. It was introduced as a voluntary practice in 2022 and become mandatory in 2023 and was based on the India Securities and

Exchange Commission National Guidelines for Responsible Business Conduct.[70] It only applies to India's largest listed companies. It is also tracking closely with the requirements outlined in the Global Reporting Initiative (GRI) and the final requirements from the Task Force on Climate-Related Financial Disclosures (TCFD). The performance metrics need to be included in an Indian company's annual report.

Reporting frameworks

At the current time, there are six major reporting frameworks generally recognized as critical to compliance reporting for sustainability. Each is listed below with a brief explanation. Leaders at a general management level need to understand the basic issues and reporting requirements involved. Leaders who have delegated responsibility for data collection and reporting need to have more detailed knowledge and must remain up to date on the multi-year implementation calendars and annual updates.

- GRI—An independent non-profit organization, it is the oldest of the major reporting sustainability frameworks, established in Boston in 1997 after the Exxon Valdez oil spill disaster. Its first reporting guidelines were published in 2000 with a focus on standards that were universally applicable to all businesses. It's stated mission is, "GRI envisions a sustainable future enabled by transparency and open dialogue about impacts. This is a future in which reporting on impacts is common practice by all organizations around the world. As provider of world's most widely used sustainability disclosure standards, we are a catalyst for that change." It was primarily known for its universal standards for most of its history, but added sector standards in 2021 to align better with the SASB, which has been primarily focused on accounting standards.
- IFRS Foundation—Independent non-profit:
  1. CDP (formerly the Carbon Disclosure Project)—The Carbon Disclosure Project was established in 2020, making it the second oldest of the major sustainability reporting frameworks.

It shortened its name to CDP in 2013. Its specific focus has been on climate impact with disclosures in the areas affecting climate change, water security, and deforestation. As such, it is much more narrowly focused than other frameworks and was established because of perceived gaps in reporting from existing disclosures. In 2012, it added the idea of planetary boundaries to its reporting and disclosure methodology.

2. International Integrated Reporting Council (IIRC)—This entity was established as the International Integrated Reporting Committee in 2009 and renamed the International Integrated Reporting Council in 2011. The key concept in Integrated reporting is to create a comprehensive and integrated picture of value creation that incorporates the idea of multi-capital formation and a short-, medium- and long-term view. A pilot project was established in 2011, the first standards published in 2013, and most recently updated in 2021. This is now a consolidated part of IFRS since 2021.

3. The Value Reporting Foundation was established in 2021 at COP26 when the IIRC and the SASB merged. The goal was to combine the best accounting practices with the ideas of wholistic Integrated Thinking (the way an organization has a dialogue on value) with best integrated reporting frameworks (the way an organization publishes its story).

4. Sustainability Accounting Standards Board (SASB)—The SASB was established in 2011 and is now part of the IFRS Foundation. The reporting is an accounting disclosure framework designed to standardize the language investors use to evaluate companies with the expanded concerns of sustainability. It is intended to identify the types of sustainability-related risks and opportunities that may affect investor interests such as business growth, loss scenarios, cash flow, cost of capital, the ability to finance operations or similar concerns.

5. Task Force on Climate-related Financial Disclosures (TCFD)—The TCFD was created in 2017 to develop recommendations on expanded disclosures. It was chartered by the Financial Stability Board (FSB) and issued its final report in 2023. "Our disclosure recommendations are structured around four thematic areas that represent core elements of how companies operate: governance, strategy, risk management, and metrics and targets. The four recommendations are interrelated and supported by 11 recommended disclosures that build out the framework with information that should help investors and others understand how reporting organizations think about and assess climate-related risks and opportunities."[71]

- Climate Disclosure Standards Board (CDSB):
  1. The CDSB is a broad directive published in 2022 by the European Parliament.[72] As with many of the document listed above, reading and understanding the directive takes some work. It covers over 36,000 words and approximately 90 pages. It has specific sections on sustainability reporting, consolidation reporting, obligations of member states, general standards, and standards for SMEs. It also makes broad statements regarding its purpose such as, "The Green Deal aims to decouple economic growth from resource use and ensure that all regions and Union citizens participate in a socially just transition to a sustainable economic system whereby no person and no place is left behind. It will contribute to the objective of building an economy that works for the people, strengthening the Union's social market economy, helping to ensure that it is ready for the future and that it delivers stability, jobs, growth and sustainable investment."[73]
  2. The newer European Sustainability Reporting Standards (ESRS) were produced by the European Financial Advisory Group (EFRAG) and adopted by the European Commission

on July 31, 2023. ESRS can be thought of as an evolution in thinking since it serves as the new compliance framework for the CDSB. It serves to standardize and enhance reporting across EU member states and adds in a new level of rigor for non-financial reporting.

- US SEC Climate Disclosure Rules—The United States Securities and Exchange Commission adopted new rules in 2024 to standardize climate-related financial disclosures.[74] The big changes are the materiality thresholds for scope 1 and 2 emissions, although there is some flexibility on the boundaries for those emissions. The rules also allow for aggregate reporting of emissions rather than a line-item level of detail. The SEC extended adoption timelines and eliminated requirements for scope 3 reporting that had been in earlier drafts. The SEC has classifications for smaller reporting companies (SRCs) and emerging growth companies (EGCs) that are exempt from reporting.

Other notable reporting frameworks include industry and function-specific frameworks such as the Supplier Ethical Data Exchange (SEDEX), and the Global Real Estate Sustainability Benchmark (GRESB).

Sector standards

Organizations like the SASB are dedicated to providing investors with accurate information to support better decision-making. They divide their compliance reporting into 77 industries across 11 sectors such as consumer goods (7 industries), renewable and alternative energy (6 industries), and transportation (9 industries). In this model, there are five main reporting dimensions for each business: the environment, social capital, human capital, your business model and innovation, and leadership and governance.

There are then 26 general issues categories. For example, in the environment dimension there are six general issues categories including air quality, energy management, and water and waste management. Each

Framework	Mandatory	Impact	Financial	Environment	Social	Governance	Sector Standards	Audit
European Sustainability Reporting Standards (ESRS)	Yes	Yes	Yes	Yes	Yes	Yes	Yes	Yes
International Sustainability Standards Board (ISSB)	Requires jurisdictional adoption		Yes	Yes		Limited	Requires jurisdictional adoption	Limited
Global Reporting Initiative		Yes	Limited	Yes	Yes	Yes		Yes
Sustainability Accounting Standards Board (SASB)			Yes	Yes	Yes	Yes		Yes
Task Force on Climate-related Financial Disclosures (TCFD)			Yes	Yes		Limited		Limited
Task Force on Nature-related Financial Disclosures (TNFD)		Yes	Yes	Yes		Limited		Limited

Figure 4.5 Framework comparison.

of the other dimensions have between three and seven general issues which are considered industry agnostic. Within each industry there will be industry-specific disclosure topics. The SASB website offers a materiality finder so you can choose your sector of interest, such as Consumer Goods, and then a specific industry such as Household and Personal Products. The materiality map will then indicate which of the 26 general issues have disclosure requirements. You can then drill down into the specific standards.

Topical standards

The GRI uses a three-tiered standard architecture of universal standards (similar to the SASB general issues), sector standards, and topical standard, of which there are a total of 120 disclosure issues. The universal standards are further subdivided into (1) foundation standards such as accuracy and verifiability, (2) general disclosures which include items such as stakeholder engagement your organizational structure and governance, and (3) material topics which align with other framework sector standards. Sector standards are currently available for 40 sectors (2023). In GRI terms, a topical standard may be on economics, the environment, and social topics.

Depending on the framework, the use of words such as general issue versus universal standards is largely a function of the organization. Sector standards are designed to be industry specific and reflect the unique aspects of the businesses in that industry. Topical standards start from a relevant category of reporting. GRI started with the idea of common reporting topics with a focus on voluntary disclosures, transparency and impact, while SASB is focused on accounting standards being adapted to sustainability with a focus on investor decision-making.

Ratings

Sustainability ratings are a form of benchmark that can be used to compare company performance. It is a standardized form of a third-party opinion based on a consistent scoring rubric. Rating scores and rating categories provide a standard upon which multiple companies in the same industry can be judged on a comparative basis. At least that's the concept. The scoring categories can be several dozen and may include industry-specific subcategories with hundreds of data points. Some companies like MSCI use a letter rating scale from CCC (Lowest) to AAA (highest), which is comparable to the credit rating scale. Other firms such as S&P Global use a scale from 0 to 100 and have category levels. CDP (formerly the Carbon Disclosure Project) offers both a framework and a rating scale of A through D. Some of the scale and rating differences are summarized in Figure 4.6.

The rating firm EcoVadis claims that since 2007 when it was founded, it has assessed (or rated) 130,000 companies.[75] According to the company, it offers, "risk mapping, actionable scorecards, benchmarks, carbon action tools, and insights guide a resilience and improvement journey for environmental, social and ethical practices across 200 industry categories and 175 countries."[76] Assessments score four categories: the environment, labor and human rights, ethics, and sustainable procurement. Companies are awarded medals and badges depending on their score (0–100). Companies such as Siemens, Fujifilm Business innovation, Signify, Omron Global, and Apollo Scientific, all have achieved the highest rating called Platinum Medal level, which represents the 99th percentile of rated organizations. EcoVadis separately produces annual recognition programs such as the EcoVadis Sustainable Procurement Leadership Award.

Many investors find the rating appealing since they are used to common rating scales like credit risk assessments; in addition, they also like the brand value of using large organizations like Bloomberg, FTSE Russell (a subsidiary of the London Stock Exchange), or ISS (Institutional Shareholder Services). The ratings or scores may be used for overall ESG performance, as evidence of long-term risk management or in some instances as evidence of policies on diversity or human rights. Having a common rating rubric makes a lot of sense; however, there is little consistency in methodologies between organizations,

Rating Company	Sustainalytics (Subsidiary of Morningstar)	MSCI (Morgan Stanley Capital International)	CDP Scores (Carbon Disclosures Project)	Bloomberg	Dow Jones Sustainability Index	Rifinitiv (Subsidiary of the London Stock Exchange Group)	ISS (Institutional Shareholder Services)
Scoring	0 (low risk) to 40+ (High risk)	AAA (Highest) to CCC (Lowest)	A (Highest) to D (Lowest)	0 (low) to 100 (High)	0 (low) to 100 (High)	0 (low) to 100 (High)	A+ (4.00) Best to D- (1.00) lowest)

Figure 4.6 Differences in various ESG ratings.

little common regulation around the world, and poor data quality in some instances. Like policy frameworks, there is some effort at harmonization, but there is also commercial interest in differentiation by individual rating agencies offering the largest ESG database, data on unique characteristics, or data that is updated more frequently.

Third-party opinions

Although a business may have impressive sustainability reporting, governments, investors, partners, and some customers may want an independent voice to verify the authenticity of any claims. Companies routinely use an outside auditor to review their financial records. Products shipped from one country to another are tested by a third party prior to acceptance. International payments from an escrow account are often contingent on the bank receiving documentation of satisfactory product acceptance testing. Having third-party documentation on sustainability issues serves a similar purpose. It suggests that your performance can be aligned and compared with industry standard practices. An example of a third-party organization that does target validation is the Science-Based Targets initiative (SBTi). The SBTi started as a collaboration among the World Wide Fund for Nature, the UN Global Compact, the World Resources Institute, and CDP. It sets standards and criteria so companies can use measurements that support the common targets on the Paris Agreement (2015). Target data can be submitted to SBTi which will validate that the submission meets all SBTi criteria.[77]

Independent opinions are also essential in products like carbon credits, which are both widely used and increasingly criticized. The global carbon market reached 949 billion USD in 2023,[78] based primarily on EU carbon allowance credits and the accompanying EU aviation allowances. The European Trading Scheme has been one of the largest global carbon markets since its inception and is based on company-submitted emissions reports that must be certified by what is referred to an "accredited verifier" under Article 3 of the Commission Implementing

Regulation (EU) 2018/2067.[79] The details of credit verification are specialist-level functional knowledge, as are other requirements related to product certification. Under the CSRD, there are different types of assurance that map to the IAASB International Standard on Sustainability Assurance 5000,[80] which is expected to go into effect in 2025, including:

- Limited Assurance—This is the basic standard that says there is nothing in the reporting that seems an obvious misstatement. This goes into effect in 2026.
- Reasonable Assurance—This is a higher level of standard that require the verifier to review the underlying documentation to any sustainability claims. This goes into effect in October 2028.

Third-party opinions are also valuable for monitoring issues associated with a broad range of international and national agreements including:

- Any issue requiring specialized scientific input and risk assessment.
- Health and safety issues on job, construction, or extraction sites.
- Vendor monitoring on health, safety and respect for forced labor regulations, particularly with migrant workers.
- Any local sites with unique permitting or policy provisions such as the reuse of recycled materials in construction or production, the use of local labor, respect for cultural heritage sites, or the permitted use of water resources.
- Security concerns in conflict and post-conflict areas as well as areas with political instability.
- Gender equity provisions, particularly if your industry or region has been cited for such concerns.
- Any situation requiring the ongoing, multi-year monitoring and verification of environmental, social, or biodiversity impact.

- Any situation with court-ordered monitoring.
- Data gathering for communities where promises have been made for remediation, adaptation, or impact assessments.
- Any issue requiring an independent audit, product certification, or recertification.
- Any biodiversity issue that requires specialized knowledge.
- Any cultural heritage issue that requires specialized knowledge.

Unintended Consequences Are Part of the Transition Process

Public policy often creates outcomes not foreseen by the policymakers. If we use domestic content laws as an example, they are intended to help local manufacturers and encourage job creation. In the textile industry, domestic content laws in the United States have created a supply chain where footwear or clothing is subdivided into component parts that are created, processed, sewn, or assembled in different countries. After circulating among three or four countries, the components are then shipped to the United States for final assembly. All of this is done to meet the legal requirements, while also meeting the cost and quality standards set for the product. The carbon footprint, the waste produced, and the logistics complexity are not the driving factors; meeting the letter of the law is!

What Do You Need to Know?

What each leader across an organization must know varies with the person's industry and role within the business. The most senior leaders have broader responsibility, more knowledge of markets, customers and strategy, and less in-depth knowledge. Functional leaders and specialists have a greater role for in-depth knowledge and an ability to engage in critical thinking with outside specialists.

The general model within a sustainable business is outlined in Figure 4.7 and is referred to a "C" model. This differs from many legacy knowledge models because of its emphasis on climate and sustainability

Climate Competencies

Horizontal bar = generalized knowledge

Core Capabilities

Vertical bar = in-depth abilities

Collaborative Credibility

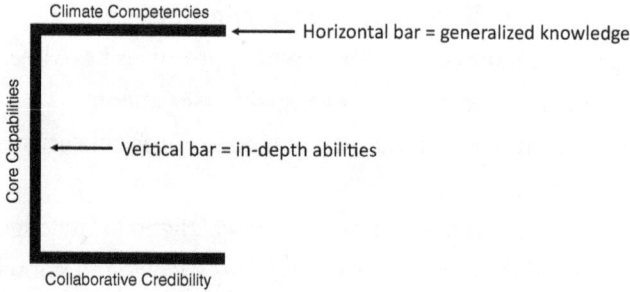

Figure 4.7 C profile.

competencies and the collaborative skills needed to work with a broader range of stakeholders.

The model illustrates that any leader in a sustainable business must have at least a generalized understanding of the basic science that is affecting their industry and the policy trends that help shape competition in their markets.

The design of a global businesses varies widely. A company can have one business unit, dozens, or even hundreds. The more diversity there is in a business, the more generalized the skill set is for executive leadership, as they focus more on the organizational design, the business strategy, capital allocation, risk management, and the like.

The large pharmaceutical company Johnson & Johnson, for example, has several hundred divisions grouped into several lines of business. The technical focus of the products and services in any one division requires the functional leader to have expertise in that product category, the science that underpins it as well as the customers, markets, and competitors. Sustainability adds another layer of boundary conditions to the existing considerations. The executive leadership of Johnson & Johnson has a different focus, which includes how issues like sustainability affect their long-term strategic choices and the major capital allocation decisions of the overall business.

The science of climate change is unlike any other traditional business concern. It will not disappear because it is expensive or inconvenient;

it is not subject to market readiness; and it will not abate because we don't have the time or resources to address the challenges. As the planet warms, there will be inevitable consequences to deal with. That forces you to either spend a lot of time on mitigation efforts or invest time to get ahead of the market by examining where opportunities exist for doing well by doing good.

The question, what do you really need to know, illustrates the idea of "working knowledge." Since the endorsement of the IPCC in 1988 by the United Nations General Assembly,[81] there has been an ever growing and accessible body of knowledge on climate change. Parallel innovations such as the United Nations Human Development Index[82] (1990), the Human Development Reports[83] (1990), the Millennium Development Goals[84] (2000), and the Sustainable Development Goals[85] (2015) have broadened the generally accepted boundaries of what we call sustainability.

The big picture issues need to be understood by any executive leader, such as the key issues in the GHG protocols that define the seven regulated GHGs. The GHG also described the idea of scope 1–3 emissions. All of this is useful information for a business leader. The details of the guidance then breakdown into the 15 categories of emissions. That level

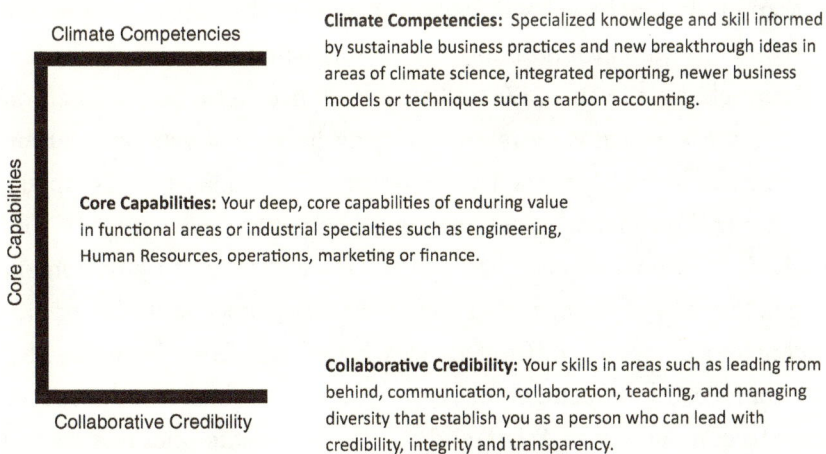

Climate Competencies

Core Capabilities

Collaborative Credibility

Climate Competencies: Specialized knowledge and skill informed by sustainable business practices and new breakthrough ideas in areas of climate science, integrated reporting, newer business models or techniques such as carbon accounting.

Core Capabilities: Your deep, core capabilities of enduring value in functional areas or industrial specialties such as engineering, Human Resources, operations, marketing or finance.

Collaborative Credibility: Your skills in areas such as leading from behind, communication, collaboration, teaching, and managing diversity that establish you as a person who can lead with credibility, integrity and transparency.

Figure 4.8 C profile competency categories.

Functional Leadership

Climate Competencies

Core Capabilities

More depth of abilities in core functional domains

Collaborative Credibility

Executive Leadership

Climate Competencies

Core Capabilities

More depth of abilities in general management domains

Collaborative Credibility

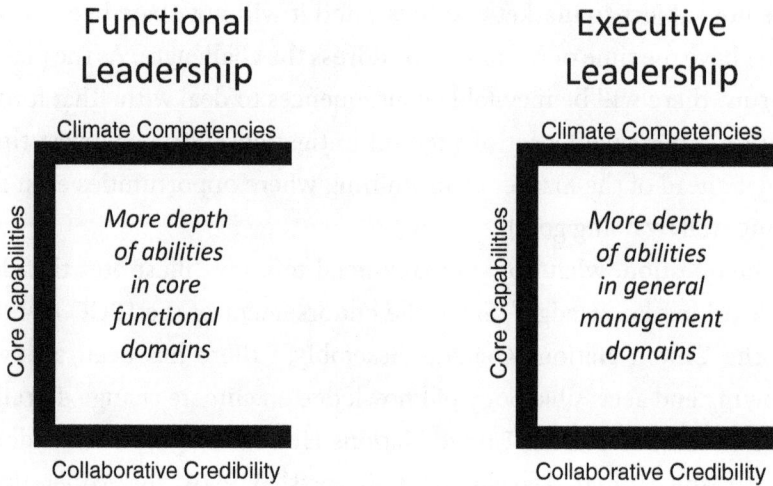

Figure 4.9 C profile for executive and functional leaders.

of detail needs to be delegated to the appropriate operating or functional leader to work through the plans on how to select, train, and collect data from vendors or to identify vendors that have the software to track the emission data.

Figure 4.10 illustrates how knowledge of the same or similar topics may delegate to different levels of responsibility and span of control.

Many individual roles will need to evolve with changes in how the markets innovate around multi-capital formation. We already see significant changes in the CFO and senior finance roles, because carbon credits are appearing on many company balance sheets and carbon pricing can be highly variable. According to McKinsey and Company, "Better carbon management can be a competitive advantage."[86] The McKinsey authors suggest that "Carbon management is highly context dependent: the challenges that a United States–based software or biotechnology company confront are clearly different from those faced by, for example, a steel, cement, or energy corporation based in Europe, or a media company in an Asian market." The leadership roles responsible for carbon management need to understand the markets, regulatory

	Narrow		Broad
Business Leader	Managing carbon pricing risk Third party opinions	ESG ratings Regional frameworks GHG strategy	Global goals NDCs Global frameworks Value creation & business strategy
Level of Authority Span of Control	Localized frameworks Customer frameworks Competitor behavior	Industry frameworks EU taxonomy Accredited verifiers	Regional frameworks Transition implementation
Function or Team	Environmental Product Certification	EU financial collateral directive EU product labeling 15 types GHG data	Functional strategy Integration with other Functions Partnerships

Narrow   Broad

Level of Responsibility

Figure 4.10 Knowledge delegation by level of authority.

frameworks, and value-creation models in order to manage the process, but more importantly, they need to develop the insights to offer business guidance on competitive differentiation and risk assessment.

In larger centralized companies, a dedicated sustainability organization may serve as a center of excellence (COE) and the coordinator of compliance activities. In more decentralized organizations, the roles described below may exist in functional, geographic, or business units. In any case, the same questions apply: What roles are needed to support our sustainability strategy and how do we organize that knowledge to get the work done? The idea of the "C" profile still applies to each role, but there is a judgment to be made regarding the depth of knowledge required for climate and sustainability capability. Examples include:

- Generalized sustainability roles: A large sustainability function may include sustainability reporting analysts and people responsible for specific market-oriented or customer-oriented reporting.
- Functional specialists: This includes roles aligned with key functional groups.

- Marketing may include roles such content creator for sustainable brands, a sustainable market research analyst, an environmental storyteller, or a sustainable brand manager.
- Human Resources may need support from a human rights officer or a specialist in diversity, equity, and inclusion.
- A finance function may add an impact assessment manager, a green bond specialist, an ESG risk manager, or a sustainability rating manager.

- Sector specialists: This may include roles aligned with an industry sector such as agriculture and include soil scientists, wildlife biologists, and land use planners.
- Topical specialties: There are certain generalized roles that may be aligned with a market, procurement, or operating group depending on the organization and industry. These may include specialists in any of the key efficiency categories such as energy, transport, material, or packaging optimization.
- Certification specialties: If your organization participates in one or more certifications at the organization or product level, then certification roles often exist as do specialists in the supporting processes such as life-cycle assessment.

Most organizations then supplement their internal functions with content specialists in areas such as LEED building consulting, and auditors or assurance specialists for environmental, energy use, carbon footprint analysis, and waste compliance.

What Is the Best Way to Learn?

I've previously tackled this challenge in the book, *Sustainability Is the New Advantage* (2019), where the following chart first appeared. The chart illustrates the different types of knowledge that need to be acquired. Rule-based knowledge has specific definitions or formula and tends to be where scientific or empirical knowledge resides. Heuristics fit the "good enough" standard that is frequently used in business and serve as the home for what we often call best practices. Social knowledge or social rituals are team-based knowledge sharing that help communicate the group we belong to, our shared purpose, or the stories that help illustrate how we should behave. Finally, the box for mental models reflects how we think. A key to change in our mental models is we need to see possibilities where we can create new products and services that do not harm the environment and that create new forms of value over time.

Figure 4.12 illustrates how some of the knowledge discussed in previous sections would apply to this model. People can generally read and understand the explicit disclosure requirements since they tend to have clear definitions and do not depend on specialized knowledge to interpret. Selling practices are different since they often depend on context and relationships and are best debriefed in a group setting to discover all of the key characteristics, steps, and options. Rituals are naturally team-based activities since it is the group dynamics that are key to the knowledge exchange. Mental models are often the hardest to define and change since they reflect implicit thinking dynamics that are hard to observe. Yet bold innovations, market disruptions, and high performance are often characterized by individuals able to see insights and opportunities where others cannot.

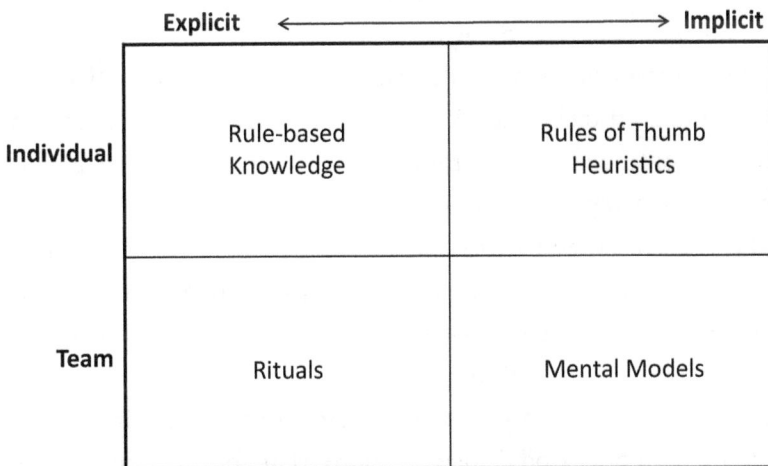

	Explicit ⟵——————————⟶ Implicit	
Individual	Rule-based Knowledge	Rules of Thumb Heuristics
Team	Rituals	Mental Models

Figure 4.11 Four box learning matrix.

	Explicit ⟵⟶ Implicit	
Individual	Disclosure requirements (ISSB) Emissions definitions (SBTi)	Practices for selling new customers products with sustainable attributes
Team	Onboarding programs that share sustainable value creation success stories and emphasize ethical decision making	Strategy dialogues on finding competitive differentiation in sustainability

Figure 4.12 Four box learning matrix with examples.

If we take the learning process one step further and ask, what techniques best apply to each learning challenge, we see the options outlines in Figure 4.13. In this chart, we have expanded the four-box matrix to a nine-box matrix to allow for a spectrum of possibilities and to distinguish group from team activities. The former being people of a common job function or level, while the latter refers to groups of people with some level of work interdependence.

Training and development are a key part of any knowledge management system as are an understanding of the most effective way to document and transmit new knowledge. In larger organizations, there may be a continuous flow of innovations and practices such as the use of mass balancing techniques in chemical companies. The business implications of a practice like mass balancing needs to be known at the senior leadership level, but there will be a cascade of operational knowledge that needs to arrive at the appropriate level of delegated authority throughout the organization.

Understanding the new ISO 22095 standard for managing the information "chain of custody" may be appropriate for the technical teams and auditors and the crediting schemes may need to be understood by

Explicit ←————————————————————————→ Implicit

	Explicit		Implicit
Individual	E-Learning Digital Learning	Apprenticeships Job Rotations	Coaching Appreciative Inquiry
Group	MOOCs	Centers of Excellence	Communities of Practice
Team	Classroom Training Cohort On-line Blended Designs	Team Events Signature Events Case Study Teams	Start-ups Action Learning Innovation Labs

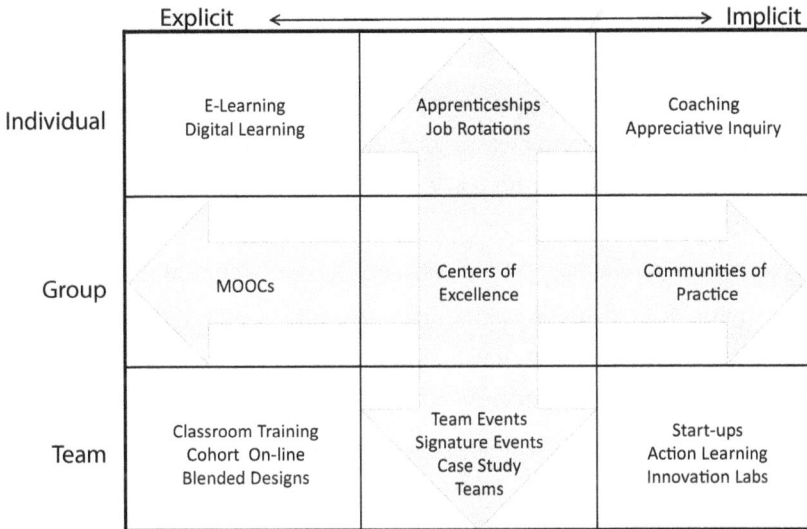

Figure 4.13 Nine box learning matrix of techniques.

key finance personnel and the product management teams. The training and development activities should vary depending on the knowledge type and its application in the value chain.

Summary

- The core requirements for any leader are to find competitive differentiation in sustainability, create recurring, long-term multi-capital value, avoid environmental and social negatives and help rebuild biodiversity and a healthy environment.
- Every organization must build its own working knowledge model. The boundary conditions of your knowledge model include science, global trends, policy guidelines and frameworks, as well as market conditions.
- The complexity of your knowledge model may include issues such as your legal, listing or tax status, as well as condition related to where you are headquartered, the geographies where you operate, and the geographies in which your customers and suppliers are situated.

- Each role in your organization can have a "C" profile that comprises their core functional capabilities, their climate competencies as well as collaborative capabilities needed to operate within your competitive space and boundary conditions.

- Scientific principles and trends are useful to establish a sense of urgency, emerging compliance issues, and possible areas of opportunity.

- Organizations can choose to lead the market with voluntary disclosures and can gain new insights with memberships in organizations that give them access to a broader range of perspectives.

- Business risk assessments and strategy scenarios are different than scientific assessments and must consider negative trends, opportunities, and weighted scenarios.

- Your business organization design involves a series of choices that influence your business boundary conditions. Optimizing your organization may require revisiting historical choices as well as making new ones.

- If you have any question about the appearance or value of a business decision, always look to subject it to a third-party opinion as part of your validation process.

Working Knowledge Reflection Checklist

Knowledge Checklist	
Is it more or less true that your organization ...	**Ranking**
1 Chose the location of your headquarters and your legal status to optimize your business opportunities to create long-term, recurring multi-capital value.	1 2 3 4 5 6 7 8 9 10
2 Has a created a process for aligning business plans with the Sustainable Development Goals and applicable international treaties and conventions.	1 2 3 4 5 6 7 8 9 10

Knowledge Checklist		
Is it more or less true that your organization ...		**Ranking**
3	Has identified all the regional sustainability guidelines and reporting frameworks in each market you choose to operate in. Those requirements have been summarized and shared, so the organization knows why it must align its behavior with the guidelines and frameworks.	1 2 3 4 5 6 7 8 9 10
4	Has delegated key sector and topical standards to the appropriate business units or functions to insure adequate analysis, planning, and reporting.	1 2 3 4 5 6 7 8 9 10
5	Created a data-collection process both internally and with vendors, so information can be summarized, reported, and discussed on a recurring basis.	1 2 3 4 5 6 7 8 9 10
6	Defined key roles both at headquarters and within each geographic area and business function that are responsible for coordinating information, reporting, and team dialogues on sustainability.	1 2 3 4 5 6 7 8 9 10
7	Created training programs to ensure knowledge transfer to all parts of the organization based on how the knowledge affects a person's ability to perform, innovate, and contribute to sustainability goals.	1 2 3 4 5 6 7 8 9 10
8	Has identified key membership-based organizations that it can join to learn more about upcoming issues, peer opinions, and changes in market adjacencies.	1 2 3 4 5 6 7 8 9 10
9	Developed a business intelligence function to monitor future reporting and disclosure deadlines, predictable changes to requirements, and trends that may be relevant for business scenario planning.	1 2 3 4 5 6 7 8 9 10
10	Developed a business-wide set of metrics that are combined with traditional business metrics to reflect the spirit of dual materiality.	1 2 3 4 5 6 7 8 9 10
Total Score		

Scoring:

- Score less than 50—A low score tends to suggest confusion about the goal or the implementation. Either one is bad. There are serious penalties for non-compliance with disclosures and equally challenging issues for business competitiveness from failing to understand the new boundary conditions and opportunities.
- Score less than 80—The sustainability domain is a low-maturity knowledge domain, which means there is constant change, and it will remain a challenge to stay current and competitive. Building depth of knowledge among a larger group of specialists and leaders is a good investment.
- Score greater than 80—A perfect score is hard to achieve, and if you gave yourself one, you may need to reexamine your scores. Knowledge of enduring value and new breakthrough ideas needs to be maintained while business heuristics need to be challenged and reexamined. However, a high score means you are on the right track.

Chapter 5

SUCCEEDING AS AN ETHICAL BRAND WITH ETHICAL LEADERSHIP

Ethics is knowing the difference between what you have a right to do and what is right to do? —POTTER STEWART, FORMER SUPREME COURT JUSTICE, UNITED STATES[1]

I t's hard to overstate the importance of ethics in sustainability. The world faces an existential crisis, and we collectively need to reinvent our economies, so we are more circular in resource use, more respectful of nature, and more understanding of the needs of communities where we live and work. Our brands must stand for something more than profit, and the pride we feel in a job well done must connect to a feeling that we are leaving the world we inherited in a better place. Those are high expectations, but necessary as a collective North Star to ensure a more sustainable future.

If you believe in the idea of ethical brands, then the pursuit of impact plays a big role in determining the opportunities a company pursues and the ways they pursue them. The goal of a sustainable business brand is to generate revenue and profits in ways that help solve climate and sustainability problems while making net-positive contributions to society. Some people have expressed this challenge as dual materiality, as a comparison or an expansion of the traditional materiality assessment done in business.

Challenges: Can a business eliminate environmental negatives and help restore environmental damage and still be successful? Are ethical concerns a legitimate consideration for a business executive? Can leaders make business decisions that are good for shareholder returns, but also good for the environment and for the communities where we live and work?

Ethics and Opportunities

Traditional materiality assessments look at risks and opportunities from a financial perspective and the short- and long-term business impact. This remains an important issue for any company. New external boundary conditions change the nature of the traditional materiality assessment since climate change and other sustainability concerns affect plans, market responses, insurance costs, and other variables. These must be added to typical concerns regarding market variations, new technology, and competitive pressures.

The modern concept of ESG begins as a project within the United Nations Environmental Programme (UNEP) that eventually became the Principles for Responsible Investing (PRI) in 2003. The use of the term "ESG" is generally credited to James Gifford, who went on to become the founding Executive Director of PRI. The original idea was to create a set of principles that would act as a bridge between the investment community and the sustainable aspirations emerging from intergovernmental organizations. ESG begins life as a tool for bringing ethical considerations into the world of business through more effective leadership and governance.

Dual materiality or double materiality emerges later. The Global Reporting Initiative (GRI) embraces the concept in its reporting but credits European Commission as being the pioneer of dual materiality reporting in 2019.[2] The concept includes traditional financial reporting perspectives but adds the idea of how the business has an impact on the larger environment and society. Do any of your business plans have an adverse impact on biodiversity, on water resources, on the communities where you live and work?

Ethical considerations are another boundary condition since they are intended to influence business decisions. If we use a variation of a model introduced earlier, we can visualize it the following way.

Leaders set the tone for sustainable change by the way they act, communicate, and manage key decisions. Leadership, ethics, and sustainable decision-making are core to the idea of sustainability, and businesses must anchor those considerations into everyday behavior by recognizing the boundary conditions described throughout this book. Ethics lay out the principles that govern our behavior. They are different than treaties, protocols, and guidelines in that they defer to a higher-order reference regarding what we think is right or wrong.

DUAL MATERIALITY

IMPACT ON BUSINESS & RESULTS	IMPACT ON SOCIETY AND THE ENVIRONMENT
↓	↓
Generate Economic Value (revenue and profit)	Avoid Social & Environmental Negatives
+	+
Add New Shared Value Streams Where Possible	Help Regenerate Natural Systems
+	+
Add New Products and Services That Are Sustainable by Design	Generate Capital to Include Financial, Manufactured, Human & Relationship, Intellectual, Natural and Social

Figure 5.1 Dual materiality.

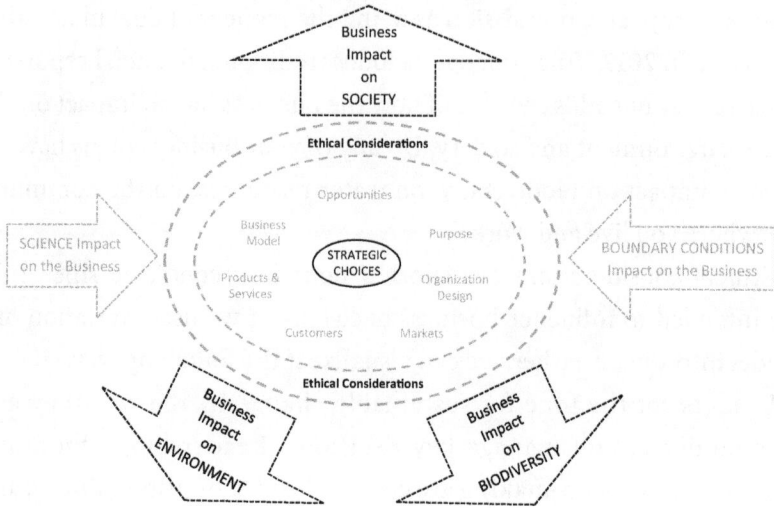

Figure 5.2 Adding ethics as a new boundary condition.

One of the best frameworks for sustainable behavior that captures the spirit of sustainability was developed by economist Herman Daly in what are known as the "Daly Rules."[3]

1. The sustainable use of renewable resources requires that consumption not be greater than the rate at which resources regenerate.
2. The sustainable use of nonrenewable resources requires that the rate of consumption not be greater than the pace at which renewable substitutes can be put into place.
3. The sustainable pace of pollution and wastes requires that production not be greater than the pace at which natural systems can absorb, recycle, or neutralize them.

These rules are simply described, clear in meaning, and focus on "what is the right thing to do?" His rules contain the elements of ethics while providing simple-to-use, prescriptive guidance on how we behave. Ethical brands have the challenge of making a commitment to such behavior and then creating an organization that translates that into the day-to-day behavior of everyone in the organization.

Several businesses have incorporated ethical considerations into their business operations by embedding the concept of dual materiality into their practices along with specific statements about how they will make decisions. For example, investment advisor Calvert Research and Management promotes themselves as "A Leader in Responsible Investing for 40+ years." The company created its own Calvert Principles for Responsible Investment: "The Calvert Principles for Responsible Investment (Calvert Principles) provide a framework for Calvert's evaluation of investments and guide Calvert's stewardship on behalf of clients through active engagement with companies and other issuers. The Calvert Principles seek to identify companies and other issuers that operate in a manner that is consistent with or promote environmental sustainability and resource efficiency, equitable societies and respect for human rights, accountable governance and transparent operations."[4] The full statement of principles is a two-page outline that highlights what each of the three ESG pillars means to them.

What Is Ethical Leadership?

Jeffrey Rosen, president of the U.S. National Constitution Center wrote a wonderful book in 2024 that examined how classical writers on moral and ethical philosophy influenced the founding of the United States, today's largest economy. Many believe that the United States leads in innovation, because each person is free to pursue his or her own vision. The individual right to the "pursuit of happiness" is enshrined in the U.S. Declaration of Independence along with rights to life and liberty as bedrock ideals. The idea that being successful makes us happy, or that success is tied to financial gain, is a very modern interpretation of business and leadership behavior. According to Rosen, "for the classical philosophers, happiness was not feeling good, but being good [...] improving your character so you can make the best use of your talents."[5] This concept ties the pursuit of individual success to the idea of doing a greater good or participating in a greater good. If we've lost the quality of this connection over the past several hundred years, the challenge of sustainability suggests that we might revisit its importance.

At the simplest level, ethics is a boundary condition based on our beliefs about what is right and wrong. The emergence of the idea that business decisions must balance environmental and social concerns with any product, customer, or market decision is new for many leaders, but it is essential for accomplishing the common goal of a more sustainable future. Is it right to mine deep-sea minerals as long as the law of the sea allows us? Or should our ignorance of the ecosystem impact of deep-sea mining cause us to refrain from such activity until the science catches up with market interest? Should our long-term business ambitions be governed by the idea that we must leave an environment for future generations that is as good or better than the one we enjoyed?

The University of Santa Clara lies at the heart of Silicon Valley California, often viewed as the epicenter of technology innovation. The University's Markula Center for Applied Ethics offers a definition of ethical behavior.

First, ethics refers to well based standards of right and wrong that prescribe what humans ought to do, usually in terms of rights, obligations, benefits to society, fairness, or specific virtues. Secondly, ethics refers to the study and development of one's ethical standards. Ethics also means, then, the continuous effort of studying our own moral beliefs and our moral conduct, and striving to ensure that we, and the institutions we help to shape, live up to standards that are reasonable and solidly based.[6]

I had the good fortune of working with the senior leadership team at MullenLowe Lintas Group in India which has a 75-year history of brand building. During dialogues with company leaders[7] we discussed the idea of ethical brands described in a company publication called "Brands to

Stands."[8] Virat Tandon, Chief Executive Officer of MullenLowe Lintas Group (MLL) reflected on brands with purpose:

"They have a following that doesn't jump camps, even on a bad day. People tend to trust and respect them much more. By following them, it's as if people are vicariously living out their own latent need to make the world a better place."[9] Chief Creative Officer and Chairmen of MLL, Amer Jaleel stated that the purpose of their "Brands to Stands" publication, "is for everyone in the world to see the magic of a thinking, beating institution that continues to sparkle and spew culture-capturing and culture defining work."[10]

The United Nations Global Compact (UNGC) weighed in on the idea of Leadership and Sustainability with its "Blueprint for Corporate Sustainability Leadership"[11] in 2010 to coincide with the 10th anniversary of the Compact being launched. The blueprint emphasized business practices that integrate the 10 principles of the UNGC into each company, the development of robust management policies, the mainstreaming of these practices into all business units and functions, and the implementation of the principles across all aspects of a value chain. It also called for a specific CEO commitment, later included in UNGC membership requirements, adoption of the blueprint by a company's board, active stakeholder engagement in the principles and adoption of the general principle of transparency and disclosure.

Figure 5.3 pulls words from these different perspectives to highlight some of the key actions implicit in many of the new protocols and frameworks. How do we expect a leader to behave? The model is a modification of an illustration first introduced in my book, *Pathways to Action* (2022).

Ethical leadership is both an individual and an organization-wide challenge. It requires a rethinking of the organizational boundary systems described previously and then communicating them clearly,

Figure 5.3 Guiding principles for ethical leaders.

so everyone can understand acceptable and unacceptable behavior. To this, we need to add both statements and stories about values and beliefs. For example, why are we engaged in this business and what impact do we want to have?

From these core ideas we need to build the support structure that supports good decision-making. It starts with purpose and the translation of policy frameworks, so everyone in the organization understands how those policies affect their jobs. Control systems are embedded into company policies and practices and major decisions require input from alternative perspectives and agreement of key stakeholders. Major decisions also benefit from post-decision reviews where the key learning can be used to help with training and development, the refinement of support frameworks, and the updating of any pre-decision practices.

To anchor this collective behavior in the DNA of the organization, two conditions are necessary.

1. Leaders must model the ethical behavior and the decision-making practices. Role models are incredibly powerful in shaping behavior. This includes leaders who ask reflective questions during

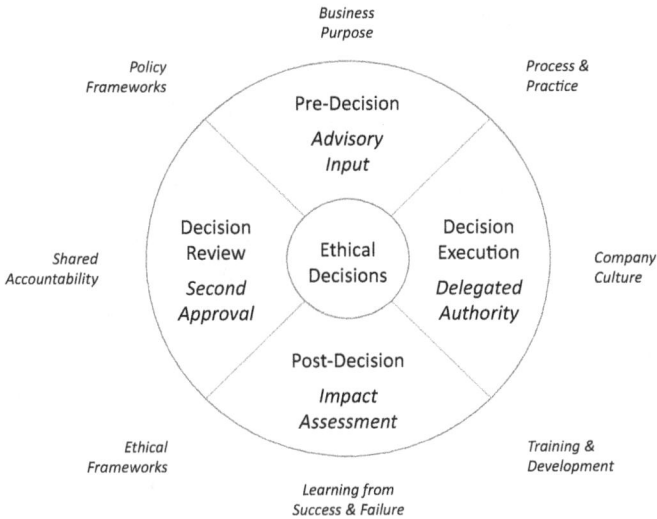

Figure 5.4 Ethical decision-making model.

meetings, who seek multiple perspectives on key decisions, who champion the right behavior, who create teachable moments from both successes and failures, who keep delegated projects on track, and who participate in training and developing team capabilities. Values must be reflected in individual decisions, but also visible in the processes and critical thinking of the organization.

2. Moving from individual leaders to organizational leadership behavior requires storytelling, strong feedback practices, and social rituals that communicate, reinforce, and embed the ethical behavior in the organizational culture. These include training programs, team events, workflow practices, and reward systems.

What Is an Ethical Brand?

Brands are about promises. What promise does your brand represent to your customers, suppliers, employees, partners, and investors? We can think of lots of popular brands that traditionally have represented promises like customer-centric design, ease of use, low cost, quality, and luxury. That is what they deliver, not how they behave. In a more sustainable future, the goal will be to deliver impact that makes a difference to society, and to do it in ways that are guided by ethical leadership and new sustainable boundary conditions.

Lifebuoy Soap in India created a marketing program to, "Help a child reach age 5," emphasizing the importance of hygiene in childhood health and mortality. Although the global focus of sustainability often emphasizes the existential threat of climate change, there are important considerations within the Sustainable Development Goals (SDGs) such as health, poverty, and access to quality health care. As part of a multi-year branding campaign across southeast Asia, Lifebuoy adopted villages in both India and Indonesia that had the highest diarrhea deaths and made use of highly personal video stories featuring a mother coping with her infant's death to diarrhea.[12] This kind of brand purpose messaging often requires educational outreach to connect the end user with both the product and the ultimate value proposition, which is a healthy life rather than the product cost or some other functional attribute.

The organization, Ethisphere, has conducted an ethical company award program since 2006. The 2024 honorees list stated, "136 organizations are recognized for their unwavering commitment to business integrity. The honorees span 20 countries and 44 industries and include 15 first-time honorees and 6 organizations that have been named to the honoree list 18 times, marking every year since its inception."[13]

The Ethisphere awards grade ethics according to several categories that collectively comprise a survey of 240 questions: (1) Ethics and Compliance Program, (2) Culture of Ethics, (3) Corporate Citizenship and Responsibility, (4) Governance, and (5) Third-Party Management.[14] These criteria rely to a degree on self-reporting and the documentation of policies and organizational structure. Those are important, although what you do and how you do it are interconnected. However, such guidelines and benchmarks are helpful since they create a model to follow when you are starting a process of improvement. Adhering to such models can have direct benefits according to Ethisphere, which tracks

A Sample of the Most Ethical Companies according to the Ethisphere Institute 2024		
Aflac Insurance (US)	Federal Express (US)	Sertecpet S.A. (Ecuador)
Covenant Health (Canada)	Groupo Bimbo (Mexico)	Schneider Electric (France)
CP Group (Thailand)	Induslnd Bank (India)	The Hartford (US)
Cementos Progresso (Guatamala)	William E. Connor & Associates Ltd. (Hong Kong)	TE Connectivity (Switzerland)
Eaton (Ireland)	Loreal Group (France)	Trane Technologies (Ireland)
HCL Tech (India)	Lonza (Switzerland)	Visa (US)
Hewlet Packard (US)	Natura and Company (Brazil)	Workday (US)
Iberdrola (Spain)	Sony (Japan)	Iberdrola (Spain)

Figure 5.5 Ethical companies—Ethisphere 2024.

the stock performance of its honorees against their competitive peers. According to Ethisphere, their index of the most ethical companies outperformed their peers by 12.3 percent from 2019 through 2024.[15]

Embedding Ethics in Core Practices

An ethical brand based on the principles of sustainability must embed the concept of ethical decision-making into its core business processes. Can the product we are developing be made in a more sustainable way? Can our products be repaired for reuse? Does our product development process respect the environment and avoid any impact on biodiversity? Is our product designed in a way so they can be disassembled for recycling at the end of life? Creating such questions depends on your industry, but they are a way to embed sustainability in key decision paths.

U.S. financial services company, Bank of the West, created a series of company policies in recent years as guidelines for its lenders and salespeople. It has explicitly stated that it will not provide lending services to companies that conduct artic drilling for oil and gas, that build coalfired power plants, or that engage in gas fracking. It will also not finance tar sands projects or tobacco companies.[16] These and other environmental statements are followed by explicit company policies on what you can and cannot do. Debating the details and making case-by-case decisions helps refine thinking and creates new heuristics.

- What if only one division of a company wants to do artic drilling? Can I lend to the parent company?
- What if the tobacco company also owns other lines of business? Can I lend to them?

Policy guidelines are an important way to translate good intentions into business decisions that a supervisor or line manager can support and help ensure that business actions are aligned with global and national goals.

Building an ethical brand based on sustainability values starts with at least one ethical leader who embodies the attributes of ethical leadership

Figure 5.6 Ethical brands link customers, employees, partners, and suppliers.

who can help communicate how the values of sustainability are good for business and how they should shape the common business goals and behavior. Ideally, the organization needs at least one leader who is also capable of modeling the ethical behavior, and recruiting, teaching, and mentoring others in the language and meaning of sustainable decision-making. Building up a core team of like-minded leaders is required to help shape the organizational changes needed to anchor the ethical attributes in the sustainable business culture.

As leaders expand their focus from building ethical leaders and an ethical brand culture, they need to be conscious of how others view the issue of ethics. The annual Edelman Trust Barometer is a widely referenced survey of issues related to institutional trust and ethics, and they use the model below by asking respondents to rank their perceptions between the two extremes of ethical and unethical behavior described in Figure 5.8 (taken from Trust Barometer 2024 Report.[17])

Leaders often deal with new situations or questions on a day-to-day business. There is no such thing as always being right, and decisions are often made with incomplete information. Stakeholder interests are not always aligned and there are frequently compromises between short- and long-term objectives. Leaders seeking to grow a sustainable business must be able to experiment, fail, and learn on the road to success.

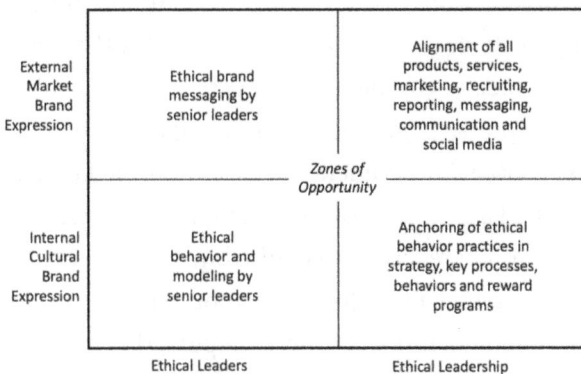

	Ethical Leaders	Ethical Leadership
External Market Brand Expression	Ethical brand messaging by senior leaders	Alignment of all products, services, marketing, recruiting, reporting, messaging, communication and social media
Internal Cultural Brand Expression	Ethical behavior and modeling by senior leaders	Anchoring of ethical behavior practices in strategy, key processes, behaviors and reward programs

Zones of Opportunity

Figure 5.7 Zone of opportunity for ethical leaders.

Dimension	Ethical Perception	Unethical Perception
Purpose-driven	Highly effective agent of positive change	Completely ineffective agent for positive change
Honest	Honest and fair	Corrupt and biased
Vision	Has a vision for the future that I believe in	Does not have a vision for the future that I believe in.
Fairness	Serves the interests of everyone equally and fairly	Serves the interests of only certain groups of people.

Figure 5.8 2024 Edelman Trust Barometer, ethical versus unethical perceptions.

Solving important problems often requires a level of perseverance to succeed with innovation. Jensen Huang, CEO of technology company NVIDIA, says that "greatness comes from character and not intelligence. Resilience matters in success."[18] A commitment to ethical leadership reflects a belief that it is the right way to lead that guides you through good times and bad. It must reside in a belief system that doing well can be achieved by doing good.

Translating Ethics into Business Actions

There are many organizations dedicated to building more ethical frameworks. Joel Rosenthal, the president of the Carnegie Council for Ethics in International Affairs says, "Ethics is not some cure-all for the world's problems, but it is an actual process for finding solutions."[19] If this view is correct, then ethics is not about pure boundary conditions that govern your behavior, but a set of principles that commit you to finding shared value to complex challenges.

In earlier chapters, I emphasized the importance of science as a driver of sustainable development because it is based on empirical evidence and exists largely as knowledge of enduring value. Because scientific observations are disconnected from market readiness, prices, or similar attributes, it provides a common basis for action that cuts across industries and national borders. In part, this is why I emphasize the importance of SDGs 13, 14, and 15 to business leaders since they are driven by a large and consistent body of evidence on climate change and biodiversity. A failure to address climate change or biodiversity challenges also has a ripple effect that is a negative influence on other goals like hunger, poverty, and gender equality.

The broader picture of sustainable development, all 17 SDGs plus the four pillars of the UN Global Compact, offers challenges to business leaders that are less easily addressed, despite our attempts to do so. National and regional practices on issues such as child labor, forced labor, or migrant worker rights, health and safety, gender equality, diversity, sexual orientation, unionization, pay scales and worker benefits are subject to much more interpretation. A significant number of organizations might agree on climate change but disagree on the unionization of their factories. Religion and cultural traditions differ widely on gender equality or sexual orientation and ultimately have a big impact on related issues such as access to education, health care, and employment. The more we see the development goals as interdependent, the more our actions need to be interconnected. Translating ethics into sustainable business action requires a common understanding of goals, the acceptance of shared boundary conditions, and a willingness to consider multiple perspectives when making strategic choices. In the current environment, ethical leaders need to be advocates for all of the SDGs.

The Ultimate Boundary—Do the Right Thing!

The pressures between marketplace demands, investor interests, and sustainability mandates are very real. The legacy automobile companies are in a difficult position. At the time of this writing, pure electric vehicle companies like Tesla are leading the industry in sales growth, EV share, margins, and stock price. The legacy automobile companies are trying to sell existing legacy brands, maintain their existing infrastructure while investing heavily in new EV products, but don't yet have the scale to be profitable. They seem to have the worst of both worlds. The Chinese company BYD shows how to grow selling pure EVs, but also hybrids and plug-in hybrid electric vehicles (PHEVs). The hybrid variants are selling well and still include the traditional internal combustion engine and drive train that the legacy companies know well. But is this the right thing to do? You will get different answers depending on how you phrase the question. Is it the right thing for investors? For the Environment? For Biodiversity? If I build cars that are right for the environment, but I lose money and the company fails, is that the right thing to do?

Many automobile companies are moving to hybrids and PHEVs because they are cheaper to build and more acceptable to the public. It makes people feel like they are doing the right thing while still allowing legacy companies to use existing capability and it greatly reduces their supply chain complexities and investor fears. But do PHEVs and hybrid vehicles solve the emissions problem? Many hybrid electric cars only have a battery pack of less than 1.5 kilowatt hours (kWh), cannot be independently charged, and the car will not drive on electricity alone. If the car could, a battery that small would only provide a few kilometers of travel. The PHEV has a larger battery pack of 20–22 kWh, but all hybrids must have two drive trains, the electric drive train and the internal combustion engine drive train. That gives them more parts, makes them heavier, and provides less performance in either the battery or gasoline modes. Is a mix of hybrids, PHEVs, EVs, and legacy cars the right solution for the market?

There are 290 million cars on the road in the European Union (2022) with the average age of cars on the road of 12.3 years. In some countries such as Greece, the average car is older at 17 years.[20] In the United States, there are 288 million cars on the road as of 2023 with an average age of 12.6 years (2024).[21] As of June 2024, there are an estimated 420 million cars and trucks on the road in China, which has a much younger vehicle fleet, averaging just 5.1 years old.[22] The decision to sell more hybrids may be a decision that customers and legacy car companies are more comfortable with, but such decisions will also mean hundreds of millions of new gasoline cars on the road that may be there well over a decade in the future.

Transitioning a large fleet can take a long time. This is a challenge for the business community, as well as a challenge for public policy and for ethical leadership. The timeline for general market acceptance may not align with what the science tells us, but business leaders can't help if they are losing money. Ethical leadership in public policy can also be judged by the "doing the right thing" standard and it implies that government and business have a need to work together to move the market along at a pace that works with the goals for climate change.

Guidelines for Ethical Leadership in Sustainable Organizations

1. Ethics must become a part of the central framework of a business guiding the development of company strategy, product development, and talent management.
2. Leaders must act, but within boundary conditions that highlight the need to do well by doing good. Leaders must model ethical behavior by asking tough questions about whether a business decision is also good for the planet, good for the communities where we live and work, and good for future generations. It also means telling the truth.
3. Ethical frameworks must be embedded in compliance and decision-making practices to provide guidelines that inform all levels of the organization about their expected behavior.
4. Leaders must continuously learn by being open, transparent, and adaptable. The science and public policy surrounding sustainability will continue to evolve and businesses must evolve with it.
5. Excellence is an aspirational goal, but businesses must often make decisions with imperfect advice and information. Positive forward progress is the desired outcome guided by a North Star Statement that grounds the organization in a sustainable purpose.
6. Leaders must be conscious of building a culture of trust, built on ethical behavior, both internally and externally.

Summary

- Ethics and sustainable business opportunities are connected since sustainability requires us to think about our impact on business results as well as our impact on the environment and society.
- Ethical leaders are guiding by principles including interconnectedness, integrity, circularity, long-term value creation, and the opportunity to have a real impact.
- Ethical decision-making involves gaining perspectives and insights from others as a way to validate decisions and operate within the context of shared values.
- Ethical brands stand for something. Ethical brands add value by finding ways to make a positive contribution to society.
- Ethical brands must survive a change in leadership, so it becomes critical to anchor ethical principles in the business strategy, key processes, and reward systems.
- Ethical behavior is part of a process and not an end unto itself. It is a commitment to finding shared value to complex challenges.
- Many sustainable business challenges require transitions and trade-offs. The ultimate ethical boundary is the idea of "doing the right thing!" Gain insights, balance the short- and longer-term value issues, and make decisions based on best available information.

Ethics Reflection Checklist

Ethics Checklist		
Is it more or less true that your organization …		**Ranking**
1	Has an ethics statement that is visible to all members of the organization?	1 2 3 4 5 6 7 8 9 10
2	Has a system of controls that prevents any one person from making a business decision that fails to comply with your statement of ethics?	1 2 3 4 5 6 7 8 9 10

Ethics Checklist		
Is it more or less true that your organization ...		**Ranking**
3	Embeds concepts of sustainable behavior and sustainable outcomes in key decision-making activities like product and process development?	1 2 3 4 5 6 7 8 9 10
4	Has one or more social rituals where senior leaders share success stories that connect sustainable results to your sustainable business mission and values?	1 2 3 4 5 6 7 8 9 10
5	Subjects major strategic decisions to a review that asks the organization to reflect on long-term value creation and the elimination of environmental and biodiversity negatives?	1 2 3 4 5 6 7 8 9 10
6	Has a process to reflect on its collective actions? Are we a force for good?	1 2 3 4 5 6 7 8 9 10
7	Aligns its innovation practices with developing solutions that reduce the business's environmental and biodiversity impact?	1 2 3 4 5 6 7 8 9 10
8	Emphasizes ethical dilemmas and decision-making solutions in its leadership training?	1 2 3 4 5 6 7 8 9 10
9	Communicates the organization's sustainable vision and values in new employee onboarding and key role transitions?	1 2 3 4 5 6 7 8 9 10
10	Designed its reward and recognition programs to incentivize doing well while doing good?	1 2 3 4 5 6 7 8 9 10
Total Score		

Scoring:

- Score less than 50—If you have a low score in any of the 10 categories, it indicates gaps in your ethical framework, either in the basic definitions or in the implementation. A few higher scores suggest you are doing something right. Your emphasis needs to be on implementing consistent, active programs and identifying accountable people for each activity.

- Score less than 80—This generally means you have strengths in some areas and working programs in all areas.
- Score greater than 80—Your organization is on the right path and needs to emphasize capability development, ongoing vendor training, and operational efforts to scale excellence.

Chapter 6

DESIGNING A TRANSITION PLAN

Change is the law of life. And those who look only to the past or the present are certain to miss the future.
—JOHN F. KENNEDY, FORMER PRESIDENT OF THE UNITED STATES[1]

The global economy exceeded 105 trillion USD in 2023, according to research published by the World Bank Group.[2] Most of that production and consumption was related to existing businesses (legacy). Each has a carbon footprint, and few were established with newer sustainability practices in mind. Each company needs to take stock of its existing business model, products and services, and market opportunities to create a transition plan that, at a minimum, puts it into alignment with sustainability compliance practices.

For those who question if sustainability has staying power or if regulations will ease over time, consider that investment banking firm Goldman Sachs predicts that the global economy will reach 227.9 trillion USD by 2050.[3] That is over 120 trillion USD higher than World Bank estimates for 2023. It also includes a population increase of 1.7 billion new people over 2023. Another way to think about it is 1.7 billion additional consumers and 120 trillion USD in new production, consumption, and waste production. If we are not meeting our climate and biodiversity goals now, how will these changes affect our ability to meet our goals?

I think it is reasonable to assume that market boundary conditions and related compliance practices will continue to evolve because market pressures will increase. As practices evolve, they will likely become more detailed and refined. It makes good business sense to explore opportunities for investments in carbon-free and carbon-neutral products and to look for returns in the sustainability sectors attracting billions of dollars in new investments.

Challenges: How do I get from where I am today to a place closer to my North Star statement? How do I plan a transition away from legacy models and practices?

Defining Your Sustainability Journey

The general model for transition plans has distinct stages and is useful for any business. Each stage can map to your change strategy, but also to your business model adoption practices, your compliance and reporting strategies, and your innovation choices. I have also worked with customers where we use a transition model to develop prospecting tools for new customers based on what type of service they might need depending on where they are in their own transition plans. The beginning of the model starts in the same place as the model for working knowledge highlighted in Chapter 4. You need to understand your legacy strategy and the impact new boundary conditions have on it. That helps you with the sense of urgency for how fast you need to move and where the opportunities are for new products and services.

The model stages are highlighted in Figure 6.2. If your organization has multiple business units as well as distinct geographic organizations, your sustainability journey can be different for each organizational unit, although your functional organizations need alignment with the

	Global Goals & Protocols	
Climate Science		*Market & Policy Trends*

OPPORTUNITIES	Legacy STRATEGY	COMPETITIVE BEHAVIOR

LEADERSHIP ETHICS	Legacy + New STRATEGY	ETHICAL BRAND PROMISES

Figure 6.1 First stages of planning a transition.

Figure 6.2 The four stage sustainability model.

fastest-moving parts of your organization and ultimately need to be integrated cross-functionally by the time you reach stage 4.

Stage 1—Become Compliant with Sustainability Regulations

The first stage requires a stocktaking exercise to ensure that your organization understands your new boundary conditions and can meet two primary goals. First, you need to ensure that your organization is following all ESG rules and reporting requirements and that you have the necessary staff accountability, policy documents, and data-collection practices. This activity begins to define your knowledge model and how that knowledge is turned into action within your organization.

Stage 1 is the "risk avoidance" stage because there can be penalties associated with non-compliance. Compliance can vary widely depending on where you are incorporated, the markets where you operate, and the size of your organization. However, some compliance activities are very straightforward. If you want to join the United Nations Global Compact, for example, you simply use the online questionnaire[4] and answer approximately sixty-four questions on your environmental, labor, human rights, anti-corruption, and governance practices. Most of the questionnaire is as simple as checking the appropriate items and then uploading an additional document, providing a link to your website, or using the space provided to fill in a bit of additional information. Then you ask your CEO to sign off on your compliance letter that the UN provides a template for online.

The compliance standards for a sample company may include the Sustainability Accounting Standards Board (SASB), the Global Reporting Initiative (GRI) Standards, and the Task Force on Climate-related Financial Disclosures (TCFD) Framework. Additional reporting may be voluntary, like the Carbon Disclosures Project (CDP) and the related Carbon Disclosures Standards Board (CDSB) Framework. It is likely that a company also has specific industry-related disclosures such as the Global Real Estate Sustainability Benchmark (GRESB), as well as market and customer disclosures to consider such as the European Union Corporate Sustainability Reporting Directive (CSRD). The market has matured to the point where many external accounting firms or consultants can give you a general roadmap for your core requirements.

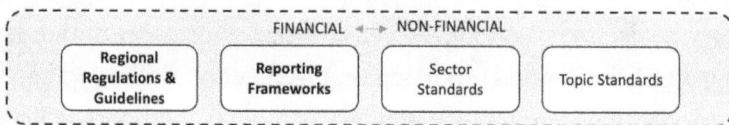

Figure 6.3 Financial and non-financial guidelines.

One reason to assign your sustainability coordination activities to a specific senior officer is that there are various implementation timelines for reporting that have programmed changes for future years. These are predictable, but it is necessary to mark your calendars and start the process of examining the business implications of future changes.

Stage 1 is also the first part of your planning stage and an opportunity to start an internal dialogue. Even if many of these directives seem cumbersome or overwhelming for your business, it is helpful to position the overall journey and the business reasons for doing so. Although compliance reporting is often the focus, the real value is in the internal dialogue and not the reporting at stage 1.

Stages 1 and 2 are about evolving your legacy organization and starting the process of understanding dual materiality and the idea of multivalue creation in your company. Standard financial planning practices have evolved over the life of the industrial revolution and current thinking on strategy and competitive differentiation have been with us for many decades, so it's reasonable that these new topics will take time to mature, and learning will happen over time. It's highly likely that none of your executive team ever had a class on sustainable business practices when they were in school. Again, the dialogue and intent are where the value lies, so it's necessary to move at a pace where your leadership team learns and matures.

Stages 1 and 2 work in tandem, since you must stay on top of current regulations and the potential for future changes. The senior team needs to discuss them as conditions that may have an impact on business strategy as well as resource allocation. The movement away from legacy value creation is also hard, since it is likely the major source of business revenue and many people will have spent their careers developing, refining, and supporting the legacy organization. The decision to experiment on new product is based on the idea that an experiment can create new "perceived value." Testing or prototyping validate that the idea has potential for scale. Only then can you see the impact on your balance sheet.

The
SUSTAINABILITY
Journey

4 – Strategic
(CREATE SOLUTIONS &
NEW VALUE)

SUSTAINABLE
VALUE

LEGACY
VALUE

1 – Compliant
(AVOID RISKS)

PERCEIVED
VALUE

NEW
VALUE

3 – Responsible
(EVOLVE
ORGANIZATION)

2 – Efficient
(REDUCE NEGATIVE
IMPACT)

Creating the
Sustainable
Organization

Evolving the
Legacy
Organization

Figure 6.4 The evolution of value creation.

Stage 2—Reduce Your Negative Impact

Stage 2 is a key part of your transition and has both more goals and a more leadership choices. This begins the process of reducing the negative impact of your business while simultaneously having conversations about a possible future direction and North Star. From my research, there are a dozen activities that companies repeatedly explore. These are valuable from a business perspective since most save money. The biggest mistake companies make is they don't simultaneously look at the potential these activities have for learning and staff development as well as building the social and political capital for future changes. The biggest barriers to scaling innovation are (1) the lack of buy-in because of perceived risks, (2) entrenched practices and mental models that favor legacy activities, and (3) the lack of internal capability and knowledge to explore the new ideas. Stage 2 activities must use projects as action learning opportunities.

Each of the activities listed below is a great opportunity to develop such resources.

1. Energy Efficiency—Audit all types of energy consumption to see opportunities for easy savings. This may be replacing outdated equipment, new insulation or the use of energy management

software. Employees can lead the way if they see the reason for the reductions. Exploring alternative energy sources, the use of localized solar energy on rooftops, parking garages and similar structures is also popular.

2. Waste Reduction—When waste has no apparent cost, it accumulates. Employee green teams almost always uncover wasteful practices. This is also a great opportunity to use incremental innovation practices and incentives to encourage reductions in waste as well as products redesign to eliminate waste at the source.

3. Water Efficiency—Water usage in certain companies is a huge challenge, but it is also an area that may have received little attention in your company. Simply auditing usage and asking if the way water is used is necessary may yield immediate savings. The key with all efficiency audits is to get a good baseline. The highest water usage may occur within your supply chain, so a more circular view on your water usage may generate a much better picture of where savings can be achieved.

4. Material Efficiency—Material efficiency is related to waste efficiency, but different groups within an organization are often tasked with elements of the process such as product design, product sourcing, product manufacturing, procurement, or product management. There may be opportunities within each element of the process as well as the overall value chain.

5. Transport Efficiency—Transportation can be a large component of both cost and carbon emissions. Choices once made when carbon emissions were not a primary consideration may not have considered alternatives. This is a highly evolving space since separate industries such as air freight, ocean shipping, rail and road shipping are developing new solutions individually.

6. Packaging Optimization—The size, shape and amount of packaging, and the choice of materials can affect many of the other efficiency strategies. Changing product packaging can reduce the weight, reduce costs, eliminate harmful chemicals, reduce

emissions, and can even introduce new sustainability attributes that may make the product more attractive to customers.

7. Process Optimization—Process improvement has been with us ever since there has been a total quality movement. It is often part of the core analytic techniques used to examine a value chain or product design effort. However, every efficiency activity will have one or more processes that can be examined and optimized and is the key to long-term savings.

8. Partner Optimization—Partnerships are a great source of knowledge and competence and can be used to explore many new types of value creation. Partners often have capabilities and insights into parts of your supply chain that will be difficult for you to map or monitor directly. It becomes increasingly important to have partners that are well aligned with your new statement of purpose and your sustainable values.

9. Recycling—Recycling, reuse, and remanufacturing are the hallmarks of a good early-stage sustainability policy. First, because practices such as recycling can be done by everyone in your organization, so they help influence behavior and create a new mental model. Second, they highlight how much waste is generated, which often leads to preventative choices, and third, recycling in some businesses can save considerable money.

10. Reuse—This is a popular practice in resource-intensive industries like manufacturing and textiles because the reuse of high-quality materials is often considerably less expensive that purchasing new virgin resources. It can also have a large impact beyond cost by avoiding additional transport, energy use, water use, or related resources.

11. Remanufacturing—Part of the attraction of remanufacturing is being driven by new laws in Europe and the United States, which require a "right to repair" for many new products. Remanufacturing is also driven by increase in solid waste disposal

costs or tariffs that make it more economical to repair equipment of office structures than it is to dispose of them properly.

12. Carbon Capture and Storage—Carbon credits, carbon capture technologies, and carbon storage solutions are increasingly part of the corporate landscape. In other instances, they can dictate land use and partnerships and be part of an environmental remediation and biodiversity initiatives supported by a company. Most carbon credits reference biological storage project, although new innovations in this space are likely to include expanded use of direct air-capture technologies and geologic storage.

Each of the practices listed above is an opportunity to save money, improve your sustainability credentials, engage your employees, and build capability. Your leadership choices will vary by the type of industry and the products and services already offered by your company, but they are generally guided by the following six principles.

1. Make production more efficient—Becoming more efficient aligns well with most existing corporate incremental innovation practices. It is also easy to design metrics that work within existing measurement dashboards. Efficiency strategies may vary for example if you are looking at scope 1 emissions where switching to renewable fuels may be a good option, or scope 2 emissions where entering into off-site power purchase agreements (PPAs) might be a viable option.

2. Decrease consumption by design—This option is a bit harder and more focused since product design is largely a dedicated functional discipline. The number of people involved is smaller and the training and focus needed to deliver results a bit harder. However, this may be one of the most important disciplines that offer significant results.

3. Use products longer—"If it's not broken, don't fix it," is an old adage, but a useful one to remember in the age of sustainability.

Part of the discipline of sustainability is to extract all the useful life from a product before disassembling, remanufacturing, or recycling. Part of the motivation to use a product longer is the idea that if you don't want to use it anymore, you are the person responsible for the end-of-life practices.

4. Increase quantity and value of resources recovered at the end of use—When you follow the practice of using products longer and know that at the end of a product's life, you need to recover as much as you can from disassembly, there is a greater appreciation for the selection or design of the products you use.

5. Minimize environmental and social harms associated with the virgin extraction of new resources—Virgin resources tend to have the largest waste and emissions footprint, and limiting the usage of virgin resources is a good practice for those reasons alone. However, there is a very strong financial case for the recycling of resources in many industries. Recycling Demin, for example, is much cheaper than processing raw cotton if you are making a pair of jeans. Many manufacturers use high-quality metals in fabrication, so reuse and recycling have much lower energy costs as well a greatly reduced carbon footprint.

6. Encourage the use and reuse, of recycled and renewable materials everywhere in the supply chain—This is one of the harder commitments since it requires you to influence organizations outside your legal boundaries. In some instances, the companies are in different countries and have different customers. They will also serve many customers, so adapting to your requirements may be a challenge. It requires ongoing communication, training, and a commitment to data collection and verification. The results can be significant because many labor, energy, or resource-intensive product components come from tier 2 or tier 3 suppliers. The more you operate in countries with strict reporting requirements for scope 2 and 3 emissions, the more important your investment in supply chain materials management and supplier training.

Stage 2 is partly about saving money and reducing your negative impact. It may be an extension of the compliance activities started in stage 1, but it is also about planning for the future. The press release for the new Corporate Sustainability Due Diligence Directive in the European Union states, "For the first time, large companies also will be required to adopt and put into effect a plan ensuring that their business model and strategy are compatible with limiting global warming to 1.5°C. This new legislation represents a significant shift from the voluntary regimes of the Organization for Economic Co-operation and Development (OECD) and the United Nations Guiding Principles on Business and Human Rights. The CSDDD establishes a civil liability regime for damages and introduces penalties for noncompliance—including fines of up to 5% of a company's global turnover."[5] In the EU, transition planning is a requirement, not an option.

Stage 2 is such a critical part of any transition planning that I have added an extra checklist as a quick test at this stage. It makes little sense to move forward with planning if the organization has not established a strong foundation.

Transition Stage 2 Reflection Checklist

Transition Stage 2 Checklist		
Is it more or less true that your organization ...		**Ranking**
1	Has a robust program on energy efficiency that includes written plans, targets and audits, and the purchase of alternative energy?	1 2 3 4 5 6 7 8 9 10
2	Has conducted process improvement programs internally and with suppliers to emphasize waste reduction, and the business measures annual improvements with transparent metrics?	1 2 3 4 5 6 7 8 9 10
3	Has audited water usage and efficiency and conducted value chain analysis to implement reductions over time?	1 2 3 4 5 6 7 8 9 10

Transition Stage 2 Checklist	
Is it more or less true that your organization ...	**Ranking**
4 Has redesigned product and service development practices to improve material efficiency and is considering substitutes that have a reduced impact on the environment or biodiversity?	1 2 3 4 5 6 7 8 9 10
5 Have audited all business transport and logistics to emphasize transport efficiency and the reduction of environmental impacts?	1 2 3 4 5 6 7 8 9 10
6 Has introduced programs to reduce excess packaging on legacy products and implemented new product development programs that actively prototype packaging optimization practices on an ongoing basis?	1 2 3 4 5 6 7 8 9 10
7 Has conducted reviews of all key processes with the goal of process optimization that link with company ESG targets for impact and improvement?	1 2 3 4 5 6 7 8 9 10
8 Have reviewed all business value chains and capability gaps and developed a program for partner optimization to address capability needs, new knowledge, risk, and other factors?	1 2 3 4 5 6 7 8 9 10
9 Communicates the need to recycle, reuse, and remanufacture, where possible, in all company processes, in supply chain activities, and with suppliers?	1 2 3 4 5 6 7 8 9 10
10 Participates in mandatory carbon allowance program and uses carbon credits to mitigate emissions with clear goals of reaching net-zero emissions consistent with global targets?	1 2 3 4 5 6 7 8 9 10
Total Score	

Scoring:

- Score less than 50—If you have a low score in any of the ten categories, it indicates the need for specific action in that activity area. Mid-level scores suggest you are doing something, and the emphasis needs to be on implementing consistent, active programs and identifying accountable people for each activity. You have considerable work to do.
- Score less than 80—This generally means you have strengths in many areas and have working programs in all areas. Audits, benchmarks, value chain analysis, and employee engagement teams are all strategies for improvement.
- Score greater than 80—Your organization is on the right path and needs to emphasize capability development, ongoing vendor training, and operational efforts to scale excellence.

Stage 3—Become Responsible and Design for Sustainability

Making the turn from stage 2 to stage 3 requires you to establish a future vision or North Star Statement that clearly articulates your aspirations for a more sustainable future. During stage 2, you have started the process of experimentation and developed a portfolio of new product prototypes. The challenge now is to take the value propositions that you have tested and start the process of scaling them into legitimate businesses. In some ways, the race is on. You can only improve efficiency and reduce costs on your legacy programs for so long before you reach a point of diminishing returns.

A company in stage 3 is characterized by new products that have been designed with sustainability in mind during the design process. Being responsible often requires a company to change core processes so there are checklists in place that ask the people in the design process to adhere to new principles. For example:

1. Can this product be designed in a more sustainable way? This may seem like a simple question, but it forces people working on the design to propose, consider, and specifically reject alternatives that do not satisfy this standard.

2. Is there a product substitute that offers better long-term sustainable performance? Product substitution is the biggest challenge in moving from stage 2 to stage 3. The initial savings from product efficiency can be addictive for a company because it often requires less long-term investment, meets compliance or disclosure requirements, and does not require abandoning legacy assets, structure, process, or capability. Creating product substitutes can create uncertainty with customer acceptance and may exceed the company's existing capability. As such, it is perceived as risky. It's the big move that many companies put off, waiting for the market to mature.

3. Have we considered end-of-product-life recycling, reuse, or remanufacturing in the design process? This type of question forces design choices about the circularity of the product before final choices of materials, production processes, or even maintenance issues are finalized.

4. Is the product designed to be reparable by the buyer or an independent resource? Many counties and localities have introduced right-to-repair laws, which make such a question relevant.

5. Have our resource and operational choices minimized our impact on the environment and biodiversity? This type of question can be further refined to speak to consideration of reduced negative impact as well as positive impact.

These types of process questions can be formulated at multiple levels of responsibility. Executives can decide to exit certain businesses, reduce exposure to certain industries, or reduce capital allocations. A question checklist can be developed for each activity. Senior functional leaders can create policy statements that specify what markets or types

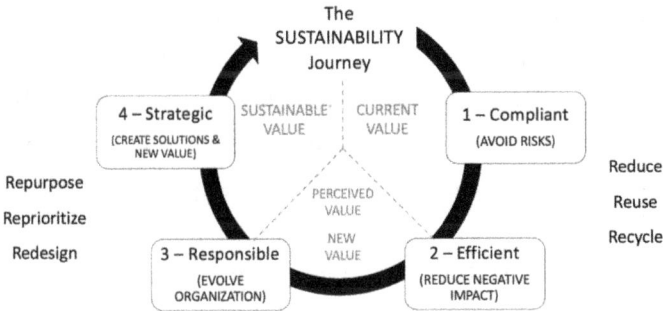

Figure 6.5 Stage 3: Becoming a responsible organization.

of products the company will or will not invest in. The follow-on is to develop a question checklist that offers guidance on how the policies are applied. More functional departments can specify operating principles and practices. Each level of decision-making must be aligned for maximum impact.

Part of the evolution to becoming more responsible involves a commitment to designing products that are sustainable from conception to end-of-life. It may also mean creating product substitutions for an existing portfolio. Companies such as BASF use a "mass balance" practice to create blended formulations of ingredients as the input source. Alternative raw materials are mixed with traditional feedstock at the beginning of the value chain so the company can produce a consistent and certifiable product. The final mix in a product for a given customer can vary based on market demand. BASF uses both mass balancing and a proprietary process known as ChemCycling for recycling and uses life-cycle assessments to determine the sustainability impact.[6]

India is a country with relatively low per capita emissions, but it is also a country that remains highly dependent on coal. It ranked as the third most polluted country based on average PM2.5 concentrations in air quality by IQAir between 2018 and 2023.[7] During the COP26 meeting in Glasgow, Scotland, the Indian prime minister announced the Panchamrit initiative.[8] The initiative pledges to "achieve 500 GW of non-fossil fuel energy capacity by 2030 and meet 50% of its energy requirements from renewables by the same year with solar energy accounting for 58% and wind about 20%. These targets align with India's broader aim of reducing its projected carbon emissions by one billion tons and decreasing the carbon intensity of its economy by 45% by 2030."[9]

Despite these plans, the global coal trade was at an all-time high in 2023 according to the IEA. "India, the second largest importer globally, showed a remarkable growth of about 21% in seaborne coal imports during the first four months of 2024. Even though India seeks to reduce the quantity of imports, new routes are being established such as the railway from Russia to India via Iran, and a trial of coal deliveries from Mongolia."[10]

India's Adani Group is one of the world's largest private developers of coal and one of the leading importers of coal in India. Coal trading and imports remain a major part of its revenue base. A strong base energy supply is seen as key to growing India's economy and helping to raise the standard of living for what has become the world's largest population. The challenge of maintaining energy supplies, reducing pollution, growing the economy, and meeting international climate commitments is a difficult balancing act. The Adani Group has been under increased scrutiny for its large fossil-fuel energy footprint as well as investor allegations of stock manipulation.[11] It seems unlikely that the Adani Group will exit the coal business based on industry reporting and company comments.

Despite these headwinds, the Group has invested in pilot solar ingot plants,[12] and has won the single largest tender for solar energy, "Adani Green Energy, part of India's Adani Group conglomerate, will build 8 gigawatts of large-scale solar capacity worth $6 billion in India over the next five years, after winning the world's largest solar energy tender award."[13] News outlet CNN reported that the plant the Group is constructing is five times the footprint of the city of Paris. "It's clean energy unit AGEL is building the sprawling solar and wind power plant in the western Indian state of Gujarat at a cost of about $20 billion. It will be the world's biggest renewable park when it is finished in about five years and should generate enough clean electricity to power 16 million Indian homes."[14] This type of business dichotomy is common in developing economies where typical business boundary conditions are also influenced by national boundary conditions for maintaining economic growth and both regional and national political considerations.

Stage 4—Pursue Your North Star

The final stage suggests that your business is now generating most of its revenue from products and services that are sustainable by design. You may still have legacy businesses and products, but you have plans to reduce their business exposure, address their sustainability deficits, or exit the business altogether. You organization has the strategic intent, the operating practices, and the people capabilities that allow you to continue evolving your business.

Many businesses have multiple operating divisions that may each be classified at a different stage. As illustrated earlier with the automotive sector, it is likely that the transport sector will continue selling legacy gas and diesel vehicles as well as servicing the existing fleet for decades to come. A major part of their challenge comes from a shrinking sales base of legacy products and the inefficiencies of scale that may become a drag on their financial performance. If the market perceives your business as being low performing, it may make it more difficult of expensive to raise new capital just when the demand for reinvestment is increasing. Simultaneously, maintenance of existing products can become a financial and capability challenge as some customers demand similar standards of care even when profitability for those services is declining.

Stuck In-Between—Fight Stagnation Between Stages

One of the biggest problems facing companies in transition is the misalignment of their new products with existing customers and market expectations. In essence, despite considerable planning effort the transition seems to go wrong. Supply and demand may be out of alignment, the pace of change may be too slow, key capabilities in short supply, the transition may be too expensive, or some unforeseen events cause unexpected changes in market conditions. The purpose of the examples listed below does not suggest that these companies are doing poorly. Many of them made ambitious plans and commitments. The examples vividly illustrate that a transition plan for any legacy company has many moving parts, and the execution of those plans can be challenging, with success determined only with a longer view.

KUWAIT HAS BLACKOUTS: The country of Kuwait is one of the largest energy producers in the world with more than six percent of the proven global oil reserves.[15] Kuwait's plans called for transitioning away from oil to natural gas for most of its electricity use as an interim step towards more renewable energy sources. They have abundant capital, centralized planning, and a well-defined geographic market. However, supply disruptions, under-investment in the transmission grid and warming temperatures have all contributed to problems. In August 2024, "Kuwait had recorded its highest electrical load in history as temperatures reached 50 degrees Celsius, or more than 120 degrees Fahrenheit, aggravated by high humidity along the coast."[16] Rolling electricity blackouts have become common as rising demand, a growing population and climbing summer temperatures make blackouts particularly painful.

LEVI's WASTELESS 511 JEANS: Levi's is a global brand known for their denim jeans and various clothing brands. In 2013 they launched a series of products made from recycled polyester blended with their traditional cotton fabrics. It was called the "wasteless 511" or the "jeans made from garbage." In the early stages of a sustainable transition, the idea seemed to make sense. Unfortunately for Levi's, the polyester/cotton fabric blend was very difficult to recycle and limited the jeans to one lifecycle before it entered the landfill. The company dropped that product in favor of their new "circular jean" in 2022 that has 40% recycled cotton. According to the company, "Choosing recycled denim content blended with certified organic cotton uses fewer natural resources and fewer chemicals to produce. We utilized our Waterless® technique for fabric dyeing and garment finishing, with zero discharge of hazardous chemicals in the finishing process."[17]

UNILEVER EXTENDS DEADLINES FOR PLASTIC PACKAGING PLEDGE: Unilever is widely recognized as an early adopter of a sustainable transition plan under former CEO Paul Polman. It had set a variety of ambitious goals including plans to reduce the use of virgin plastics by 50% by 2030. Those plans have been adjusted in a Bloomberg News article, "ESG Poster Child Unilever Waters Down Green Pledges."[18] The suggestion is that scaling back pledges is due to both the technical difficulty and investor backlash at the costs for non-financial impact projects.

THE UNITED KINGDOM MANDATES ZERO EMISSIONS VEHICLES: Starting in 2024 the UK announced that 80% of new cars and 70% of new vans would need to be zero emission vehicles (ZEV) by 2030 and be 100% zero emissions by 2035. The program will be phased in with requirements for 22% ZEVs in 2024, 33% in 2026 and 52% in 2028.[19] The government has spent billions of pounds building out charging infrastructure to support the transition. The financial penalties for failure to meet the new law can be severe. Companies will either have to trade certificates crediting their excess sales with companies under quota or be fined 15,000 British pounds per non-compliant car sold. Unfortunately for the UK government, the Society of Motor Manufacturers and traders (SMMT) has testified before House of Commons' Transport Select Committee[20] that the industry will be well below the targets this year. The June data from the SMMT suggests that new car sales of all electric zero emission vehicles between December 2023 and June 2024 was 16.6%.[21] One problem may be the type of home ownership in the UK. Lloyds Bank recently released a study suggesting that only 56% of British homes can support an electric charging point and that 30% of people applying for a new mortgage in 2024 will not have a garage or dedicated parking spot where they can charge.[22]

CROC FOOTWEAR EXTENDS IT NET ZERO PLEDGE: The company known for its branded footwear has promised to reach net zero emissions by 2030 and had been making positive progress. However, business expansion decision in 2021 led to the acquisition of casual footwear brand HEYDUDE.[23] The acquisition substantially increased the company's value chain emissions, its baseline emissions calculations, and led to a change in its new zero emissions target to 2040, according to its 2023 Corporate responsibility and Sustainability Report.[24]

COLGATE-PALMOLIVE MAY MISS SOME PACKAGING CIRCULARITY TARGETS: The company had committed to a 2025 target date to make all its packaging recyclable, reusable or compostable by 2025. The company suggests it has achieved 89.5%[25] of its targets but that certain packaging was proving very difficult to convert. As of year-end 2023, it had reduced plastic packaging by 21.4% (vs 2025 target of 1/3) and reduced post-consumer recycled plastic in packaging by 18% (vs 2025 target of 25%).

MICROSOFT EMISSIONS INCREASE DESPITE PLEDGES TO BE CARBON NEGATIVE BY 2030: Microsoft has been a sustainability leader among high technology firms but has experienced new challenges as artificial intelligence has pushed up demand for data centers. Microsoft states in its year end 2023 report, "In aggregate, across all Scopes 1–3, Microsoft's emissions are up 29.1% from the 2020 baseline. The rise in our Scope 3 emissions primarily comes from the construction of more datacenters and the associated embodied carbon in building materials, as well as hardware components such as semiconductors, servers, and racks. Our challenges are in part unique to our position as a leading cloud supplier that is expanding its datacenters. But, even more, we reflect the challenges the world must overcome to develop and use greener concrete, steel, fuels, and chips. These are the biggest drivers of our Scope 3 challenges."[26]

REINSURANCE COMPANIES SCRAMBLE TO STOP LOSSES: 2023 was the hottest year on record and follows a trend of overall global warming that has accelerated in the past 20 years. According to the Swiss Re Institute, global losses from extreme weather events like heavy rains, hurricanes and thunderstorms exceeded $280 billion USD with a record 142 catastrophic events. "Swiss Re echoes other studies in finding that climate change will play an increasingly large role in driving future costs."[27] Many home and mortgage owners in coastal areas are finding costs increasing every year. The insurance losses are also expected to increase as new zoning and building codes drive up the costs for new construction and renovations and the increasing populations in coastal areas are also driving up the value of assets in those areas. Reinsurance companies have traditionally been able to spread the risks, but with so many areas affected by the same conditions, it's becoming harder to price products that customers can afford where companies can make a profit.

Finding Success in Transition

Despite missteps, setbacks and challenges, there are success stories among larger companies in transition. Tesla has successfully created one of the largest new automotive companies in the world and has helped usher in a new era in electric vehicles. Over the last decade Tesla has expanded manufacturing operations around the world, solved many of the challenges of EV manufacturing and operating at scale, developed global partnerships, redesigned sales channels, and continues to launch new products.

Global retailer IKEA announced as early as 2015 that, "all cotton used for its products—from furniture to towels, bedding and other home textiles—comes from more sustainable sources; specifically, from farmers that use less water, less chemical fertilizers and pesticides, and are also able to increase their profits."[28] IKEA has committed to reducing emissions from its supply chain by 50 percent, reaching net zero by 2050 and is working toward a more circular economy model from its operations.[29] In 2023, IKEA was the seventh most valuable retail brand in the world and made a gross profit of 14.7 billion Euros.

Other companies like Vestas Wind Systems benefited from an early start at transition. The company was founded in Denmark in 1945 as a manufacturer of appliances. It is starting in the wind energy business in 1979 on a part-time basis and then transitioned to full-time focus within 10 years. It later merged with other wind turbine manufacturers to become the largest wind turbine manufacturer by the early 2000s. The company has successfully managed several business downturns and the market crash of 2007–2008. Today, it operates in 83 countries with more than 25,000 employees.[30]

Understanding customer needs and market acceptance is an important part of any business transition. Are my existing customers onboard with product changes? Are they accepting and want more? Do my sustainable product changes open up completely new markets and customer segments? Figure 6.6 illustrates some of the possibilities.

Start-up companies have the advantage of targeting new customer segments and have the ability to create a brand story that aligns perfectly with their new value proposition. A legacy business often needs to maintain an existing customer base, and its revenue stream, while it discovers a new product mix capable of supporting a similar revenue base and growth model. If a legacy business is not careful, it can

ZONES OF INNOVATION

	Evolutionary Growth (need to reduce variability – focus on improving existing success models & customer relationships)	Revolutionary Growth (need to introduce variability & rethink, re-educate, re-design people, processes & capability)	
New	**POTENTIAL CUSTOMERS** (same customer characteristics – existing product ideas) KNOWN MARKET SEGMENTS & SIMILAR VALUE PROPOSITION	**NON-CUSTOMERS** (new opportunities with new customer characteristics – new products) NEW PRODUCT FOR NEW MARKET OR NEW CUSTOMER SEGMENT	New
Current	**EXISTING CUSTOMERS** (same customer characteristics – existing product ideas) PRODUCT SUBSTITUTIONS OR SIMILAR PRODUCTS WITH NEW FEATURES	**CONFUSED CUSTOMERS** (mis-alignment yields poor results and impact) SAME CUSTOMER BUT VALUE PROPOSITION CHANGES OR SELLING POINT MOVES	Current

CUSTOMER SEGMENTS (left side)

Incremental	Radical

PRODUCT CHANGES

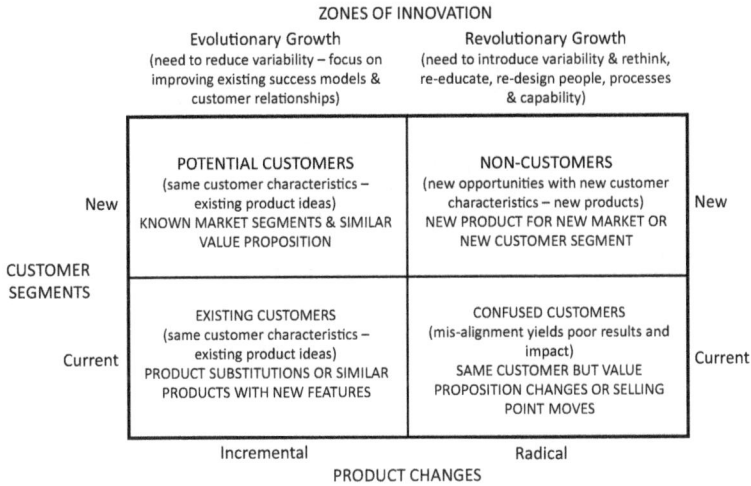

Figure 6.6 Product evolution and customer acceptance.

confuse its customers or move too slowly as it carries the operating costs of a shrinking base of existing products while adding costs for new segments. Figure 6.7 converts the previous chart into key questions.

What is typical at this stage of an industry transition is you see both challenges and successes. Ford is noted above for significant losses in its fledgling EV business, but it has done very well in other areas of its sustainable business strategy. According to Ford, "Since 2000, Ford has achieved a 76.2% reduction in absolute freshwater use, accounting for a cumulative 186.3 billion gallons of water saved. In 2022, Ford used 22 percent less water globally, the equivalent of providing a year's worth of water to 1.7 million homes."[31] The Carbon Disclosures Project (CDP) provides Ford with an A rating for water stewardship, and it was the only automotive company to receive an A grade in both the water and climate categories in 2023.[32]

Transition plans need to be adaptable to changing conditions. As some of the brief examples above illustrate, change needs to involve product development, prototyping and testing as well as talent development

ZONES OF INNOVATION

	Evolutionary Growth (need to reduce variability – focus on improving existing success models & customer relationships)	Revolutionary Growth (need to introduce variability & rethink, re-educate, re-design people, processes & capability)	
New	Can I expand my market share with current products by adding new sustainability attributes?	Are there new, underserved customer segments that will be attracted to a new sustainable value proposition even if its radically different than my existing offers?	**New**
Current	Can I retain current customers by evolving products with new sustainability attributes?	Are my current customers confused by my new sustainable value proposition, its pricing or attributes?	**Current**

CUSTOMER SEGMENTS

Incremental   Radical

PRODUCT CHANGES

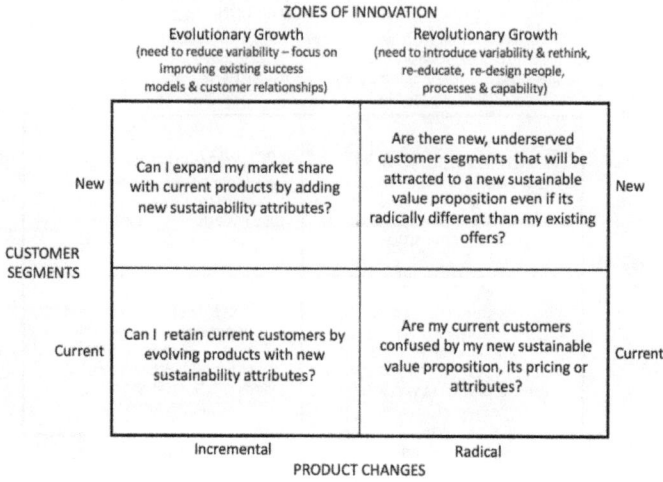

Figure 6.7 Product evolution and customer segment questions.

and process changes. New products may also need alignment with both existing customers and non-customer segments to see where the new products are best introduced. There are also potential challenges on the buy-side if you are a supplier, if your buyer incentives are not aligned with your new unique selling proposition. That may require you to find a new point of entry into traditional customers where the sustainability attributes you are selling are more valued.

A simple change such as using recycled plastic for small beauty product bottles, which may require food grade quality, or changes in product packaging, which may affect customer perceptions, needs to be prototyped and tested for customer reactions. The challenge may not be in the product or packaging, but in customer education.

Dr. Ayana Elizabeth Johnson, co-founder of the Urban Ocean Lab and author of *What If We Get It Right?* (2024) states, "We already know how to electrify transportation, produce energy in a clean way, how to shift our agriculture to make that more sustainable, to insulate and green our buildings and infrastructure, to protect and restore ecosystems, to look to photosynthesis as the magical climate solution that it is."[33] "We need to have creative conversations with experts from other perspectives that can help you see futures and well as barriers preventing us from getting there and what roles are important to fill."[34]

The key with the most innovative and successful transitions are they often emphasize taking educated risks and "failing forward," a term coined by author John C. Maxwell.[35] This means that change always come with the possibility of failure, but you learn, improve, and ultimately succeed. You also benefit from the knowledge and capability you develop in the process.

Summary

- Transitions are an essential part of any move to a more sustainable future.
- Transition planning can be modeled as a four-stage process that evolves from a focus on compliance with disclosure standards and frameworks, to improvements in operating efficiency related to key sustainability challenges, to more responsible behavior characterized by producing products that are sustainable by design to the final stage of strategic sustainability where the plans, capability, core processes, and capital allocation are all aligned with sustainable business practices.
- Each stage from 1–3 has common practices that can be implemented to make positive forward progress. Efficiency gains, based on legacy practices and fossil fuel dependence, will have limits on how much additional efficiency can be achieved without the complete substitution of alternative energy or more radical changes.
- It is common to find the transition from stages 2 to 3 to be difficult as companies work to emphasize new sustainable products while maintain the revenue streams from legacy operations.
- Starting early, dealing with setbacks, and adjusting to market changes are part of the new business reality. Leaders need to remain focused but must also deal with rebalancing efforts to keep all stakeholders on board.

Transition Planning Reflection Checklist

Transition Planning Checklist	
Is it more or less true that your organization ...	**Ranking**
1	Has a North Star Statement that has been shared with the organization?	1 2 3 4 5 6 7 8 9 10
2	Has developed a sustainable business strategy and goals for when it hopes to achieve net-zero status?	1 2 3 4 5 6 7 8 9 10
3	Created a business transition steering committee to coordinate change management activities?	1 2 3 4 5 6 7 8 9 10
4	Created a master transition plan organized into stages with key milestones for each stage?	1 2 3 4 5 6 7 8 9 10
5	Creating a planning process to assess all disclosure and performance requirements for sustainability in the markets where the business chooses to operate?	1 2 3 4 5 6 7 8 9 10
6	Assessed both market competitors and adjacencies to identify possible sustainable business opportunities?	1 2 3 4 5 6 7 8 9 10
7	Identified key leaders to work on prototyping teams to design and test new product and service opportunities?	1 2 3 4 5 6 7 8 9 10
8	Aligned data collection and reporting to ensure the organization can communicate its sustainable business activities to all necessary stakeholders?	1 2 3 4 5 6 7 8 9 10
9	Communicated with key partners about the new business vision and the plans for business transitions?	1 2 3 4 5 6 7 8 9 10
10	Evaluated business capabilities and talent needs based on the timing and needs of the transition plans?	1 2 3 4 5 6 7 8 9 10
Total Score		

Scoring:

- Score less than 50—The scoring on this checklist is more sequential than the other checklists, so it is necessary to look at both the overall scores and any individual question with a very low score. A low score tends to indicate either a very early-stage planning effort or a process that has been understaffed or inadequately staffed. There is a lot of work to be done.
- Score less than 80—Again, the prescription depends on where the low scores are. If you score high on the early questions and lower on the latter questions, that suggests good planning, but perhaps not enough time to fully execute the plans. This is where visible senior-level support and good change leadership are essential.
- Score greater than 80—Things are looking positive. This is a self-scoring assessment, so multiple perspectives are helpful to ensure that the scoring is not inflated. Even great planning must be executed strongly and then maintained for several business cycles to ensure that key process and capability changes take hold.

Chapter 7

ENABLING A CULTURE OF SUSTAINABILITY-ORIENTED INNOVATION

I think the only way we're going to achieve climate goals that have been set is through innovation. I mean, that's the only way forward. We have to innovate our way out of it. CHAD SYVERSON, PROFESSOR OF ECONOMICS, UNIVERSITY OF CHICAGO BOOTH SCHOOL OF BUSINESS[1]

T he great management theorist Peter Drucker once observed that "every single social and global issue of our day, is an opportunity in disguise." It is generally accepted that key markets like transport, housing, shipping, utilities, and others are in transition. However, as Johnathan Ive, the former lead designer at Apple has said, "It's very easy to be different but very difficult to be better." Past market transitions have taught us at least two lessons: First, if you are a legacy business, you must adapt and evolve, or you will be left behind. Second, if you are a new business, you must be future-focused and relentlessly pursue new value creation.

Challenges: How do we reorient innovation practices to deal with issues of sustainability? How do new boundary conditions affect our approach to innovation? How do we re-align those practices with functions and roles to achieve the best results?

Opportunities in Disguise

The transport industry is a good example of a sector in transition that is heavily concerned with innovation challenges. Legacy car companies have invested huge amounts of capital in electric vehicles (EVs). Reports suggest that "vehicle manufacturers and battery makers plan to invest $860 billion globally by 2030 in the transition to EVs. Nearly a quarter, $210 billion, is expected to be invested in the United States, more than in any other country."[2] That is a huge opportunity, not only for the companies making the new cars, but the supply chain, the dealers, the repair centers, and spare parts companies. The significant level of investment is matched by enthusiasm among investors. "The combined market capitalization of pure play EV makers boomed from USD 100 billion in 2020 to USD 1 trillion at the end of 2023, with a peak over USD 1.6 trillion at the end of 2021."[3]

Early evidence of a market transition not only includes the high levels of investment but also broad-based product introductions and significant market share growth. The International Energy Agency (IEA) reports that, "Electric cars accounted for around 18% of all cars sold in 2023, up from 14% in 2022 and only 2% 5 years earlier, in 2018."[4] Given those conditions, you might expect companies to be earning good profits. But that's not the case. Analysis by the Boston Consulting Group indicates that most EV makers lost about $6,000 per vehicle in 2023.[5] This is despite 65 percent of the global car market reaching an adoption rate described as mass adoption (>15 percent) or a tipping point adoption (5–15 percent).[6]

Ford Motor Company is an interesting example. It remains one of the oldest legacy car makers in the world in continuous operation since 1903. In 2018, they announced plans to invest over $11 billion USD to develop and roll out 40 new EVs by 2022.[7] Unlike other auto companies, Ford also announced a restructuring in 2022 to separate its EV products from its internal combustion engine vehicles by establishing the "Ford Model e" division.[8] One of the innovation challenges of launching a completely new set of products within a legacy company is that old ways of thinking and old business practices can be barriers to innovation. Ford's goal in creating the new division is to accelerate the transition and increase the rate of innovation.

That reorganization is one of the reasons I can use Ford as an innovation example. A separate business division means you have separate financial reporting that allows analysts to break out EV sales and costs from traditional products. Despite some great new product reviews, "Ford Model e reported a full-year EBIT loss of $4.7 billion on sales of 116,000 EVs, or an average of $40,525 per vehicle (2023)."[9] That was certainly bad enough news, but it gets worse for 2024. "Ford's electric vehicle unit reported that losses soared in the first quarter (2024) to $1.3 billion, or $132,000 for each of the 10,000 vehicles it sold in the first three months of the year, helping to drag down earnings for the company overall." "Ford said it expects Model e will have EBIT losses of $5 billion for the full year."[10]

Legacy Success Can Be a Barrier to Change

Part of the challenge is changing a legacy business and the core processes and behaviors that have led to previous success. Ford Motor Company's annual revenue was over 176 billion USD in fiscal year 2023.[11] If the market is moving away from fossil fuel vehicles, then Ford's transition plan must include replacing those 176 billion dollars in annual revenue, plus add more for growth. That is a considerably different challenge than launching a small company that may be evaluated on achieving high growth numbers based on a very small installed base.

The only EV maker in the United States making money on EVs is Tesla, which was the first successful new automobile company in the United States in decades and one that reimagined its production and supply chain from Day 1. It is the most profitable of any global car company and has the highest market capitalization. Despite making fewer cars, Tesla has enjoyed a larger market capitalization of any car company as of Q1 2024.[12]

It's hard to say at this point in time that Tesla is a success and Ford is a failure. Transitions take time and companies must continuously prove their value in the marketplace. A first mover advantage helped Tesla build up its production capacity by selling to early adopters willing to pay a premium for its products. Those early buyers may never have been traditional Ford customers, and Tesla marketed itself in part by being different. As important to Tesla was the benefit it received from its manufacturing location in California and the state cap-and-trade scheme as well as the California Zero Emissions Vehicle (ZEV) program. This illustrates two boundary conditions that are relevant to transitions.

- Selling to early adopters and non-customers—Early adopters are customers who want the new product because they value having the first version, the new innovation, or the status of early adopter. There is a limit to the size of this audience, but it is frequently a key part of a new product launch where costs may be higher. The second audience is comprised of non-customers. A non-customer is a person or an organization who feel they can benefit from a technology innovation based on benefits or value that was traditionally not available to them. This a major strategy for companies selling early digital camera products and for current companies selling hydrogen fuel cells to long-haul truckers or to battery companies selling their products to niche markets like airlines
- Incentives and subsidies—Government subsidies are often designed to help companies transition and keep employment and business tax revenue in the host market. They are key to innovation because they reshape the cost/value equation and can also reframe the innovation practices that work during a transition. For example, Chinese government subsidies for EVs allow Chinese

companies to use older battery technology or use government subsidized ecosystems so they can sell a cheaper mass market car that drives scale. As such, reverse engineering techniques may dominate in that market over more disruptive strategies in markets where local investors bear all product launch costs.

Government subsidies can have a transformative effect on a market. They can favor new or existing players, they can influence the type of innovation or the standards that dominate, and they can reshape markets and capital allocation for years to come. At an executive level, the levers of control used by executives to influence are limited, so they must be allied differently to each situation.

Remaining with the automotive industry as the example, governments respond with subsidies because the industry employs millions of people worldwide, is a massive addressable market, and it connects to many other strategic industries like steel, aluminum, plastics, chemicals, and fuels. Whether you agree or disagree with the use of subsidies, any business leader must consider them as a significant business driver that influences its transition and innovation planning.

The ZEV credit system that Tesla used in California says that every car maker must make an increasing number of ZEVs as a percentage of its overall sales in the state. If they do not, they must buy ZEV credits to offset their portfolio deficit. Who has excess credits? Tesla of course,

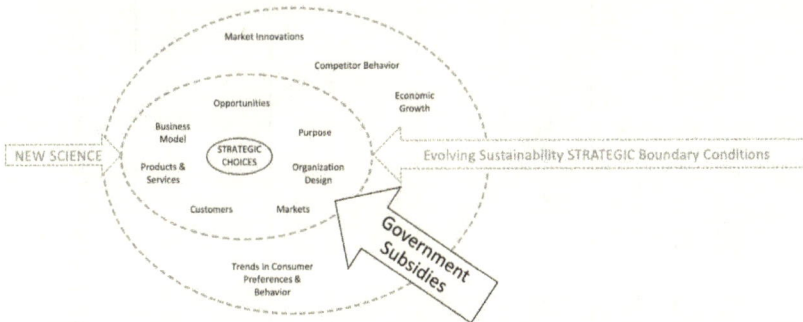

Figure 7.1 Subsidies can transform market dynamics.

Example-Executive Levers of Control	Legacy Approach	Disruptive Approach
Capital allocation	Additional capital is allocated to the largest and most successful product categories with the highest margins.	Capital is allocated to new ideas with the largest addressable markets, with the most disruptive potential.
Organizational design	Structured hierarchies and clear division of labor with specialized functions dedicated to key products and services.	Flexible design with many leaders serving in multiple roles as needed. Few rigid hierarchies.
Leadership	Hired for experience managing large systems and good market communication and influence skills.	Hands on leaders who can be the chief sales evangelist as well as a hands on problem solver.
Key hires	Specialized hires with an emphasis on past experience managing operations at scale.	Hire for enthusiasm, energy and willingness to be adaptable. Often over hire to ensure growth potential.
Key processes	Clear process development to maximize efficiency.	A focus on best available practices. Core processes evolve over time as needed.
Incentives	Continuous top and bottom line growth and continuous innovation. Limit surprises and risk issues.	Adaptable. New growth in markets, customers and product acceptance is often emphasized over profitability. Team success is often prized as is radical innovations that are brand defining.

Figure 7.2 Examples of executive levers of control.

because they made all their early EVs in California, and made a lot of them. Since the credits were first introduced in 2017, credit sales of all types (ZEVs and carbon credits) have been a major feature of Tesla's balance sheet. They have sold more than $100 million USD in carbon credits every quarter since Q1 of 2019. In Q4 2023, Tesla sold $890 million in carbon credits, its most ever.[13] This has allowed Tesla to invest and innovate by redesigning key components of the EV car and by investing in new technology such as self-driving, AI, and battery technology. Early-stage government subsidies can have great value, but they can create friction between trading partners over the level and type of subsidy. Carbon credits were first introduced under the UN Kyoto Protocol, Article 17, in 1997.[14]

Competition among major markets like the European Union, the United States, and China changes the way capital supports innovation. The use of subsidies, tariffs, tax advantages, free services, or subsidies has become part of the sustainable business transition and cannot be ignored by any business. Again, the EV market is a good example because of its perceived importance in all of the major global markets. China has emerged as both the largest market for vehicles and the largest market for new vehicle start-ups. The Chinese government has encouraged new company formation with over 100 new EV and hybrid brands emerging including brands like BYD, Nio, and XPeng and international brands owned by Chinese companies like Volvo, Lotus, and Polestar. It is estimated that between 2009 and 2023, the Chinese government (national, provincial and city) provided over 225 billion USD in subsidies to EV makers.[15] This includes tax breaks, direct support, and reduced costs for services and components. The European Union is investigating the Chinese EV makers for possible tariffs[16] and the United States has already announced a 100 percent tariff on Chinese vehicles.[17]

Sometimes legacy practices have been so successful that they prevent people from seeing new possibilities. Hydroelectric dams have harnessed water energy since the early days of the industrial era. They are well-understood technologies for offering cheap electricity, but the value proposition is based on financial value creation. If you examined the issues of environmental and social negatives or the destruction of other sources of capital like fish and wildlife habitats, then the value proposition becomes more problematic. Although traditional large-scale hydroelectric dams are still being installed around the world, there are newer innovation solutions like Ocean Power Technologies' PowerBuoys [18] that offer sustainable energy without the environmental negatives. The PB3 buoys float in the ocean and generate energy from wave and tidal action. Carnegie Clean Energy has been developing equally innovative solutions such as its CETO technology that uses floating generators to capture wave and tidal energy.[19]

When and How Fast to Innovate

Tesla has gone through phases of trying to vertically integrate several components like castings and motors but has also partnered in areas like batteries with companies such as Panasonic and CATL. Over the past several years Tesla battery technology, a core component of vehicle cost, has not been the most advanced. It was reliable and good, but several other companies beat them with higher energy density and efficiency. Yet Tesla became the best-selling manufacturer of EVs in the world. BYD of China also lays claim to that title, but only when you include EVs, hybrids and plug-in hybrid vehicles together. Tesla does not manufacture in the latter two categories. Despite the presence of many large incumbent automobile companies with decades of experience, hundreds of thousands of employees, and tens of millions of vehicle unit sales per year, the EV industry is now dominated by one United States and several Chinese start-ups that did not exist before the turn of the century.

The issue of innovation timing was first introduced by Everett Rogers back in 1962 with his book, *Diffusion of Innovations.*[20] He outlined five types of companies including the innovator (the company creating the new idea), the early adopter (a company that can capitalize on getting to market quickly), the early majority (companies that add similar products after initial market acceptance and growth), late majority (companies that respond to the competitive actions after market growth), and laggards who have largely missed the innovation and are playing catch up. As discussed earlier, this is a type of heuristic knowledge. It may not be empirically tested, but it seems to accurately capture market behavior about the introduction of new products in a marketplace.

Tesla was started as a car company in 2003 and went public in 2010, a year in which it sold approximately 1,000 cars and had full-year revenue of ~110 million USD.[21] It launched its new flagship product that year, the Tesla Model S, and accepted $5,000 USD deposits from 2,000 customers to help finance the cars development costs.[22] Fast forward and Tesla sold 1.81 million pure EVs in 2023, a 38 percent growth rate over 2022. Tesla's success has attracted many competitors, and its innovation strategy has evolved with the size and scope of its operations. Gone are the days when 2,000 customer deposits would excite investors or the general public. Now the question becomes can they continue to grow at double digits from a base of almost 2 million units.

In 2024, Tesla announced the use of innovative new batteries in several models to include breakthroughs in energy density, increased range, and reducing weight.[23] The condensed battery design from CATL[24] was originally made for the airline industry, but they are now applying the same concept to mass-produced car batteries. Tesla has apparently kept it eyes on market adjacencies and partnerships as potential sources of strength. Its innovation strategy appears to lead the pack at times, lag in in others, and includes both incremental improvements as well as breakthroughs. That makes them a unique and very challenging competitor for the legacy car companies.

From an innovation perspective, it raises questions for the rest of the EV industry. The new Tesla, CATL battery partnership is based on a graphene aluminum-ion battery formula. Ford Motor Company made plans to open a $3.5 billion USD battery plant in Michigan based on licensing Chinese lithium-ion battery technology.[25] Owning the factory guaranteed Ford a dedicated source of batteries, but it also committed the company to a large investment and a type of technology. It has now scaled back those plans both for political pushback because of US-China tensions and because of its growing losses in the EV market.[26] Will changes in battery technology complicate matters? Will delays in choosing new battery designs make their EVs less competitive? What about the existing investments in lithium mining, lithium recycling, and other applications for lithium battery suppliers? Will a radical change in energy density promised by aluminum-ion batteries create a market disruption?

Timing and level of commitment are two additional elements of innovation that must be balanced, particularly if your timing and level of commitment restrict your ability to be adaptable in future years.

There are two key insights developed by innovation pioneers over the years.

1. Breakthrough ideas often start small by serving customers who are often willing to pay a higher premium for their unique application. These sales almost always start small, which is why they are less attractive to large companies that don't see how such innovation address the needs for large revenue substitutions. The advantage to this approach is that initial commitments can be small. That allows the profitable sale of early-stage innovation while the company works out the issues of scale and cost reduction.

2. Disruptions seem to appear quickly, although they have often been in plain sight for many years. The difference is, they first appear or are incubated in adjacencies or new markets. Smart companies often explore low-cost partnerships with non-competitive industries as a way of learning about the potential of new innovations. While timing may appear fast to current market players, the disruptor has often been working on the new products ideas for years and has the advantage of experience that governs and mitigates their risk assessment.

Large legacy companies often approach incremental and radical innovation very differently based on their different capabilities. A small start-up or mid-sized company has more line-of-sight management and can adapt quickly. Leaders can know everyone in the company by name and mobilizing the company for change can be more immediate. Large legacy companies have the advantages of scale, established customers and brand recognition, but their processes are designed to limit risk. As such, many legacy companies defer radical innovation to the market and choose to observe market changes with the hope of investing in, merging, or acquiring a more innovative peer at a later date.

Example - Executive Levers of Control	Legacy Business	Start-up or High Growth SME
Approach to radical or disruptive innovation	Defer to the market. Observe market behavior and attempt to buy minority positions in non public companies or merge or acquire public companies at a later date.	Disruption helps to define new brands and is a source of attraction for more capital, key staff and customers.
Approach to incremental innovation	Incremental innovation is essential to continuously offering your customers new features or improvements in performance. That is why customers buy again, renew or remain loyal	Disruption focuses on "good enough" products or products that are better than what the market offers rather than perfect. Incremental innovation comes later as the products and markets evolve.

Figure 7.3 Approaches to incremental versus disruptive innovation.

Organizational Tensions Affect Your Innovation Practices

The challenges of sustainability have become prominent for most businesses at a time when national competitiveness, global tensions, and the speed of innovation are happening in parallel. Additional market tensions have been created that make executive decisions more complex. The broad range of intergovernmental treaties and regional public policy changes have challenged traditional market drivers because

of deadlines, penalties for non-compliance, and reporting requirements. These policy changes have been supported in some instances by
increased tariffs, taxation schemes, and subsidies that serve to redirect
capital allocation and the development of new products and services.
Each of these factors can create a new innovation tension that influences or redirects innovation activities. Figure 7.4 highlights the five
primary innovation tensions that need to be balanced or resolved by
any organization trying to become more sustainable by design.

More vs. Less Variability Market Tensions: Part of the challenge for a
legacy company is the tension that exists in a mature business that has
rode a wave of success for years or decades. When a company finds a
successful model for products and services, it tends to cut back on other
products and devotes its energy to evolving its most profitable and
enduring efforts. More risky investments are less favorably received,
and the innovation focus becomes one of continuous improvement.
Variability is often the enemy in a mature legacy business where it
implies added cost. Alternatively, it may be prized as an asset in a disruptive business.

Organizational tension creates a paradox for managers trying to support both practices. On the one hand, incremental innovation is about
teams all working in unison with common goals, structure, and practices. Radical innovation allows for improvisation and divergent thinking and benefits from a diversity of perspectives, whereas incremental
innovation values the consistency of structure and practice. The two
different innovation streams require different management approaches,

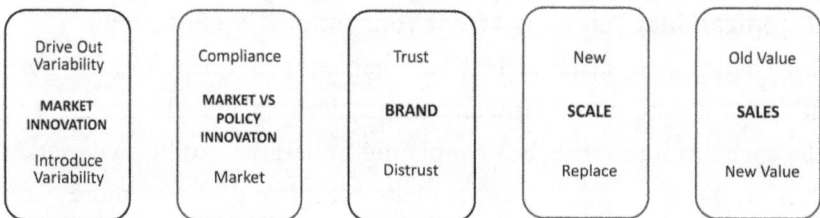

Drive Out Variability	Compliance	Trust	New	Old Value
MARKET INNOVATION	**MARKET VS POLICY INNOVATON**	**BRAND**	**SCALE**	**SALES**
Introduce Variability	Market	Distrust	Replace	New Value

Figure 7.4 Summary of innovation tensions.

and some companies choose to physically separate such efforts to avoid negative influences.

Japanese auto companies are closely associated with the ideas of total quality, originally developed by W. Edwards Deming.[27]Kaizen (continuous improvement) was popularized in the United States and Europe by Masaaki Imai[28] and Six Sigma is often credited to Motorola engineer Bill Smith, who developed the early process methodologies. Radical innovation techniques became popular in the United States with Michael Hammer and James Champy's reengineering programs in 1993,[29] Clayton Christensen's research on disruptive innovation in 1997,[30] and design thinking, most closely associated with the Stanford University Hasso Plattner Institute of Design,[31] established in 2005.

A good example of a strategy to manage the tension at a large legacy company can be seen again at Ford Motor Company. In an article in which the Ford CEO Jim Farley discussed the competitive challenges of Chinese EV companies, "Bill Ford and I shook hands and agreed that this one we're going to have to get it right from scratch, and that's why we created the 'Skunk Works' team because I felt that the institution of Ford would have a really hard time competing with BYD. So,

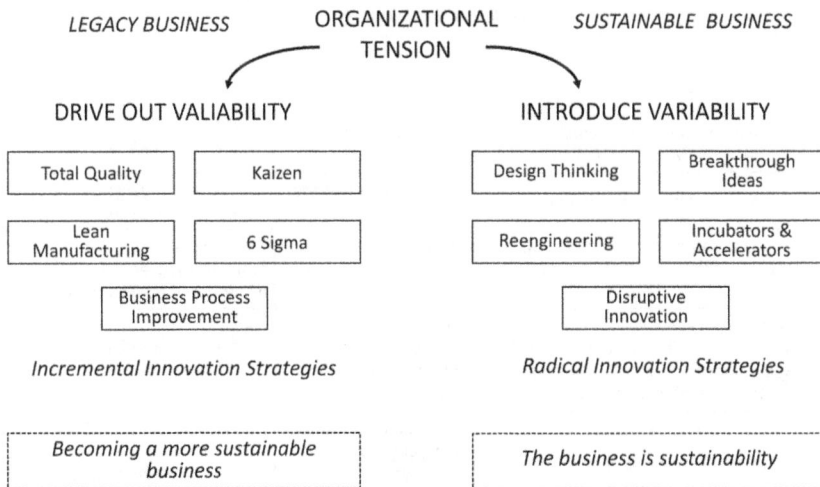

Figure 7.5 Two innovation streams and organizational tension.

we built a ground up team with a similar approach to Kelly Johnson's SR-71 Skunkworks in California."[32] The team includes individuals from Tesla, Rivian, Lucid, and Apple, who can operate in California, according to their own rules and practices, completely separate from Ford's Dearborn Michigan headquarters.

Market-Driven vs. Policy-Driven Tensions: The three large global markets in the United States, China, and the European Union have different policy frameworks as well as subsidy and taxation schemes. As described in Chapter 2, these schemes which include Chinese subsidies in the form of forced technology transfers, preferential administrative procedures, and public procurements European Union programs such as the Cross Border Adjustment Mechanism (CBAM) and the United States Clean Technology Tariffs. All are designed to influence executive decisions on new product development, facility locations, supply chain practices, and intellectual property development. A tension is created when the direction of such subsidies differs from choices that would be made from pure market feedback.

Trust vs. Mistrust Brand Tensions: Social media has become highly influential as a driver of public opinion regarding trust in corporate

What is Common or Different about the Two Innovation Streams		
Common to Both	**Unique to Incremental Innovation**	**Unique to Radical Innovation**
Clear problem statements	Focus on constant improvement from established success	Focus on a fresh perspective and a new way of doing things
Acting with a sense of urgency	Building on what already works	Seeking out game changing ways of doing something.
The need for an environment of trust and an acceptance of intelligent failure	Training team members on standard methodologies and tools.	Focus on deep dives, brainstorming and an allowance for out of the box thinking.
Telling stories about your successes and failures that convey the type of change you want to create and your commitment to innovation.	Delighting existing customers with excellence and constant improvements.	Discovering new value with non-customers.
	Often embedded within existing organizational structure.	Teams often separated and even relocated to allow for unique environment.

Figure 7.6 Innovation characteristics that are common and different.

brands. Advocacy groups and the use of lawsuits and public shaming campaigns have also influenced corporate commitments to ESG topics. The "Clouds of Misinformation" referenced in Chapter 1 emphasize the issues of "greenwashing" and "green gaslighting" that may be attributed to company behavior, but also the idea of "woke washing" that comes from political and social disagreements about the type and pace of social change. All of these labels can be bad for brand engagement and create distrust in a company's public commitments or actions. These brand tensions can lead to a dilution in public sustainability commitments.

Large vs. Small-Scale Tensions: Larger legacy firms enjoy certain advantages of business scale. They have established market presence, may have a loyal customer base and substantial people and intellectual property assets. However, several of the innovation tensions described above such as large market subsidies as well as differences in reporting disclosures and mandates can diminish the value of scale. If a company needs to build separate products or have separate documentation for different markets, then costs may be multiplied. Manufacturing and supply chain decisions made years or decades ago now be advantageous if they were made solely because of costs and did not account for emissions reductions or domestic content rules. In certain markets, the scale tension will also be driven by policy requirements such as Zero Emission Vehicle Rules that penalize a company by certain dates if the company's product mix does not contain the right ratio of sustainable products versus legacy products. In this case, scale works against the company since they must invest in replacing the legacy sales with sustainable products while simultaneously introducing sustainable products by design and overall year-to-year growth. This may lead to substantial up-front costs, greater risks, and lower overall returns on investment. The tensions may restrict newer innovations and can lead to both staff turnover and brand trust issues.

Old Value Proposition vs. New Value Proposition Tensions: The final tension is seen at the operating or sales level. The executive team may support the introduction of new products with enhanced sustainability attributes that may be ahead of customer readiness. Higher prices or new selling propositions may face resistance. Despite regulatory mandates, the question remains, "Are my customers willing to buy?" This final tension is often complicated by a misalignment of internal practices, incentives, or marketing programs which are still designed for legacy products.

Who Is Winning the Automobile EV Transition and Why Is Toyota on the Sideline?

It can be difficult to determine if a company made the right strategic decisions in the middle of a market transition. In the auto industry, Toyota has shied away from pure EV vehicles and emphasized hybrids, plug-in hybrids, and hydrogen fuel cell technologies. Toyota's strategy to avoid market leadership in EVs had many analysts questioning their approach over the last five years.[33] They were, after all, the early green pioneer with the Toyota Prius hybrid model released in 1997. Did they cede their market advantages to Tesla and the Chinese start-ups or are they pursuing a different strategy? With so many peers losing money on EVs, is Toyota smart to avoid losses while waiting for investments in fuel cells and solid-state batteries to mature? At the moment, they make money on hybrids that offer limited green functionality, but at more competitive price point. Is this good for Toyota investors, but bad overall for the environment, since it does little to solve the climate crisis?

The issue for Toyota during most decades would be determined by market and customer acceptance. Getting the timing right would reward the company with market share and improved profitability. Since the current market is driven by the science of climate change and biodiversity, it remains imperative for all market participants to plan their transition. Toyota will still need to build EVs if it hopes to sell cars in many markets where mandated changes are already law. It has also bet big on hydrogen fuel cells, which have not yet found significant market acceptance. Time will tell if their choices allow it to remain a large global player.

Toyota and other Japanese companies had a reputation for high quality and Japan, for a time, could reasonably consider itself the master of gasoline autos. Today, many analysts call China the home for the best-built EVs. They cite companies like BYD, which has been the clear global challenger to Tesla's former dominance in EVs. They cite the Chinese markets growing ecosystem of support companies and BYD's rapid product development, manufacturing efficiency, and cost advantages. Some analysts indicate that build quality for similar Tesla models is best at its Chinese factory as compared to its factories in Germany and the United States.

All of this may or may not be true, since it only highlights a point in time. BYD's ascent is similar to comments about Tesla's innovation excellence or Toyota's early advantages with hybrids. High-growth companies often lose at least temporary control over costs or product efficiency as they rapidly add talent or expand facilities. Achieving high growth as a small start-up is not the same as doing it when you are a large market leader. Competitive advantages are won and lost and must be constantly refreshed through the process of innovation. Achieving excellence is hard, but maintaining it over time is how organizations ultimately succeed.

BYD, despite its significant growth and record of success, is discovering it is not immune to the challenges of managing a larger business. A Chinese automobile analyst firm called 12365auto conducts ongoing surveys of new car complaints and BYD had 6 of the top 10 nameplates with the most complaints[34] in July of 2023. A trend that has been growing as the company has expanded sales. The same surveys show Chinese-built Tesla models as having the fewest complaints for new models. BYD will likely face ongoing challenges as it opens new factories in Thailand, Mexico, and Vietnam. Winning the war for market innovation is a hard task and requires diligent leadership support, continuous training, and adjustments in the level of organizational design and control to maintain a leadership position.

Creating a Culture of Innovation Takes Time

One of the reasons to create a culture of innovation is to establish the internal ecosystem that teaches, supports, encourages, and rewards innovative behavior. Innovation is largely a team practice and is easily stifled if there is not a general acceptance of experimentation, reflective inquiry, teamwork, and a willingness to learn from mistakes. That takes time, funding and active leadership support. That means the executive levers of control need to be adapted to the company purpose and the culture that will support it over time.

Good innovators start with a question that needs to be answered or a market need. The question may come from a briefing about market adjacencies, a green team tasked with investigating a challenge, a leader participating in an industry forum, a supplier observation or research co-created with a partner. Senior leaders cultivate such sources in high-innovation companies because they see it as their role to feed the innovation pipeline with ideas. They help with the dialogue and debriefing so there are always ideas under discussion and a portfolio of experiments in progress. Innovative companies have simplified and easy processes for teams to get together to investigate an idea. In some instances, this is an expectation for functional and business unit leaders. Innovative companies also look at team activities as development opportunities for emerging leaders where they gain experience and insights into the process of innovation.

The team approach capitalizes on the fact that describing a great idea is different than being able to prototype that idea, scale it, or continue the process of incremental improvements. It is also true that sometimes it's necessary to separate innovation streams because they offer different opportunities, require specialized skills and possibly different practices, leadership, and incentives. They may each use a similar process of observation, ideation, prototyping, execution and improvement, but the boundary conditions of an existing product with defined customers and work streams is different than a new breakthrough.

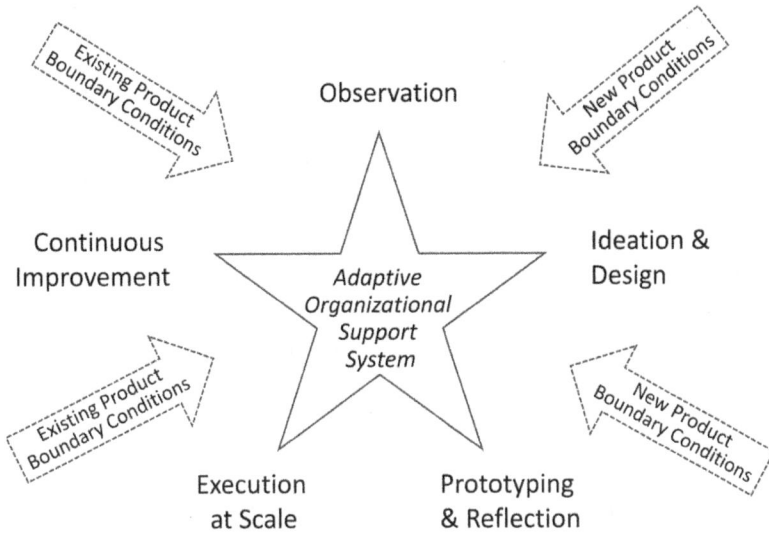

Figure 7.7 The adaptive organizational support system.

Embrace Challenge-Driven Innovation at Every Level

Developing a culture of innovation requires translating the big goals and concepts into practical issues that people can act upon. This means connecting your sustainable purpose and ethical frameworks with each product and service in ways that everyone understands. Everyone must feel part of a greater whole but also see how they can have an impact. Specific tools are helpful, role-based training is essential, cross-functional alignment of processes makes life easier, and the engagement of leaders is necessary to build a strong culture. Figure 7.8 highlights some examples of how different roles innovate.

The CEO may get to determine sustainable corporate policy, such as a bank not lending to companies that invest in artic drilling. While the branch customer service representative or the teller in the bank doesn't get to make that decision, the local branch may be engaged in operating more sustainable facility and helping customers understand sustainable investment products or a credit card offer that tracks personal emissions. Some techniques like value chain analysis, causal loop modeling,

Role Examples	Examples of Where this Role Innovates	Examples of Innovation Strategies
Executives as well as senior business, functional and geographic leaders	Business models, financial instruments (e.g., green bonds), corporate policy, organizational design, North Star Statement, partnerships, Incentives, culture development, communication strategies, capital allocation.	Co-creation, reverse innovation, reengineering, disruptive innovation, incremental strategies.
Marketing	Brand, channel, product and product system development and customer experience, partnership development, messaging	Co-creation, reverse innovation, disruptive innovation, incremental strategies.
Human Resources	Incentives, corporate rituals, training, culture development, employee experience	Co-creation, reverse innovation, incremental strategies.
Finance	Cost, policy, risk analysis, scenario planning, measurement, integrated reporting, multi-capital value modeling, carbon credits, offsets, dual materiality, renewable energy credits	Value chain analysis, causal loop modeling, future scanning
Supply Chain	Supply chain, product design, efficiency, partnerships	Value chain analysis, causal loop modeling, circular product assessment, Environmental product declarations, third party opinions
Technology	Efficiency, automation, workflows, cost and quality improvements, process improvements, network improvements	Breakthrough technologies and Incremental improvement strategies.
Key Individual Contributors	Cost and quality improvements, performance improvements	Ideation, prototyping and Incremental improvement strategies.

Figure 7.8 Innovation roles. Note: Peter McAteer, *Sustainability is the New Advantage: Leadership, Change, and the Future of Business,* Anthem Press, London, page 92.

or scenario planning may be applicable to many people in an organization because they allow for incremental innovation across a workflow. Other techniques like circular product assessment, or choices to seek third-party opinions to validate ideas, may fall to mid-level or senior functional roles.

When you are trying to enable sustainable change throughout an organization, it moves faster if you can articulate several easy ways for people to participate tomorrow. As each individual gains experience and learns innovation techniques, they begin to see new opportunities. Peers then learn from peers as well as from leaders and trainers and the process begins to self-reinforce.

If we apply some real-world examples to the model illustrated above, we can see how role-based innovation works in action.

- Executive Leader Innovation: Open AI was created by a series of investors who envisioned an artificial intelligence (AI) research firm. Originally created as a non-profit, it is now seeking new investors to raise billions of dollars in new investments to build-out massive new AI data centers and energy systems to power them.[35] CEO Sam Altman is reportedly meeting with representatives of UAE investment funds as well as partners like Taiwan Semiconductor and the U.S. Government to explain his plans.[36] These innovation ideas potentially include new financial instruments, multiple partnerships, and a new global vision for AI. This scale of the proposals, the money involved, and the engagement need to make the partnerships work suggest that this can only be done at the most senior level.

- Business Unit Leader Innovation: Bank of the West in California decided to create a range of bank policies that limited their lending: No lending to tobacco firms, artic drill, and fracking companies. Because of the ways banks are regulated, and risk is managed, such policies need to go through a series of senior-level reviews with approval by the senior-level bank risk committee.

- Functional Leader Innovation: Ben Stuart, chief marketing officer at Bank of the West negotiated a partnership with "1% for the Planet."[37] His marketing product teams managed the design of an account that tracks your carbon footprint of all customer purchases. The detail design of the product was the innovation of partners Mastercard and Doconomy.[38]

- Broad-based Incremental Innovation: Companies like Dell introduced plant-based packaging as far back as 2011 and today is a leader in using ingredients like bamboo in sustainable packaging solutions.[39] Puma, the global footwear company has long been committed to reducing the paper and cardboard in its shoe boxes. In 2021, it launched the "PUMA circular Lab" to anchor the ideas of circular innovation in the DNA of the company. Its recent sustainability report claims that 80 percent of products were made of certified or recycled materials in 2023. Many of these solutions are the result of employee ideation or specific work teams focused on is sustainability goals.

- Broad-based Regulatory Inspired innovation: This is a type of forced innovation model where a government policy like Europe's Waste Electrical and Electronic Equipment regulations requires companies to consider the costs of compliance versus alternatives. Companies across the EU must rethink their products to consider the waste stream compliance costs in the design phase or as an adaptive strategy since the regulation change their cost models. Everyone will participate and learn from competitive and non-competitive peers and common, best-in-class solutions will emerge.

Many innovations are driven by existing company technologies or practices that are repurposed. BASF, one of the world's largest chemical companies, partnered with Carbon Minds, to expand its database for chemicals and plastics with associated product carbon footprint (PCF) data.[40] This provides thousands of companies a standard way of calculating some of their scope 2 and scope 3 emissions.

Although innovations are often associated with physical products, a great many sustainability-oriented innovations are occurring in the areas of investment and financing. The traditional private equity businesses, as an example, were focused on extracting value and generating liquidity and cash flow. Today, global finance markets have become more attuned to sustainable business principles and long-term sustainable value creation. Part of this change is due to the design of carbon credit markets which are now closing in on one trillion USD.[41] This represents both a new and attractive asset class as well as a model for managing environmental negatives. The carbon market is driven by regulated markets and cap-and-trade schemes, but the model is also being considered for a range of other issues like pollution, plastics, and biodiversity as well as collateralized instruments for general finance.

Several examples highlighted by European law firm Fieldfisher are[42]

- loans secured by emissions allowances;
- repurchase transactions on emissions allowances;
- spot purchase of emissions allowances coupled with a cash or physically settled forward;
- funded collar transactions on emissions allowances; and
- total return swaps on emissions allowances.

Challenge-driven innovation takes a boundary or idea and asks everyone to innovate solutions using the boundary as the starting point. Having multiple teams approach the same boundary from different perspectives often results in different ideation patterns. Each new idea can serve as a pathway for additional layers of discovery. For example, if we use circularity as our boundary challenge, we ask all teams to identify solutions using that concept as the core boundary. A team with mixed perspectives will often create solutions that leverage their diversity in service of the larger goal. For example, a person with a finance background may have ideas about shared ownership or leasing or buyback schemes, while a person with a supply chain background may innovate around product transparency, certification, or shared procurement. Alternatively, they may be able to take someone else's idea and offer strategies to operationalize the financing or purchasing options. Something as simple as a word cloud of ideas may open an innovation discussion to bolder thinking. A sample word cloud for circularity is shown in Figure 7.9.

Embrace Intelligent Failures as Teachable Moments

Amy Edmondson, professor at Harvard Business School and author of, *Right Kind of Wrong*, says, "A healthy failure culture rewards intelligent failure. Without I, there can be no innovation. Without innovation, no organization can survive over the long term."[43] The key issue is the engagement of senior leaders. If they are involved in sponsoring,

Functional Supply Tenders   Designed for Repair & Reuse

Revenue
Sharing   Multi-use
Land strategies   Upcycling   Refurbished
Resales

Co-tenancy   Designed for
Long Life   Biodegradable
Components

Mass Balance
Feedstock   Demand
Reduction   Downcycling   Sell &
Buy-back

Waste to Energy   Pay to Use
(No Ownership)   Reverse Logistics

Recycled
Feedstock   Circular
Substitutions   Parts
Harvesting   Virtual
Substitution

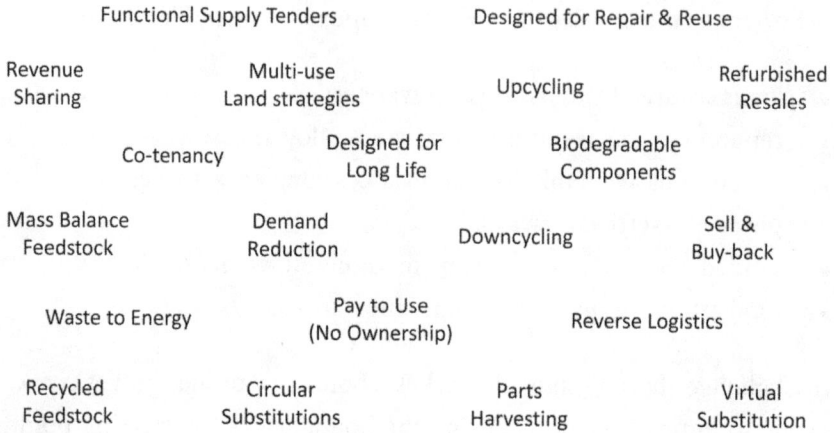

Figure 7.9 Circularity word cloud.

supporting, and coaching the teams that fail, then they share the journey and help the team learn from the process. An organization that is actively experimenting with new sustainable solutions has a portfolio of ideas that are simultaneously being developed. The goal is to have the portfolio of projects lead to positive outcomes. Those outcomes may include new products to scale, new learning about customers, markets and technologies, possible partnerships, staff development, and other new capabilities. Failure is part of the process, but it needs to be managed intelligently so the organization and the people involved all make positive forward progress from the experience. Examples:

1. Nike launched a brand of shoes called "Considered" in 2005 with a boot made of hemp fibers.[44] An eco-friendlier shoe has merit, but the execution didn't work with Nike's customers and sales never took off. Nike has had other successes from designing sewing machines that use less electricity to using more recycled plastics in footwear to redesigning the assembly process. Over time, they also learned lessons on how to introduce new products that fit better with their sustainable brand messaging.

2. Amazon is one of the largest retailers in the world with a global network of distribution centers. Customers posted online images of Amazon orders (UK 2020) arriving at their door, with each item arriving in a separate box.[45] Although Amazon had worked hard to make the individual boxes and packaging more environmentally friendly, their order management system was not designed to limit overall packaging on each order. Amazon has made progress in intervening years to improve the sustainability of individual packages as well as the overall order.

3. McDonald's replaced plastics straws used with beverages with paper straws in the United Kingdom in 2019. This seems like a great idea since McDonald's UK reportedly used 1.8 million straws per day.[46] Unfortunately, the straw design thickness made them difficult to recycle with their UK waste management partners and they typically ended up in the general waste. Since then, McDonald's has engaged with recycling efforts at many levels. It works with the Recycling Partnership with grants to expand recycling innovations and is part of the Polypropylene Recycling Coalition.[47]

4. Philips Lighting Company introduced its Earth Light extended-life fluorescent bulb back in 1992. The concept and performance of the bulb allowed it to replace incandescent bulbs and save energy over the life of the product. Unfortunately, the initial price of $15–20 per bulb made it a difficult purchase decision for most customers. The product launch became the subject of academic case studies,[48] since it raised interesting questions about product launches and marketing of sustainable products. Philips is a good example of an early adopter company that worked continuously to create more sustainable products. It still makes its Earth Light brand and has current commitments to design 100 percent of its products in line with its EcoDesign requirements and to a quarter of its revenues by 2025 from circular products and services.[49] According to Philips, "The difference between EcoDesign and conventional design is

the clear goal—right from the start of the innovation and design process—to reduce the total environmental impact."[50]

The key with each example is not that the product, product launch, or customer targeting was less successful than desired, but that each company remained focused on the objective, learned from the experience, and is currently more capable as a result.

Use Social Rituals to Reinforce a Cultural of Sustainability-Oriented Innovation

Social rituals are group events used to reinforce a sense that each person is part of an organization with a common purpose. Sustainable development is already framed as a common purpose for all humanity and is easily translated into benefits for the communities where we live and work. This makes connecting a company purpose with broader global goals easier. . Most surveys find that employees are highly motivated to work at purpose-based organizations.

Social rituals become a critical part of anchoring a culture of sustainability because they use existing role models and stories to transfer knowledge to the rest of the organization. A social ritual is also an opportunity for networking and for creating personal bonds with fellow team members. Such rituals may include orientation programs for new employees, promotional transition programs for first-time managers, annual award and recognition events or team meetings to plan and generate buy-in with new initiatives.

If you break down the words "social" and "ritual," both parts are important. The social element is key to creating emotional connections and shared memories. Social rituals are about sharing, learning, and co-creating. The ritual element is about the recurring nature of an event that gives it significance in the company culture. It is something that helps define the annual company calendar and is a common element that everyone can participate in. In some instances, it is also a rite of passage, such as when all new managers are required to serve on

standing sustainability committees as part of promotional consideration, or if all leaders are expected to teach in the new employee orientation program to help convey the company culture.

Summary

- Changes in boundary conditions create what are referred to as "opportunities in disguise," because we are not used to seeing opportunities within social and environmental challenges or in multi-capital formation.
- Organizational tension is a normal occurrence in organization with both large legacy businesses and newer disruptive businesses. Although normal, the tension must be managed so different types of innovation can evolve simultaneously.
- Organizations need to create an adaptive organizational support system to be certain its innovation practices evolve with changing boundary conditions. It is much easier to train everyone to be adaptable then to be always right. Mistakes are opportunities for learning as long as the organization fails forward.
- Innovation practices can be tailored to the type of business objective and to the role and level of the people doing the work. The more the innovation tools and training allow people to have impact, the more engaged they will become.
- Sustainability requires a business culture that can allow a legacy business to become more sustainable, while developing new products and services that are sustainable by design or that serve a market niche created by sustainable demand. Particular emphasis must be given to training, leadership support, and key activities that support the innovation process.
- Challenge-driven innovation is essentially a forced innovation model. Your task is to provide a specific challenge and boundary limitations and then develop best-in-class solutions. Sustainability offers a range of such opportunities where we are creating industry alternatives that all support net-zero emissions or circular resource model.

- Failure is part of innovation. That is not an excuse for poor decisions, but the expression of reality when a company is exploring new ideas and experimenting with possible solutions. Leaders must embrace opportunities to learn and leverage such situations for future success.

SOI Reflection Checklist

SOI Checklist		
Is it more or less true that your organization ...		**Ranking**
1	Assessed the competitive pressures and opportunities facing the organization?	1 2 3 4 5 6 7 8 9 10
2	Has taken planning steps to separate legacy transition activities from new product and service programs?	1 2 3 4 5 6 7 8 9 10
3	Identified key high-potential leaders to participate in key "Green Teams" charged with solving key innovation issues?	1 2 3 4 5 6 7 8 9 10
4	Assessed partnership opportunities where the organization can learn new strategies and build capabilities for sustainability-oriented innovation?	1 2 3 4 5 6 7 8 9 10
5	Designed and provided training programs on sustainability-oriented innovation that are targeted at both the business challenge and the employee level, so you provide tools for everyone to participate in innovation?	1 2 3 4 5 6 7 8 9 10
6	Evaluated the reward and recognition systems for different parts of the organization so they are aligned with the innovation challenges?	1 2 3 4 5 6 7 8 9 10
7	Established clear expectations for senior leaders who will mentor and support each innovation effort to allow for "failing forward" as the organization embraces innovation?	1 2 3 4 5 6 7 8 9 10

SOI Checklist		
Is it more or less true that your organization …		**Ranking**
8	Created a large enough portfolio of sustainable innovation ideas to allow for comparable and competitive assessments of the best new ideas?	1 2 3 4 5 6 7 8 9 10
9	Established one or more social rituals that celebrate sustainable innovations as the way forward for the company?	1 2 3 4 5 6 7 8 9 10
10	Incorporated innovation capability in the organization's talent planning, recruiting, and promotion schemes?	1 2 3 4 5 6 7 8 9 10
Total Score		

Scoring:

- Score less than 50—Focus on your low scores to determine what part of the process is weak. SOI only succeeds when all aspects are aligned and working together. Weaknesses in capability or leadership support can kill an otherwise good program.

- Score less than 80—Innovation requires a lot of positive energy. The idea of learning from intelligent failures is also a difficult skill to master. Keep the focus on creating small successes and a balanced approach. It is better in larger organizations to build one business or geographic unit at a time so there are centers of expertise to leverage.

- Score greater than 80—You likely have some strong capability, although it may be limited. Moving from initial success to ongoing success is a challenge of moving to scale and leadership commitment.

Chapter 8

FINDING VALUE WITH TEAMS, PARTNERSHIPS, AND VOLUNTARY MEMBERSHIPS

Great things in business are never done by one person: they're done by a team of people. —STEVE JOBS, FORMER CEO OF APPLE[1]

The speed of a business transition can often feel too fast if stakeholders are not confident in the change process and willing to support the transition. The organization must feel the collective sense of urgency and work to bridge any gaps in knowledge or capabilities among staff, partners, and the business ecosystem. False starts may increase the resistance to change and the appearance of chaos may lead to a loss of confidence in the executive team.

Challenge: How do teams, memberships and partnerships help us learn more, leverage our strengths and reduce risks?

There are a number of resources at the organization's disposal. Teams, external memberships, and partnerships offer opportunities for learning new capabilities, filling knowledge gaps, and accelerating innovation. Such strategies can accelerate action by validating assumptions and identifying market trends that reinforce your transition plans.

Teams Are Sources of Problem-Solving and Innovation

Teams are an indispensable part of any transition strategy. They add perspective, unleash energy and innovation, and are a source of problem-solving, learning, and capability building. Some organizations call them "green teams," others use standard project management terms. Teams can be assigned projects like decreasing energy use or reducing waste. In these instances, the business is engaging staff in developing a sense of accountability. In other instances, teams are used to assess and develop solutions to customer-facing products and services and solve specific sustainability challenges like product packaging, vendor data collection, or waste reduction.

Teams are the ultimate tool for challenge-based innovation. The team can be organized, chartered, and provided resources and time to solve a specific issue, problem, or opportunity. The narrowness of the charter, the fixed time to reach a recommendation, and the creative tension that produces almost always produce something of value.

In organizations with a very strong legacy culture and well-entrenched products or services, it may be necessary to separate the teams physically from the mainstream operations. This idea has given rise to companies placing teams in partner organizations or selecting a division or geographic location with a leadership team ready to support the ideation process. In organizations with a more developed ideation portfolio, you may see innovation incubators that serve as empowerment hubs, or accelerators that provide training or services designed to speed up the process of bringing good ideas to market.

To avoid disconnects between the core organization's culture and teams operating with joint ventures, vendors, or partners, it is necessary to involve everyone in select social rituals connected to the organization's North Star Statement and values. Operating practices can vary greatly between big mature organizations and small start-ups, but values can be a connecting bridge. Senior-level transparency and support is important, as is consistent, ongoing communication. All parts of the business are part of the transition solution and have a potential role to play within social rituals. Teams offer levels of speed and adaptability that more established organizational structures may struggle to match.

Voluntary Memberships Are Sources of Learning

The unique challenge of sustainability as a business driver is that the goals are based on common global problems that are beyond the reach of any person, business, or country to solve on their own. Creating a more sustainable future requires collaboration, shared accountability, respect for multiple perspectives, and a level of broad-based innovation not seen before. So where can you listen to new perspectives, access information about evolving standards, and learn about broader industry or international innovations? Memberships in networks, industry associations, or communities of practice are easy, low-cost, and readily available solutions. The biggest investments are frequently time and energy.

The United Nations helped sponsor the UN Sustainable Development Solutions Network in 2012. The initial work to set up the network was done by then Secretary-General, Ban Ki-Moon, and Columbia professor, Jeffrey Sachs, who served as an advisor to several UN leaders. The goal of the network is to "mobilize the world's universities, think tanks, and national laboratories for action on the Sustainable Development Goals (SDGs) and the Paris Agreement."[2] Today, the network has over 1,900 member institutions and almost 60 national and regional sub-networks.

Memberships can be found for general management as well as functional and industry groups. Memberships should be approached as sources of value where an individual or organization can contribute ideas and find sources of fresh inspiration and learning. Figure 8.1 offers examples.

Membership Focus	Organization
Senior Leaders	• World Business Council for Sustainable Development (WBCSD) • Alliance of CEO Climate Leaders (World Economic Forum) • CEO Action Network
Financial Leaders	• CFO Coalition for Sustainable development • World Sustainable Finance Association (WSFA) • CFO Leadership Network – Accounting for Sustainability • The Sustainable Banking and Finance Network
Marketing Leaders	• The Global Sustainability Council (International Advertising Association) • World Federation of Advertisers (Planet Pledge) • Sustainable Brands (SB)
General Leadership	• Association of Climate Change Officers (ACCO)
Engineering Leaders	• Engineers for a Sustainable World • European Society for Engineering Education (integration of sustainability in engineering education)
Technology Industry	• CleanTech Alliance and CleanTech Leaders Roundtable
Agriculture Industry	• Field to Market • AgTech Founders Network
Consumer Goods	• The Sustainability Consortium (TSC) • Sustainable Packaging Coalition (SPC)
Women	• Women in CleanTech and Sustainability (WCS) • Women of Renewable Industries and Sustainable Energy (WRISE)

Figure 8.1 Membership organization examples.

Which membership is right for you? Keep these questions in mind.

1. Do you have a clear goal in mind? For example, brand visibility, knowledge acquisition, ability to influence industry policy, or networking.
2. Does the membership organization align with your goals and interests?
3. Are there other alternative memberships that you can compare and contrast?
4. Do you have access to other members so you can ask questions about activities and purpose?
5. Does the membership organization of interest have any brand risks?
6. Can you add meaningful value as a member?
7. How much time is required to add value to the membership organization and achieve your goals?

8. Is there a term limit to membership so you can participate for a specified period of time and then either leave on good terms or renew your membership?
9. Do you have a company sponsor who supports your participation?

Ecosystems Can Be Your Competitive Advantage or Your Barrier to Growth

How do you work with your suppliers and partners, particularly SMEs, to insure they can support your plans? During research interviews for my first book, *Sustainability Is the New Advantage*, conducted in 2018, a number of senior leaders indicated that the biggest barrier to growth was the lack of alignment or support they had with their extended supply chain or ecosystem. Since I was conducting those interviews only 2–3 years after the Paris Agreement, perhaps that is not surprising since many small- to medium-sized firms were not required to do ESG disclosures and there was no formal requirement for larger companies to disclose water, waste, or emissions data from suppliers in many parts of the world. Yet for this book, I received very similar feedback.

Part of the feedback reflects the issue that most small- to medium-sized businesses lack the capital to invest in more sustainable business practices. It's a big risk factor for a smaller organization. Another aspect of the problem is the lack of cross-functional alignment in larger companies so systems and business practices at lower levels of the organization evolve to support the supply chain or partnerships.

So how do you improve the ecosystem alignment with your sustainability goals? One strategy is to emphasize the need for data collection, collaborative skills, and the value of multiple perspectives. The latter is important to sharing data that is relevant to the needs of each major constituency and to satisfying the needs for compliance and for execution of a purpose-based mission. For example, the supply chain organization of Lowes Home Improvement conducts webinars for suppliers that teach suppliers how to identify, collect, and organize information about scope 3 emissions.[3] They also offer product pitch events for new product ideas, and publish a series of videos, guides, and tutorials to aid suppliers in supporting their goals.[4]

Open versus closed ecosystems

Should you build an open or closed ecosystem? Technology companies like Apple are famous for developing a closed ecosystem that offers several benefits such as better security, integration, and quality control. The term "ecosystem," however, is used broadly across many industries such as agriculture, textiles, transport, and housing. In some instances, major subcontractors and suppliers service major competitors, although in other instances suppliers aggregate around a select group of large customers and maintain exclusivity. "A main concern around an open vs. closed ecosystem is the protection of proprietary intellectual property and the associated social or relationship capital."

The balance of evidence for sustainable development and low-maturity markets suggests a more open ecosystem, but the choice is not the same for all companies and is not an either-or choice. One of the key considerations is where are you competitively? If you are an early adopter, the choices may be different than if you are competing against companies with existing market share and an established customer base. An open ecosystem is often preferred for developing partners, for learning and for improved adaptation in markets with greater ongoing innovation. It is also the case with technology companies that regulators in both the United States and Europe have looked at technology ecosystems as potentially anti-competitive. That is less the case with many other industries, where the ecosystem is considered less of a "product system" and more of a "supply chain." The ecosystem as a competitive product advantage can be seen with application stores or in music services where they serve as the access portal to customers. This allows the ecosystem owner to define how participants behave, what they offer, how much they charge, and how they appear in customer searches.

Partnerships Reduce Your Risks and
Fill Big Gaps in Knowledge

One of the earlier boundary conditions described in Chapter 2 was the company's legal status. Where a company chooses to place its headquarters or its operating units can have an effect on its tax and governance structure. Another aspect of legal status is an ownership position of less than 100 percent that allows a company to work with partners to gain insights, access to more capital or capability. Engaging in a partnership can have a variety of value considerations that determine the duration of the partnership, the funding and the governance structure. Some of the more common partnership value options are listed in Figure 8.2.

Raven SR, a global waste to energy firm was launched in 2018. According to the firm, "we are revolutionizing the way the world uses waste. We take any organic waste and convert it to clean hydrogen and synthetic Fischer-Tropsch fuels through our patented Steam/CO_2 Reforming process."[5] Raven SR partnered with Chevron New Energies,

Figure 8.2 Partnership value options.

a subsidiary of Chevron Corporation and Hyzon Motors on a project to produce green hydrogen from waste in Northern California[6] in a project called Raven SR1. The project also involves another local partner Republic Services that barters space at its landfill in Richmond California in exchange for Raven SR to remove ~75–90 tons of green waste from Republic's landfill each day. Raven SR1 is expected to produce 2,000 tons of renewable hydrogen per year. Chevron New Energies 50 percent stake in the partnership gives them rights to 50 percent of the green hydrogen which it intends to sell for green hydrogen fuel cell vehicles. Chevron also gains by aligning its brand with a green alternative energy start-up. Raven SR reduces its financial risks and gains new value creation. Republic reduces financial risks and builds new relationships. Each of the partners has a different, but well-aligned partnership value proposition.

There was a time when large charities, NGOs, and even intergovernmental organizations shied away from corporate partnerships. This has certainly changed in the last 20 years with major NGOs with the best green credentials embracing partnerships as a way to improve impact. The Nature Conservancy has total asset of over 9 billion USD with over a third held in its endowment and long-term investment funds.[7] Nature Conservancy now partners with corporate firm like Kellogg and Syngenta on more efficient farming practices for irrigation and water conservation.[8] Since 2011, the Nature Conservancy has partnered with Dow Chemical examining how nature-based solutions can have a benefit for nature as well as for business. Dow has created a Valuing Nature Goal which "sets out to achieve $1 billion in net present value through projects that are good for business and better for ecosystems."[9] U.S.-based Walmart, one of the world's largest retailers and online sellers partnered with the Nature Conservancy on the Pacific Island Tuna project to create an end-to-end tuna supply chain. Walmart now buys, "Pacific Island Tuna's Marine Stewardship Council-certified, fish aggregating device-free, canned skipjack tuna for its in-house brand, helping make a responsibly produced protein source widely accessible within the U.S. and supporting the communities of the Marshall Islands."[10] Walmart, the Walmart Foundation, and The Nature Conservancy have since partnered on various projects to reduce the environmental impact of global food sourcing.

Partnerships Create Value for Mutual Gain

As is often the case with corporate interests, when a partner becomes known for effective practices and value creation, they attract new partners. The Nature Conservancy has successfully partnered with companies as diverse as Coca Cola, Whole Foods, The Walt Disney Company, T-Mobile, General Mills, Shell, and many others.[11] Many have worked with the organization for over a decade.

Some partnerships become long-term relationships when a company finds a good solution to one of its sustainability challenges and decides it is better to work with a like-minded organization over time. Pizza Hut is a restaurant chain with more than 20,000 locations in 2023, owned by parent company Yum! Brands. Reducing emissions from agricultural activities is a major challenge. Unlike energy production, where you can potentially switch to an alternative fuel, emissions products from any type of animal-based activity requires a different approach. Pizza Hut reported that it had cut emissions from its supply chain, including beef, poultry, dairy, and packaging by 6 percent in its 2023 sustainability and citizenship report.[12] In 2022, Pizza Hut partnered with the "Dairy Farmers of America (DFA), a farmer-owned cooperative owned by more than 10,000 farm families, to provide select farmers in the U.S. with technology and data to help reduce on-farm greenhouse gas (GHG) emissions. The collaboration is producing positive results among participating farmers including a 10% decrease in GHG emissions intensity from the milk used in the production of Pizza Hut cheese."[13] Based on positive U.S. results, Pizza Hut has launched a two-year project in the United Kingdom and three-year project in New Zealand. The projects all use data and software to spot efficiencies and shared learning across its global network of partners.

Sometimes partnerships develop among industry competitors when they discover an issue that is too big for any one company to solve. The chemical industry provides products and services to most industries. Such products are often linked to scope 3 emissions and are deeply integrated in the global supply chain. Solving challenges like circularity and net-zero emissions are in every industry player's interest, but the costs are significant. Encouraged by events at the World Economic Forum, industry leaders from companies including BASF, Mitsubishi Chemical Group, SABIC, Siemens Energy, Clariant, Covestro, LyondellBasell, Sabanci, Syensqo, and SUEZ joined forces to create the Global Impact Coalition. According to the Coalition's website,[14] "The challenge is too big for any single company alone to solve. The Global Impact Coalition provides a platform and safe space to exchange ideas, develop new business models and create proof-of-concept pilots." The Coalition borrows expert talent from within the industry and also partners with outside organizations such as engineering company Linde and Dutch innovation company TNO. Part of the role of the Coalition is to identify high-impact projects based on a series of agreed goals:[15]

- Reduce emissions with high global warming potential.
- Reduce process carbon emissions.
- Enable the energy transition.
- Increase circularity of polymers.
- Utilize alternative carbon sources.
- Increase chemical safety and reduce pollution.
- Promote end-to end transparency and certification.

The Global Impact Coalition (GIC) also demonstrates the value of executives voluntarily participating in international events like the World Economic Forum and Conference of the Party (COP) meetings that served as the spark for the GIC. These global events serve to incubate ideas and offer networking opportunities for key decision-makers.[16]

Another good example of multisector partnerships involves the draft of a new net zero standard introduced by the International Organization for Standardization (ISO) in 2024. The draft standard grew out of a collaboration introduced at the COP27 meeting in Egypt and resulted in staff from Intel, Meta, Amazon, Federal Express, Google, Mars, and McDonald's, participating in a working group to generate the draft standards. The output of that group will now be used for input from national standard bodies across the globe with a public consultation to be launched at COP30 to be held in Brazil in 2025.[17]

Mergers and Acquisitions Allow Fast Followers to Rapidly Build Scale

Some companies see merger or acquisitions as a better way to scale than starting and building new businesses. The logic of this approach allows a company to observe the market of new innovators to see how they progress and if any company separates itself as a market leader. The trade-off is the higher cost of investing in such a company as the market-leading companies rise in value.

The artificial intelligence (AI) space may be the fastest growing new opportunity anywhere and it is expected to have enormous implications for sustainability. Broadcom, one of the current leaders in AI, starting life with a series of mergers, the most significant being the merger of Avago industries with Broadcom in 2015.[18] The merger, then valued at 37 billion USD, created a leading company in the wireless communication and semiconductor industries just as the AI industry started its accent. Eight additional acquisitions occurred between 2018 and 2023[19] creating a platform company that is a key player in data center networks. Broadcom's stock price has increased over 2,900 percent since 2015 with an increase of over 600 percent in the last five years including dividend reinvestment.[20]

The merger and acquisition strategy is an acknowledgment by some market players that their legacy company is not good at starting and nurturing new businesses. Leading a start-up is very different than leading a large span of control so the leadership team may not be prepared to help solve small start-up problems. Larger acquisitions or mergers are frequently done when a company's stock price allows the acquiring company to make a competitive offer with upside to the existing investors. This strategy depends on making the acquisition work and making decisions on how the combined company creates more value than the companies do separately.

Summary

- Teams are the internal organization tool for problem-solving and quick, challenge-based innovation.
- Memberships offer a range of opportunities to learn from business peers and business adjacencies in a low risk, low-cost environment. Enthusiasm, openness to learning and time are the primary investments.
- Ecosystems can be a competitive advantage or barrier to growth. Suppliers and partners must be aligned for purpose, capability, and data collection to ensure reporting, compliance, and competitive advantage are all advanced.
- Partnerships can be innovation multipliers and provide access to capabilities not found in the parent organization. The options for partnerships are almost endless because all you need is a common interest in a sustainability challenge.
- Mergers and acquisitions are an alternative to creating an internal portfolio of new businesses but require substantial capital and a clear plan for how to merge, leverage, and manage the combined businesses.

Team, Partnership, and Membership Reflection Checklist

Team, Partner, and Membership Checklist		
Is it more or less true that your organization ...		**Ranking**
1	Creates internal green teams to continuously innovate around key business sustainability goals?	1 2 3 4 5 6 7 8 9 10
2	Encourages senior leaders to participate in external membership organizations dedicated to solving common sustainability challenges?	1 2 3 4 5 6 7 8 9 10
3	Encourage key staff at all levels to participate in business networks that share best practices and ideas for sustainable business innovation?	1 2 3 4 5 6 7 8 9 10
4	Provides vendor training on data collection so the accuracy and availability of scope 2 and scope 3 emissions are available?	1 2 3 4 5 6 7 8 9 10
5	Assessed the value of open versus closed ecosystems and how each may benefit the organization's sustainability efforts?	1 2 3 4 5 6 7 8 9 10
6	Has active partnerships in areas of high potential and risk designed to push the envelope on innovation and create new organizational options of growth?	1 2 3 4 5 6 7 8 9 10
7	Link team leadership and team memberships to the organization's talent planning and development efforts to increase staff capabilities with direct experience solving sustainability problems?	1 2 3 4 5 6 7 8 9 10
8	Require senior leaders to support a portfolio of staff development, team and partners programs designed to enhance organizational capability?	1 2 3 4 5 6 7 8 9 10
Total Score		

Scoring:

- Score less than 40—A low score suggests that you have not embraced teams, memberships, and partnerships as a strategic business advantage. The senior team needs to define high-priority areas and make the effort to model the benefits of participation, and then work to engage key leaders.
- Score less than 60—Your organization likely has several initiatives, but the efforts are inconsistent, not well understood, or supported only by parts of the organization. Assess your best practices and key leaders and develop a strategy to create a more broad-based effort.
- Score greater than 60—The goal now is to continue the practice, rotate leaders and key individual contributors across multiple teams or memberships, and refine your key learning to evolve your strategy going forward.

Chapter 9

TELLING YOUR STORY

When your organization needs to make a big change, stories will help you convey not only why it needs to transform, but also what the future will look like in specific, vivid terms. —FRANCES X. FREI AND ANNE MORRISS, CO-AUTHORS, MOVE FAST AND FIX THINGS[1]

Telling your story has always been part of building a successful company. If you are a new business, you're communicating your value proposition and results to new customers and investors. If you are an ongoing concern, those conversations continue as you expand your customer base, enter new markets, and seek partnerships. For the publicly traded company, sharing your story is a quarterly and annual ritual as you seek to convince stock analysts, investors, and customers that you have met or exceeded expectations and the future looks bright. With the age of sustainability, those conversations include reporting on your ESG obligations and how your business will evolve and participate in a sustainable future.

> **Challenge: What is the typical evolution of reporting that matches your transition plan? How can good reporting enhance your brand and your business?**

The importance of the environmental, social, and governance factors for investors can be traced to a program called "Who Cares Wins (WCW)," initiated by the United Nations in collaboration with the UN Global Compact (UNGC), with funding from the Swiss government. It involved a series of invitation-only events for members of the financial and investing communities where the case was made for the routine assessment of ESG risk and opportunities. There was certainly reporting on environmental and social factors before this program was introduced, but the WCW program gave new impetus to ESG reporting on the back of other international agreements and the emergence of pilot programs for the carbon credit markets. These meetings continued through 2008 and included a series of influential reports including:[2]

- *Connecting Financial Markets to a Changing World* (2004)
- *Investing for Long-term Value* (2005)
- *Communicating ESG Value Drivers and the Company-Investor Interface* (2006)
- *New Frontiers in Emerging Markets Investment* (2007)
- *Future Proof? Embedding ESG Issues in Investment Markets* (2008)

As the titles indicate, they address many of the issues with ESG analysis and reporting that are still relevant today. The WCW program also coincided with the first United Nations Global Compact Global Leaders' Summit, chaired by UN secretary-general Kofi Annan in 2004.[3] It should be noted that the first Executive Director of the UNGC was George Kell, who led the UNGC from its inception until 2015, which concluded the era of the Millennium Development Goals (2000–2015). George Kell became chairperson of the Anglo-German asset management company Arabesque Partners in 2017,[4] after leaving the UN Global Compact, succeeding Professor Robert Eccles, who is very much associated with the idea of Integrated Reporting. It's a small world.

The United Nations' Principles for Responsible Investment (PRI) were published in 2006. The early signatories to the PRI were many of the attendees from those early WCW meetings. This kick-started what has become a growing market for sustainable investing assets by establishing standard ESG criteria to be included in financial evaluations. These six foundation principles[5] are as follows:

1. We will incorporate ESG issues into investment analysis and decision-making processes.
2. We will be active owners and incorporate ESG issues into our ownership policies and practices.
3. We will seek appropriate disclosure on ESG issues by the entities in which we invest.
4. We will promote acceptance and implementation of the principles within the investment industry.
5. We will work together to enhance our effectiveness in implementing the principles.
6. We will each report on our activities and progress toward implementing the principles.

Each principle has three to seven sub-activities that help guide investment and financial managers. The PRI proved to be a huge success with ever larger number of investment managers signing on to support the principles as part of their investment practices. The PRI now has two United Nations partners, including both the United Nations Environmental Program Finance Initiative and the United Nations Global Compact. The PRI has steadily gained in acceptance and memberships as the global standard for ESG investing. Today it has more than 5,300 signatories including asset managers, business owners, investment managers, and investment service providers that collectively represent over 128 trillion USD under management.[6]

ESG reporting as part of telling your company's story is significant in terms of attracting new investment. For example, if you are a large and publicly traded firm, by virtue of your inclusion in a potential ESG asset class, it opens the door for possible new investor interest. If you are a smaller firm or listed on a regional exchange, the PRI Principles still allow you to operate in ways that may offer you an ESG rating for your efforts.

If we follow the four-stage transition model introduced in Chapter 6, we can begin to think about the type of reporting we want to model.

Stage 1—Compliance and Common Practice Reporting

Compliance reporting has become much easier than earlier in the 2000s when many efforts were voluntary. There were significant efforts in harmonization starting in 2021 at the Conference of the Parties (COP21) meeting in Glasgow, Scotland, which included the establishment of the International Sustainability Standards Board (ISSB) and led to improved cooperation among major markets and listing exchanges. Depending on the markets where you operate, compliance may be an extension of financial materiality that has been updated to include ESG elements and the PRI Principles. Other markets already require some type of dual materiality. In either case, the goal of compliance is to ensure you are participating in a process bounded by your market

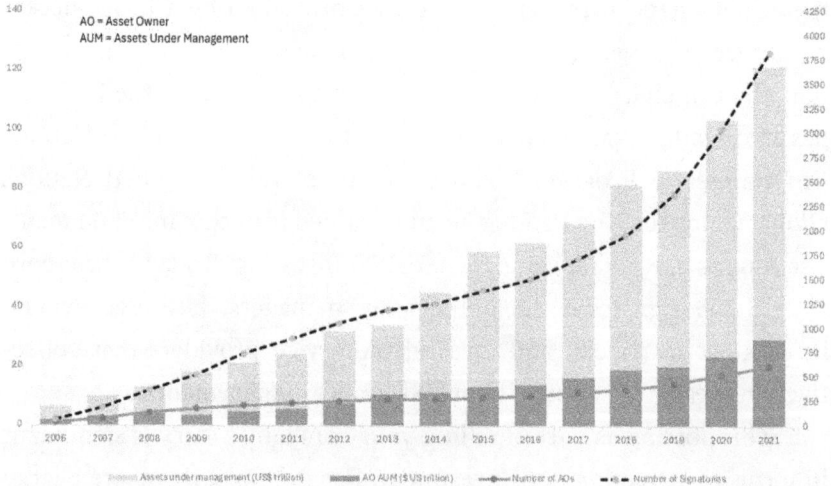

Figure 9.1 PRI Growth 2006–2021 *Note*: PRI Growth 2006–2021, About the PRI, Principles for Responsible Investing website, https://www.unpri.org/about-us/about-the-pri, accessed 30 August 2024.

regulatory authorities and have started the internal practices of collecting information, discussing the data, summarizing it into standard categories, comparing your data to competitive peers and putting it all down on paper (or on your website). As described in Chapter 4, you need to develop your working knowledge model by considering issues such as the markets you operate in, your customer locations, your exchange listing, and the business legal status among other choices such as voluntary memberships and industry associations in developing your full reporting model. A simplified example of how reporting can change is exhibited in Figure 9.2.

The early stages of reporting compliance often start by using one of the many training programs or case studies now available from any of the primary reporting organizations like GRI, or from your listing exchange. If you are a specialized organization like a Benefit Corporation, then it is a simple matter to look up similar companies that are generally required to post their sustainability and financial reports online. One of the first reporting decisions is whether a company creates a separate sustainability report or a blended business report. I use the word "blended" rather than "integrated," because many companies

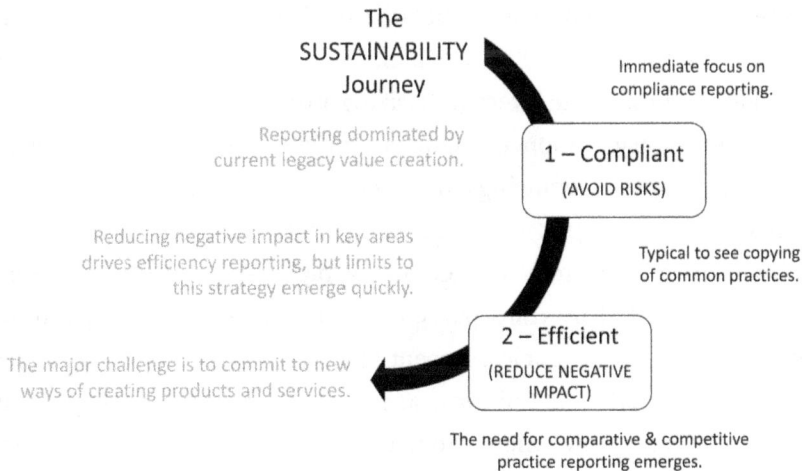

The
SUSTAINABILITY
Journey

Immediate focus on
compliance reporting.

Reporting dominated by
current legacy value creation.

1 – Compliant
(AVOID RISKS)

Reducing negative impact in key areas
drives efficiency reporting, but limits to
this strategy emerge quickly.

Typical to see copying
of common practices.

The major challenge is to commit to new
ways of creating products and services.

2 – Efficient
(REDUCE NEGATIVE
IMPACT)

The need for comparative & competitive
practice reporting emerges.

Figure 9.2 Reporting changes at the first two stages of transition.

at this stage develop their sustainability reporting as a separate report, or as add it as a separate section in one document rather than fully integrating the content.

Stage 2—Comparative and Competitive Practice Reporting

Moving from stage 1 to stage 2 depends a bit on the content you have to work with. If you are essentially a legacy company working on early-stage efficiency activities, then your reporting will tend to evolve as you work your way through the annual process of reducing your water consumption or waste by some percentage. In most cases, you are concerned about how you look relative to your competitive peers more than anything else. If you put yourself in the position of an external analyst looking at your report side-by-side with a competitor, which report looks most informative and impressive? Producing a high-quality, professional-looking sustainability report is not hard to do any more. There are many good examples readily available and a small army of consultants willing to help with the writing, infographics, and formatting.

The challenge is to enhance the quality of the content in your report, which is a reflection of the work you have done as a senior team evolving the business strategy and the sustainable transition plans. This is the stage where many companies violate the idea of making a report concise and complete by adding in too many color photos of beautiful trees and landscapes, while overemphasizing project concepts rather than results and impact. Sooner or later, such embellishments may catch up with the company, requiring a need to restate your results or reporting that an ongoing project is less significant than expected.

If you are a large and visible company, big claims of impact will tend to be investigated by third-party advocacy firms that do a good job of exposing inconsistencies. Recent changes in greenwashing regulations, sustainability definitions, and labeling requirements, particularly in the European Union, can make errors or misleading statements costly. Stage 2 reporting is also where companies experience their first brush with diminishing returns if they have not started experimenting with products that break the connection between growth and emissions or between increased sales and resource consumption. You can only reduce your existing emissions so far, if you are still dependent on fossil fuels. The same goes for most packaging or material efficiency. Early successes can be quite positive, but you eventually reach a point where you are near peak efficiency, unless you commit to more radical changes.

Stage 3—Integrated Reporting

The third stage in the transition cycle is where you tend to see more innovation and personalization in reporting and the beginning of true integrated reporting. As key functional, geographic and business leaders are engaged in data collection, change management and sustainable business dialogue, there are changes to the market messaging, single and dual-use websites, various sub-reports from partnerships, and extensive storytelling. The messaging is directed not just to investors and regulators, but also to partners, suppliers, customers, prospective customers, employees, and communities. The need for conciseness and transparency on a common reporting framework is maintained in regulatory filings and in standard labels and packaging to comply with the law, but a great deal of creativity is seen at this stage in how a company embraces sustainability as an opportunity and in what ways the company tells its story to different audiences.

As illustrated in Figure 9.3, reporting becomes dominated by the new products and services which may have higher growth rates or profitability over legacy products. The emphasis on reducing negative impact eventually becomes less newsworthy because you can only cut or reduce so far. There are better stories to tell.

The International Integrated Reporting Council was established in 2010 to address deficiencies in corporate reporting that traditionally did not include social and environmental impact considerations that investors may find relevant. The goal was to take the best of current reporting practices and add in the concepts of (1) multiple capital formation,

The
SUSTAINABILITY
Journey

Integrated Reporting AND
Integrated Thinking

4 – Strategic
(CREATE SOLUTIONS &
NEW VALUE)

Reporting dominated by new solutions,
new products and transition successes
over time.

Early Stage
Integrated Reporting

The focus on reducing negative impact
gives way to new areas of multiple capital
value formation.

3 – Responsible
(EVOLVE
ORGANIZATION)

Best Practice
Reporting

Promising experiments emerge that
match business purpose. A large portfolio
is often enhanced by partnerships and
strategic investments.

Figure 9.3 Reporting changes in the final two stages of transition.

(2) the organization's interaction with the external environment, and (3) the idea that value creation for the organization is interconnected with value creation for society. The IIRC established the first integrated reporting (IR) framework in 2013, based on guiding principles and shared reporting elements. It was updated in 2021.

In 2022, the International Financial Reporting Standards (IFRS) Foundation took control of the IR Framework as part of ongoing harmonization efforts. The current guiding principles include the following:[7]

1. Strategic focus and future orientation—What is the company's strategy and how does it intend to create value in the short, medium, and long term?
2. Connectivity of the information—The goal is to show how all aspects of value creation are interconnected and how the relationships work.
3. Stakeholder relationships—All stakeholders have unique interests so the reporting should reflect that knowledge and how those relationships work in a mutually beneficial manner.

4. Materiality—Anything that directly affects the organization's ability to create value in the short or longer term is relevant and should be included in the reporting.

5. Conciseness—Although some corporate reports can be lengthy, the goal of IR is to provide all relevant information in brief form, so it can be consumed and understood as the key insights reflecting the organization's value creating performance and potential.

6. Reliability and completeness—The IR report should be concise, as described above, but also thorough, balanced, and accurate.

7. Consistency and comparability—An IR should follow a common format that remains consistent over time. Commonality is also designed to allow external stakeholders and investors to compare reporting.

Shared content elements of an Integrated Report are based on the following questions (from 2021 framework[8]):

- What does the organization do and what are the circumstances under which it operates?
- How does the organization's governance structure support its ability to create value in the short, medium, and long term?
- What is the organization's business model?
- What are the specific risks and opportunities that affect the organization's ability to create value over the short, medium, and long term, and how is the organization dealing with them?
- Where does the organization want to go and how does it intend to get there?
- To what extent has the organization achieved its strategic objectives for the period and what are its outcomes in terms of effects on the capitals?
- What are the challenges and uncertainties the organization is likely to encounter in pursuing its strategy, and what are

the potential implications for its business model and future performance?

• How does the organization determine what matters to include in the integrated report and how are such matters quantified or evaluated?

Stage 3 integrated reporting is a substantial accomplishment. Many of the executives I have interviewed over the years tell me the same story. Although the organization embraced the ideas and practices, it really took years for the leadership behavior to change. The quality of the organizational dialogue, the levels of stakeholder engagement, the annual process changes, and the evolution in business culture really made a difference in mental models. Great-looking reports and compelling stories give way to a difference in how the organization thinks about their business purpose.

Stage 4—Integrated Reporting and Integrated Thinking

Integrating Reporting is the act of creating written documentation to satisfy a set of compliance requirements and communication objectives. It is a required output of business leaders charged with governance decisions and oversight of the business. It is meant to follow certain key practices and answer common questions relevant to stakeholders.

Integrated Thinking is bit different. It suggests the organization is trying to bring together both mature traditional business considerations like financial reporting, strategy and risk assessment with the newer, less mature considerations of circular strategies, social and environmental impact, and multi-value creation. Integrated Thinking is designed to take the IR Framework and incorporate the SASB Standards. Leaders must embrace ideas like transparency and consider how to gain input from key stakeholders and link that to issues of materiality. They also must reflect on the idea that all these requirements have a real purpose linked to goals for a sustainable future. The compliance requirements are someone's written expression of the intent. A well-written report is great, but real impact is what matters.

Integrated Thinking requires an organization to collectively bring together all relevant information (data, perspectives, and insights) so they are given due consideration within the sustainable purpose of the organization. That is followed by cascading the insights into decisions that translate purpose into strategy, innovation, culture, governance, risk assessment, and performance management. In the best of circumstances, this is a self-reinforcing circular model. Making integrated Thinking a standard business practice takes time and often requires the use of independent third parties to infuse the dialogue with questions, examples, new information, and critical feedback.

Summary

- Transitioning a business from a legacy enterprise to a business with sustainable purpose, products, and processes requires careful transition planning.
- The four stages of business transition provide a framework for reporting that matches the business strategy and the stories that a business can tell.
- The first two stages in a sustainability transition are an opportunity for a business to consolidate its regulatory filings, engage the leadership teams in dialogue on multiple-capital creation, and begin the process of experimentation to establish new sources of revenue and profits that comply with key sustainability practices and principles.
- The third stage in a sustainability transition is where individual company creativity emerges. It is evidence of engagement and an acknowledgment of the business opportunity.
- The final stage of a sustainability transition is where integrated reporting connects with Integrated Thinking. This final stage is evidence of the underlying ideas of sustainability, the development of an ethical brand and the practices of ethical leadership becoming embedded in mental models and the business culture.

Telling Your Story Reflection Checklist

Telling Your Story Checklist		
Is it more or less true that your organization ...		**Ranking**
1	Has a strategic focus and future orientation tied to sustainable solutions?	1 2 3 4 5 6 7 8 9 10
2	Engages in ongoing dialogue about all aspects of value creation for the organization?	1 2 3 4 5 6 7 8 9 10
3	Solicits feedback from all stakeholder groups related to sustainability to ensure such perspectives are reflected in the ongoing operations of the business?	1 2 3 4 5 6 7 8 9 10
4	Developed and communicated short-, medium-, and long-term goals related to sustainable value creation?	1 2 3 4 5 6 7 8 9 10
5	Compares business performance and impact with competitive peers and leading organizations regarding key ESG performance indicators?	1 2 3 4 5 6 7 8 9 10
6	Assesses ESG risks that are material to the business and has articulated how those risks affect short-, medium-, and long-term goals related to sustainable value creation?	1 2 3 4 5 6 7 8 9 10
7	Evaluated its business model and incorporated changes to that model in its future-oriented transition planning?	1 2 3 4 5 6 7 8 9 10
8	Develops and maintains several messaging platforms that feature stories and customized sustainability content for each key stakeholder group?	1 2 3 4 5 6 7 8 9 10
9	Builds a concise annual integrated report for investors that accurately reflect IR best practices?	1 2 3 4 5 6 7 8 9 10

Telling Your Story Checklist		
Is it more or less true that your organization ...		**Ranking**
10	Practices Integrated Thinking across all levels of management from business to geographic to functional organizations, and the dialogues are fully integrated, summarized, and shared across the organization?	1 2 3 4 5 6 7 8 9 10
Total Score		

Scoring:

- Score less than 50—A low score may indicate that you are at the beginning of your transition strategy to a more sustainable future, or it may suggest a lack of emphasis on sustainability and reporting.

- Score less than 80—Creating an ongoing dialogue on multi-capital formation takes some work since it is not in the normal experience or training of most executives. A mid-range score can also indicate a bias toward only some activities or a difference between reporting between organizational units.

- Score greater than 80—A higher score suggests that you are at least keeping pace with industry best practices. The challenge is those practices continue to evolve so your organizational efforts must evolve as well.

Chapter 10

AVOIDING DERAILMENT AND THE PRESSURE TO COMPROMISE YOUR VALUES

Increasic makes markets more efficient and economies more stable and resilient. —MICHAEL R. BLOOMBERG, CHAIRPERSON, TASKFORCE ON CLIMATE-RELATED FINANCIAL DISCLOSURES (TCFD)

What Is Derailment?

The term "derailment" is frequently used today to describe the downfall of a senior leader who encounters one or more events that make continuing their job untenable. Dennis Kozlowski, the former CEO of Tyco International, was considered a good CEO during his early years at the helm of the firm, as he built the company into a $40 billion powerhouse. Unfortunately, he was found guilty in 2005 of misusing company funds and spent over eight years in prison.[1] Jeff Skilling, former CEO of Enron, was convicted in 2006 of crimes including lying to auditors, fraud, and insider trading. He eventually spent 12 years in prison.[2] Ramalinga Raju, the founder and chairman of Satyam Computer Services, was found guilty of fraud in 2009 by overstating the company's revenue, income, and cash balances so it appeared more profitable to investors.[3]

One of the more recent cases of executive derailment was Elizabeth Holmes, the CEO of blood diagnostics company Theranos. The company was once considered a revolutionary business that promised to greatly reduce the cost of medical blood diagnostics and help prevent diseases with non-invasive and cheap testing. If true, this was a major milestone in democratizing access to quality preventative health care. Unfortunately, the CEO and other senior leaders were accused of misrepresenting the company's products and finances to investors. The company was once valued as much as 9 billion USD. In 2022, after a lengthy court trial, Holmes was found guilty and sentenced to 11 years in prison.[4]

In each case, the executives involved were successful, well-compensated, and talented individuals. Had they been transparent and honest with stakeholders, they may have experienced some failures but would have retained the ability to learn from their mistakes and reinvent their careers. Instead, each chose to engage in behavior that eventually led to their career derailment.

Challenges: Why does derailment happen to otherwise capable and successful organizations? How do you avoid the risks of overpromising on sustainability performance and maintain accuracy and transparency in your business decisions, messaging and marketing?

Behavior leading to derailment is not a new issue for leaders and companies. Meta boss Mark Zuckerberg has reportedly fired several highly paid staff for abusing meal credits and vouchers. According to *Fortune Magazine*, "Meta reportedly fires staffer on $400K a year for spending $25 meal credits on toothpaste and tea."[5] Someone making that much money does not need to abuse an expense and benefit system. Derailment is an abuse of trust and a failure of controls designed to prevent behavior inconsistent with company or public values. Sustainability offers new avenues where challenges and opportunities can lead to failure if ethical boundaries and business controls are not in place.

I first became aware of the term "leadership derailment" during the 1980s from the work of V. Jon Bentz, a vice president of human resources at Sears Roebuck and Company, who did a 30-year study of failed managers in the 1970s.[6] The idea of analyzing management failure was later extended by individuals such as Morgan McCall, Michael Lombardo, and Ann Morrison, then at the Center for Creative Leadership, which resulted in their excellent book, *The Lessons of Experience* (1988).[7] There has been extensive work on leadership derailment from a failure perspective, as well as from the lessons learned. Michael Watkins's excellent book, *The First 90 Days* (2013)[8] describes the key practices needed to start a new position that helps lead a more successful career.

Yet despite decades of research on what is needed for effective leadership, transparency in communication, and appropriate product marketing, the challenges of sustainability have brought forth new scandals that diminish brands and disrupt careers. There has been so much misinformation generated about sustainability or issues like climate change that we have generated an entirely new vocabulary with terms like impact washing, greenwashing, green hushing, green gaslighting, green bleaching, woke washing, and blue washing to describe some of the misguided efforts.

The Importance of Handling Adversity and Ambiguity

I have noted in my other books the challenges associated with a low-maturity knowledge domain like sustainability. Although the history of various sustainability topics can be traced to the nineteenth century and certainly to post-World War II, there remains a lot of change in knowledge, public policy, and competitive solutions. Making the wrong bet on an energy technology, choosing a capital-intensive solution that limits future flexibility, or moving too slow on new product introduction are just a few of the leadership choices that can slow growth or limit productivity. When boards of directors confront slow growth, poor stock performance, or a lack of competitive positioning, changes to the senior leadership team are often the result. For many executives, moving too fast or slow on sustainability initiatives can be their key derailment challenge.

Asoka Wöhrmann was CEO of DWS Group, one of Europe's largest asset managers, and 80 percent owned by Germany's largest bank, Deutsche Bank AG. Asoka started with Deutsche Bank in 1998 and was named CEO of the DWS Group in 2018. In June of 2022, "German authorities raided the Frankfurt offices of Deutsche Bank and its investment arm DWS today, deepening the greenwashing concerns that have surrounded the company for the past several months. According to statements from the Frankfurt prosecutor's office, the search had been triggered by media reports that DWS overstated the green or sustainability-related aspects of financial products and following examination of evidence leading to suspicion of 'prospectus fraud.'"[9] Asoka stepped down as CEO the next day amid the growing scandal.

DWS was ultimately investigated by both the U.S. Securities and Exchange Commission (SEC) and Germany's financial regulator. In 2023, DWS settled with the SEC and agreed to pay a fine of $19 million, which is the largest greenwashing penalty ever imposed on an asset manager by the SEC.[10] The problems for the bank caused a loss of confidence, and a loss of business in addition to the financial penalties. The European Union also increased scrutiny of greenwashing through the work of the European Securities and Markets Authority (ESMA) and the EU's Sustainable Finance Roadmap.[11]

In its 2022 Climate Check survey, Deloitte also stated, "greenwashing" has become a major concern for companies, with two-thirds of executives saying it has become a serious concern in their sectors. Greenwashing also topped the list at 41% of climate-related issues that executives felt should receive the most attention globally, second only to national and international security risks from changing weather patterns, at 50%.[12] Deloitte's 2024 annual CXO Sustainability report emphasized the importance of sustainability as a growing priority for executives and boards. One of the major findings from the survey of 2,100 executives in 27 countries "shows that climate change remains a top three issue for global C-suite level business leaders (CxOs), surpassing political uncertainty, competition for talent, and the changing regulatory environment, among others."[13]

Examples of Country-Level Misinformation

In 2021, the U.S.-based *Washington Post* published an analysis[14] of the greenhouse gas emissions reported by each country to the United Nations in their Nationally Determined Contributions (NDCs).[15] The NDCs were part of the Paris Agreement stocktaking exercise (2015, Article 4, paragraph 2) with the first country reports to be submitted by 2020. *The Post* reported, "An examination of 196 country reports reveals a giant gap between what nations declare their emissions to be vs. the greenhouse gases they are sending into the atmosphere. The gap ranges from at least 8.5 billion to as high as 13.3 billion tons a year of underreported emissions."[16]

The Post reporting called out the country of Malaysia for claiming, "Malaysia's trees are absorbing carbon four times faster than similar forests in neighboring Indonesia."[17] *The Post* analysis concludes, "It is the result of questionably drawn rules, incomplete reporting in some countries and apparently willful mistakes in others—and the fact that in some cases, humanity's full impacts on the planet are not even required to be reported."[18]

Countries don't derail the same way as individuals and companies do, but negative press affects politicians also and no delegation to a major conference wants to lose the trust and respect of their fellow negotiating parties. Country-level misinformation gets noticed by the major intergovernmental organizations like the regional development banks and the World Bank Group as well as major foundations that have a say in development funding in emerging markets.

Product-Level Misinformation

Product marketing practices have been with us for as long as there have been commercial transactions. In parallel, there have been ongoing efforts to provide consumers and buyers with greater accuracy and transparency on the products they buy. The first food labels were introduced in the United States in 1850, and the U.S. Pure Food and Drug Act of 1906 made it illegal to make false claims. Europe has a longer history with standard package labeling dating back to at least the 1700s. The more modern European Union requirements govern most products in the EU. Current food labeling dates back to 1978 and nutrition labeling to 1990.[19] Pretty much everything you can buy has some type of regulatory component, often driven by buyer complaints over deceptions and inaccuracies. There are also numerous independent databases such as the EWG Skin Deep database that provides data on the risks associated with cosmetic chemicals in over 110,000 products.[20] Product-level misinformation may result in heavy fines.

The Price of Overpromising

Overstating, exaggerating, or underdelivering on sustainability claims can cost your company money as well as cost the responsible business leader their jobs. There are new rules on taxonomies, product labeling. Partners and investors are increasingly wary of sustainability claims and the risks they may impose on your business. There are also investigative agencies like Canada's Competition Bureau, the United States Securities and Exchange Commission, the United States Border Protection Agency, and the European Commission, all of which investigated, fined, or banned companies and products.

As recently as October of 2024, the United States Commodities Futures Trading Commission (CFTC) charged the former CEO of a major carbon credit project developer with fraud. The complaint charges that the "CEO and majority shareholder of a carbon credit project developer, engaged in a fraudulent scheme that involved reporting false and misleading information to at least one carbon credit registry

Company	Issue	Fine	Fined by
Volkswagen	Systems that helped to falsify emissions data on car tailpipe emissions	4.3 billion USD	United States[1]
		502 million Euros	European Commission[2]
		125 million USD	Australia[3]
DWS (part of Deutsche Bank)[4]	Marketing of ESG funds that did not meet the sustainability standards associated with their marketing	25 million USD	United States
Goldman Sachs[5]	Misleading customers on ESG investments	4 million USD (2022)	United States
Keurig Canada[6]	Misleading claims about the recyclability of their single use coffee pods	3 million CAD	Canada

[1] Volkswagen AG Agrees to Plead Guilty and Pay $4.3 Billion in Criminal and Civil Penalties; Six Volkswagen Executives and Employees are Indicted in Connection with Conspiracy to Cheat U.S. Emissions Tests, Pres release, US Department of Justice, 11 January 2017, https://www.justice.gov/opa/pr/volkswagen-ag-agrees-plead-guilty-and-pay-43-billion-criminal-and-civil-penalties-six, accessed 20 August 2024.

[2] Antitrust: Commission fines car manufacturers €875 million for restricting competition in emission cleaning for new diesel passenger cars, Press Release, European Commission website, 8 July 2021, https://ec.europa.eu/commission/presscorner/detail/en/ip_21_3581, accessed 20 August 2024.

[3] Court orders Volkswagen to pay record $125 million in penalties, Media release, ACCC website, 10 December 2019, https://www.accc.gov.au/media-release/court-orders-volkswagen-to-pay-record-125-million-in-penalties, accessed 20 August 2024.

[4] Deutsche Bank Subsidiary DWS to Pay $25 Million for Anti-Money Laundering Violations and Misstatements Regarding ESG Investments, US Securities and Exchange Commission website, Press release, 25 September 2023, https://www.sec.gov/newsroom/press-releases/2023-194, accessed 22 August 2024.

[5] SEC Charges Goldman Sachs Asset Management for Failing to Follow its Policies and Procedures Involving ESG Investments, US Securities and Exchange Commission, Pres release, 22 November 2022, https://www.sec.gov/newsroom/press-releases/2022-209, accessed 16 August 2024.

[6] Keurig Canada to pay $3 million penalty to settle Competition Bureau's concerns over coffee pod recycling claims, Competition Bureau Canada, Government of Canada website, 6 January 2022, https://www.canada.ca/en/competition-bureau/news/2022/01/keurig-canada-to-pay-3-million-penalty-to-settle-competition-bureaus-concerns-over-coffee-pod-recycling-claims.html, accessed 12 August 2024.

Figure 10.1 Examples of regulatory actions.

and third-party reviewers, among others."[21] Charged in the complaint are the company, CQC Impact Investors LLC (CQC), the former CEO and former COO.

Such enforcement mechanisms are significant in that they demonstrate a trend of more active enforcement that affects not only companies and brands, but also key leaders. "The order requires CQC to pay a $1 million civil monetary penalty, cease and desist from violating the applicable provisions of the CEA and CFTC regulations, and comply with certain conditions and undertakings, including the cancelation or retirement of voluntary carbon credits sufficient to address the violative conduct. CQC admitted the findings of the order and acknowledged that its conduct violated the CEA and CFTC regulations."[22] The impact on the named executive is unclear, but this type of action implies a major career derailment event. It also makes it difficult for the company to participate in the voluntary carbon markets in future years.

Regulatory Changes and the Growth in Penalties and Punishment

Lawsuits have increased in recent years as climate and sustainability advocacy groups see lawsuits as a significant tool for holding companies accountable. The law firm Baker McKenzie conducts an annual survey of senior dispute lawyers are large firms to gauge their concerns about the year ahead. According to the company's 2024 Global Disputes Forecast, "Respondents cite ESG disputes as the top litigation risk to their organizations in 2024 (up from second place in 2023). The breadth of ESG disputes is a growing challenge, as human rights and social issues are increasingly incorporated into the ESG agenda."[23] A company does not have to lose all lawsuits for the issue to become concerning. Lawsuits when filed, bring unwanted press coverage that may be damaging to a brand, increase litigation costs, and affect key stakeholder perceptions.

Legal and press activity tend to encourage political reviews and may result in new legislative actions. Most new regulations are designed to create both transparency in product offerings and to rein in the use of misleading and vague terminology. Terms such as ethical investing, 100 percent sustainable, or socially responsible have no formal meaning in most markets and their use is to be avoided. Terms or statements that promise a "Green," "Positive," "Sustainable," or ESG impact, without specific details, are likely to be viewed as misleading by regulatory authorities. Consider the definition of the term "greenwashing" by the Australian Securities and Investment Commission: "In relation to investments, 'greenwashing' is the practice of misrepresenting the extent to which a financial product or investment strategy is environmentally friendly, sustainable or ethical."[24]

One way to avoid misrepresentations is to test your methodologies and practices early. The EU Corporate Sustainability Reporting Directive is set to be implemented over several years from 2025 through 2029. The auditing aspects of the reporting will follow new guidelines from International Auditing and Assurance Standards Board with different type of auditing programs going into effect between 2025 and 2028. Companies like AstraZeneca, for example, plan to prepare a CSRD-aligned report in 2025 to ensure readiness for compliance, in what the company calls a "dry run."[25]

Building a Sustainable Derailment Firewall

Many of the previous chapters on topics like ethical leadership and innovation provide ideas on how companies can introduce practices that help avoid misinformation and derailment. Internal controls such as having multiple leaders participate in an approval process is one step, as are ensuring there are pre-decision consultations, planning reviews, clear policies, and after-action reviews that take advantage of multiple perspectives. A tolerance for intelligent failure is also needed. Derailment often occurs when individuals feel excess pressure to meet or exceed expectations. Deceptions often occur when decisions lack transparency, and bad decisions begin to accumulate. In such situations, the pressure increases, which often leads to the choices leading to derailment.

Ethical frameworks, teaching case examples of problem resolution, including descriptions of company controls in training and social rituals all help. We need to understand sustainable boundary conditions for what they are—a body of principles within which we are asked to operate and behave toward common goals. Ethical leadership is essential to building multi-capital value and a cornerstone of a sustainable future where we avoid social and environmental negatives and help restore some of what we have already degraded. Asking ourselves, is this the right thing to do, sounds simple, but it is the ultimate guiderail to avoid derailment.

Summary

- Derailment refers to an otherwise good leader or company taking actions that cause a policy, legal, or performance-based disaster that come to the attention of customers, regulators, or auditors.
- Derailment is mostly the result of poor choices rather than unexpected events.
- Strong company cultures, ethical frameworks, and business controls are designed to prevent such poor choices.
- Sustainability regulations have become more detailed and harmonized and failure to manage compliance exposes organizations to reputational risks.
- Corporate behavior is subject to jurisdictional compliance in every geography and market you operate in. The details do matter.
- Overpromising on the attributes of a product or service may be tempting, but increasingly carries severe penalties for misinformation or non-compliance.
- Sustainability regulations now cover products and labeling, which offer new risks for derailment and reputational risk.

Derailment Reflection Checklist

Derailment Checklist	
Is it more or less true that your organization ...	**Ranking**
1	Has a senior leadership team known for its ability to handle adversity and ambiguity?	1 2 3 4 5 6 7 8 9 10
2	Has a system of checks and balances in place for senior-level decision-making on matters of sustainability?	1 2 3 4 5 6 7 8 9 10
3	Ensures that major sustainability investments are subject to third-party opinions?	1 2 3 4 5 6 7 8 9 10
4	Has operating controls in place to handle issues of corruption and bribery in markets with higher risks for such behavior?	1 2 3 4 5 6 7 8 9 10
5	Does your leadership team review country-level examples of derailment and misinformation that relate to competitive peers or keystone players?	1 2 3 4 5 6 7 8 9 10
6	Ensures that leadership teams review product and service-level examples of derailment and misinformation that relate to competitive peers or keystone players?	1 2 3 4 5 6 7 8 9 10
7	Is socializing new market guidelines related to greenwashing claims?	1 2 3 4 5 6 7 8 9 10
8	Has market guidelines for product certification and labeling that are well understood by your product management and marketing teams?	1 2 3 4 5 6 7 8 9 10
9	Bases its greenwashing and sustainability practices on the markets with the most robust regulations?	1 2 3 4 5 6 7 8 9 10
10	Does your organization conduct test runs of new regulations before they become mandatory, to ensure your organizational controls and practices meet standards?	1 2 3 4 5 6 7 8 9 10
Total Score		

Scoring:

- Score less than 50—Low scores suggest you have risk exposure. Immediate attention needs to focus on developing a plan that is supported with third-party inputs and guidance.
- Score less than 80—It only takes a few mistakes, even unintentional, to have a negative brand impact. As greenwashing and sustainability practice guidelines become more detailed and penalties more severe, the organization must conduct a gap analysis and insist on both improvements and regular reporting. The senior-level team is responsible and accountable regardless of how misjudgments happen.
- Score greater than 80—Building on strength involves audits and benchmarking to insure you maintain capabilities and use them to enhance your company, product, and leadership brands.

Chapter 11

FUTURE-PROOFING YOUR ORGANIZATION

Knowledge is always a good thing because it empowers you to react and to do something if something needs to be done. —NEIL DEGRASSE TYSON, ASTROPHYSICIST

As a leader, future-proofing your organization means that you and your team are staying in touch with market trends and anticipating issues that lead to competitive opportunities or new compliance requirements. Some of this is easy. For example, if you had read the Paris Agreement in 2015, you would have been aware of the 2020 timeline for Nationally Determined Contributions (NDCs) and the timeline for the Enhanced Transparency Framework (ETF), which went into effect between 2022 and 2024. Depending on your status, developed countries need to submit their first ETF by 2022 and by the end of 2024 for developing countries. Although these are for countries and not companies, there is a connection between national actions and public policy, and that does affect companies. It is reasonable for leadership teams to find time on their calendars to explore the implications, particularly when there is such advanced notice.

Challenges: How do you understand the direction of disruptive markets? How do you build transparency and accuracy with corporate reporting, while anticipating new changes in years to come?

There is a need to keep an eye on changes in any of the primary boundary conditions that affect your business. For example, keeping an eye on science climate modeling affects the design of insurance and financial risk models. Everyone in the organization does not need to do this, but you need to have a dedicated sustainability specialist position or subscribe to a service that does market scans for new information. For example, if you are in a food service or fishing business, you may be aware of the issues of permafrost melting, but it does not seem to have a direct effect on your business. Will it influence higher methane emission, yes? Will it influence businesses in the far north, also, yes? But if that is not where your business is located, this seems like an interesting bit of information but not essential. However, if you missed the recent research suggesting that increases in permafrost melting may also yield increases in mercury,[1] you may have missed an important issue. When mercury is released into the air or freshwater streams it can migrate long distances and is highly toxic to life on land and life in the water. Given the scale of permafrost melting and the unknown impact of higher temperatures on mercury migration, you might be well served to keep an eye on future research in this area. Scanning information for general awareness does not take much time.

Observe Changes in Technology and Science

If we reflect back on our model of scientific drivers from the earlier chapter of this book, we'll see terms like tipping points, planetary boundaries, and accelerating glacial melt. The climate science discovery process is an ongoing effort and important to business planning on a long-term basis. For example, recently published results from a six-year study (2018–2024) by the International Thwaites Glacier Collaboration concluded that, "Thwaites has been retreating for more than 80 years, accelerating considerably over the past 30 years, and our findings indicate it is set to retreat further and faster."[2] The complete melting of this glacial system is widely recognized as a keystone system and a global tipping point for sea-level rise.

This type of information is globally important and of concern to everyone. The fact that it may be irreversible once started should be a wake-up call for urgent action and new public policies. The question for any business is, can we help? Is there a scenario where we can take action that makes a difference? These sorts of big global changes are difficult for any one company to react to, but they offer an important context around which business leaders can reinforce their statement of purpose.

Science drivers are important to a shared sustainable future because new technologies offer the chance to leverage your impact. Recent breakthroughs in anode-free sodium solid-state batteries,[3] are examples, as are advances in solar cells using perovskite technologies and new cell construction techniques using super-thin cells and stacking techniques.[4] These are of great interest to anyone in the energy generation, energy distribution, transport, and building industries for several reasons. The breakthroughs have been tested in reputable laboratories (validation), commercial and university partnerships have tested production techniques (reliability), and the innovations promise greater efficiency (attribute differentiation), possible use in distributed systems (new customers), lower weight (reduced costs and improved performance) as well as other factors.

A sustainable business intelligence practice gathers information from your direct industry, industries aligned with your business ecosystem, and from various business adjacencies that serve different markets and customers. Where are new technologies emerging? What customers can make use of the advantages today? How likely is the technology to scale and become more affordable? Here are some examples of typical business considerations for scientific research:

- Do the scientific results constitute an evolutionary change in an existing technology or a breakthrough in a new technology?
- Does the result offer a major change in attributes for existing customers?
- Does the result imply possible applications for new products and non-customer acquisition?
- Are companies in any market using the technology so it can be observed, regardless of the application or customer?
- Can possible new product ideas be prototyped easily?
- Do we understand how to repeatedly produce the innovation benefits at scale?
- What type of investment is required to bring new products innovation to market?
- What is the timeline from a "strategic yes" to market availability?

Although some large companies maintain their own substantial R&D organizations, many organizations partner for new technologies or license technologies from firms specializing in intellectual property. For example, companies like Intel design and manufacture their own microchips, while others like Broadcom do the design, but outsource the manufacturing to specialists like Taiwan Semiconductor. For a smaller firm like Transfertech, who are part of the global supply chain, the issue may be understanding breakthroughs, so they understand who to partner with, or which companies offer the best long-term relationships.

Track the Keystone Players for Sustainability Policy

Keystone players dominate markets and specific industries. Examples include California in the United States and the European Union (EU). What do discussions around California Senate Bills 251 and 263 tell us about future directions? California has long been a U.S. Keystone, but the rest of the U.S. market does not always follow its lead. Markets like India are intriguing on a long-term basis, but they are playing catch-up with mandatory reporting.

Overall, the best keystone market for sustainability public policy is the EU. The 27 member EU countries are the biggest export market for 80 different counties and account for ~16% of the world's imports and exports.[5] The EU member countries also account for about one-sixth of global GDP trailing only China and the United States.[6] The exit of Great Britain from the EU in 2020 also seems to have strengthened the resolve of other EU members. Although the EU has competitiveness issues, it has the most stringent sustainability requirements and has been good with harmonizing policy with industry-based frameworks. It maintains the best at integrating policy from the country level to the product level and has one of the strongest regimes of penalties and enforcement mechanisms. That does not make it perfect by any means, but it is the clear market leader in the areas cited and is likely to remain the keystone market leader between now and 2030.

The EU sustainability leadership includes the Corporate Sustainability Reporting Directive (CSRD) and the European Sustainability Reporting Standards (ESRS). These initiatives focus on all large companies and any small- to medium-sized businesses listed on a stock market. They require dual materiality assessments, mandatory verification (third-part opinions), and some level of sector-specific standards and offer some written guidance to help with implementation. They also have mechanisms for receiving feedback and offer annual updates on standards and guidance. It is reasonable to assume those practices will continue. As pressure mounts to harmonize standards, it is likely that other countries will move closer to the EU model.

Part of the EU's leadership on sustainability is by design. Europe has a long history with carbon reduction and credit schemes, a willingness to try carbon taxes and cross-border adjustment mechanisms and a regional governance process that has been developed since 1992 with the signing of the Maastricht Treaty.[7] More recently Europe's sustainability leadership has expanded in response to the conflict between Russia and Ukraine, the first war on the European continent since World War II. It is a sad failure of international diplomacy, but it did

European Financial Reporting
Advisory Group (EFRAG)
(Private organization)

Advice

European Commission

Core Regulations

NFRD
Non-financial reporting Directive
2014

Increases Regulation
Scope and Detail

Corporate Sustainability
Reporting Directive (CSRD)
January 2023

Adds

European Sustainability
Reporting Standards
(ESRS) July 2023

General Requirements &
Disclosures

Environment

Social

Governance

Sustainable Finance Package

EU Taxonomy
+
Sustainable Finance Disclosure
Regulation (SFDR)
+
CSRD

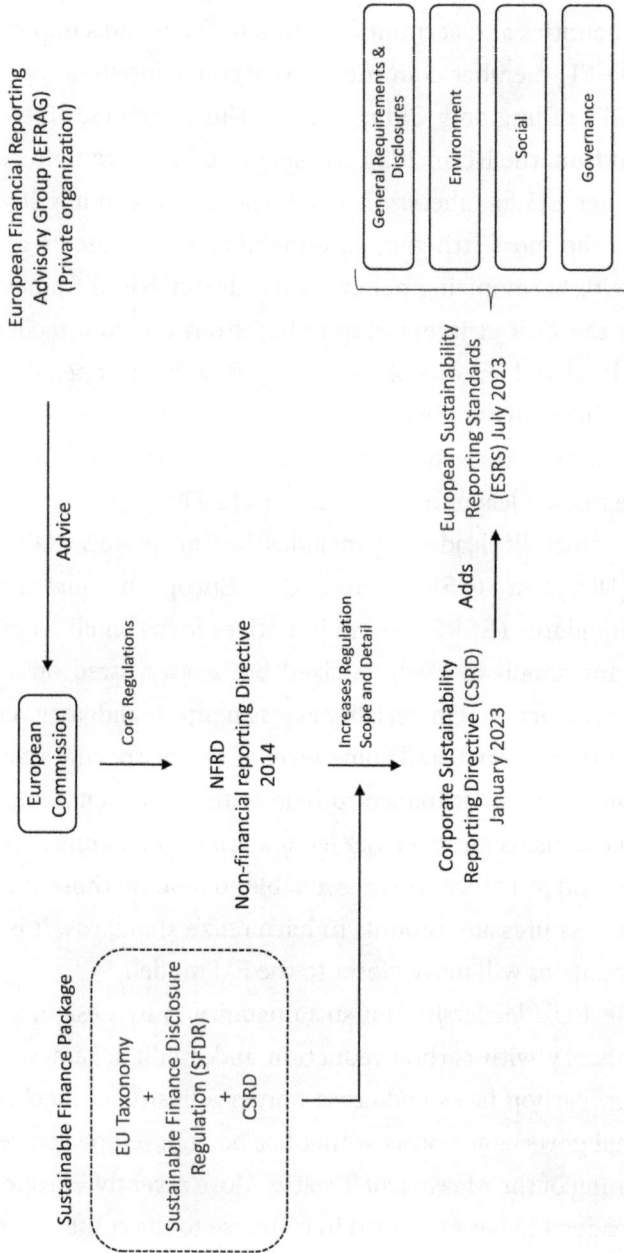

Figure 11.1 Evolving European model.

spur an acceleration of action on energy independence and sustainability practices. Despite occasional pushback from member states and calls for more innovation and less regulation, the EU has consistently led from the front on issues of sustainability.

The EU's stability as a keystone market leader is partially due to its unique governance structure. The EU has the benefit of two levels of authority since each country in the EU signed off on major international agreements like the Paris Agreement (2015), but the EU is also a separate party to the same agreements. That allows for enforcement mechanisms locally, in each country, as well as on a multiparty EU basis from EU headquarters in Brussels. That is unique in the world.

The EU also has the EU Taxonomy for Sustainability Activities and an outline of Sustainable Finance Regulation Definitions that aid in clarifying language differences between markets and improves standardizations. The Greenwashing Directive of 2024 imposes perhaps the clearest rules on green claims and establishes penalties and fines to enforce the rules. The EU has also been a world leader in such areas as the "right to repair," which aids in reuse and remanufacturing and has required Environmental Product Declarations (EPDs) since 2022. Although as a company you can operate in many other countries under less robust compliance regimes, keeping an eye on the EU's policies and practices give you an idea of where the world is headed. The new ESRS is already well aligned with ISSB and GRI to offer more harmonized global sustainability standards.

A look at the categories of the ESRS in Figure 11.2 shows how comprehensive the disclosure requirements are. The general disclosures include impact materiality and financial materiality (SBM-3, IRO-1 and IRO-2) as well as disclosures about business models, internal controls, and stakeholder views.

The environmental (E) disclosures are shown in Figure 11.3. They contain items such as resource use and circular economy and some depth on biodiversity.

ESRS 2	BP-1	BP-2	Gov-1	Gov-2
General Disclosures	General basis for preparation	Specific circumstances for preparation	The composition and role of management	Sustainability information provided to management
ESRS 2 (continued)	Gov-3	Gov-4	Gov-5	SBM-1
General Disclosures	Incentive schemes	Sustainability due diligence	Risk management and internal controls	Market position, strategy and business model
ESRS 2 (continued)	SBM-2	SBM-3	IRO-1	IRO-2
General Disclosures	Stakeholder views and interests	Material impacts in relation to strategy	Materiality assessment process	Material topics included and omitted
ESRS 2 (continued)	DC-P	DC-A	DC-M	DC-T
General Disclosures	Policy Content requirements	Action plan requirements	Metric requirements	Target requirements

Figure 11.2 ESRS 2 general disclosures.

S4	S4-1	S4-2	S4-3	S4-4
Consumers and end users	Policies	Process: consumer engagement	Process: remediate impacts	Taking action on impacts
S4 (continued)	S4-5			
Consumers and end users (continued)	Targets			
G1	G1-1	G1-2	G1-3	G1-4
Business conduct	Corporate culture	Supplier relationship	Corruption & bribery detection	Corruption & bribery incidents
G1 (continued)	G1-5	G1-6		
Business conduct (continued)	Political influence activity	Payment practices		

Figure 11.3 ESRS 2 environmental disclosures.

The Social (S) disclosures are illustrated in Figure 11.4. The categories continue the Policies, Guidelines, Targets and Effects model that is consistent throughout the disclosure program.

The continuation of the Social (S) categories and a final Governance (G) series is shown in Figure 11.5.

The thoroughness of the disclosure program is strong, and it incorporates a broad range of items from previous guidelines and is more workable for companies. It also overlaps well with many of the predecessor frameworks so there is less redundancy. The biodiversity challenges are less pronounced, which may be expected since that work stream has received less attention since the original framework Conventions on Climate change and biodiversity were introduced in 1992. I would expect the biodiversity area to see additions in the future as better data and monitoring becomes available.

Be Aware of Potential "Wild Cards"

China continues to invest heavily in sustainable technologies, but its reporting and transparency requirement are still limited. As of 2024, most analysts would say that China's ESG requirements lag the other large markets, although as the world's largest exporter, Chinese companies must comply with the due diligence and data reporting requirements of its larger customers and markets. China has been a country that is both a major innovator in sustainable industries and one that continues to expand carbon-intensive industries. It has also a mixed track record in recent years regarding ecosystem destruction and biodiversity loss. How will the Chinese market and major companies evolve in the coming decades?

Recent press releases from China's National Development and Reform Commission, the State Administration for Market Regulation, and the Ministry of Emergency Management indicate that, "China has released a comprehensive plan to standardize carbon emission calculations across key sectors to meet its carbon reduction targets. By the end of 2024, China will publish ~70 new national standards on carbon accounting, footprint measurements, carbon reduction, capture, utilization and storage, covering all key sectors and companies. In 2025, a standardized calculation and evaluation system will be established for businesses, projects, and products. This system will ensure key sectors and products meet world-leading benchmarks for energy consumption control."[8]

E1	E1-1	E1-2	E1-3	E1-4
Climate Change	Transition Plan	Policies	Actions & resources	Targets
E1 (continued)	E1-5	E1-6	E1-7	E1-8
Climate Change (continued)	Energy consumption	GHG 1-2-3 emissions	GHG removal projects	Internal carbon pricing
E1 (continued)	E1-9			
Climate Change (continued)	Financial effects			
E2	E2-1	E2-2	E2-3	E2-4
Pollution	Policies	Actions & resources	Targets	Pollution of air, water and soil
E2 (continued)	E2-5	E2-6		
Pollution (continued)	Substances of concern	Financial effects		
E3	E3-1	E3-2	E3-3	E3-4
Water and marine resources	Policies	Actions & resources	Targets	Water consumption
E3 (continued)	E3-5			
Water and marine resources (continued)	Financial effects			
E4	E4-1	E4-2	E4-3	E4-4
Biodiversity and ecosystems	Transition Plan	Policies	Actions & resources	Targets
E4 (continued)	E4-5	E4-6		
Biodiversity and ecosystems (continued)	Biodiversity metrics	Financial effects		
E5	E5-1	E5-2	E5-3	E5-4
Resource use and circular economy	Policies	Actions & resources	Targets	Resource inflows
E5 (continued)	E5-5	E5-6		
Resource use and circular economy (continued)	Resource outflows	Financial effects		

Figure 11.4 ESRS 2 social disclosures.

S1 Own workforce	S1-1 Policies	S1-2 Process: worker engagement	S1-3 Process: remediate impacts	S1-4 Taking action on impacts
S1 (continued) Own workforce (continued)	S1-5 Targets	S1-6 Employee characteristics	S1-7 non-employee characteristics	S1-8 Collective bargaining
S1 (continued) Own workforce (continued)	S1-9 Diversity metrics	S1-10 Adequate wages	S1-11 Social protection	S1-12 Persons with disabilities
S1 (continued) Own workforce (continued)	S1-13 Training and skills	S1-14 Health and safety	S1-15 work-life balance	S1-16 Compensation metrics
S1 (continued) Own workforce (continued)	S1-17 Human rights incidents			
S2 Workers in the value chain	S2-1 Policies	S2-2 Process: value chain engagement	S2-3 Process: remediate impacts	S2-4 Taking action on impacts
S2 (continued) Workers in the value chain (continued)	S2-5 Targets			
S3 Affected communities	S3-1 Policies	S3-2 Process: community engagement	S3-3 Process: remediate impacts	S3-4 Taking action on impacts
S3 (continued) Affected communities (continued)	S3-5 Targets			

Figure 11.5 ESRS 2 additional social and governance disclosures.

The statements on China's proposed regulations suggest they intend to address carbon accounting and reductions in industries such as electronics, plastics, and construction materials as well as improve their cap-and-trade system for carbon emissions. That is a lot of new regulations for everyone to understand and integrate into their business practices. The challenge for China has been that bold statements are not always followed by consistent actions or enforcement. The "wild card" for planning purposes is how the rhetoric matches reality.

The "wild card" notation is also relevant for major public policy individuals like U.S. president Trump who suggests dramatic shifts in established policy. Although statements about withdrawals from international treaties are significant, are they matched by changes in operating practices? Do actions match the words? Actions like layoffs, loss of staff capability, suppression of science-based publications, promotion of misinformation, budget cuts or agency elimination, harassment of thought leaders, grant suspension, and advocacy litigation are more significant than any public statements and create challenging business issues for business leaders trying to create a more sustainable future. "Wild cards" can act as a significant accelerant in global trends.

Follow Both Thought Leaders and Practice Leaders

Five categories of information leadership are worth following.

1. Thought leaders are those that publish or speak on key areas of interest. As a general rule, when you find someone who can articulate complex issues in simple terms or who can offer insights when other offer reams of data, follow them. Social media makes it easy to find and track thought leaders and the best of them, when you listen over time, offer good and memorable ideas.
2. Practice leaders can be easy to identify but finding true insights into their competitive secrets may be more difficult. They are always worth paying attention to, both at large incumbent companies and also at the smaller fast-growing start-ups. Practice leaders in different markets are worth observing even if they are not direct competitors.

3. Conferences can be a good source of information, but you need to be selective. The general issue here is, when smart people in your industry get together, what do they want to talk about? What questions are of greatest concern? The key is to find the conferences that attract decision-makers or that offer a good cross section of industry and public policy experts.

4. Investment leaders in both start-ups as well as M&A activity provide insights into market potential. I always found capital market conferences interesting as well as conferences that focused on business plan competitions. In each instance you get to see a snapshot of ideas, business plans, and funding activity.

5. Awards—Awards from reputable organizations provide third-party opinions on the perceived quality or impact of new practices. There are awards on almost every sustainability topic as well as regional and industry awards. For example, there is an award program for sustainable transformation in packaging,[9] awards for innovations in residential air conditioning,[10] and big picture awards like the Earthshot Prize that provides money to innovators in five categories: (1) Protect and Restore Nature, (2) Clean our Air, (3) Revive our Oceans, (4) Build a Waste-Free World, and (5) Fix our Climate.[11] Intergovernmental organizations like the United Nations Environmental Program recognize "UNEP Champions of the Earth"[12] in an annual ceremony. Individual companies may also provide awards to their employees or vendors that can be adopted to your organization. DBS introduced it Daredevil Award in 2019, "to recognize those within the bank who dare to experiment and try without the fear of failing. It aims to encourage employees to constantly experiment and push the boundaries of innovation."[13]

Invest in and Socialize Your Sustainable Business Intelligence

Business intelligence practices are essential to future-proofing your business to gain advantage from new changes in policies and competitive activity.

Key strategies

1. Compliance Automation—Digital technologies and artificial intelligence will greatly improve reporting and forecasting in a host of industries. Investing in compliance software and working on alignment of data with your vendors is a smart practice. Increased harmonization as well as newer transparency regulations, the standardization of label laws, taxonomies, and definitions is a boon to the software development companies and will likely reduce the burden of reporting moving forward. Software as a subscription models will increase, so annual software updates becomes part of the services offered to firms.

2. Digital Twins—This is another aspect of digital technology, but it deserves its own focus since digital twins promise to revolutionize forecasting and scenario planning. Creating a virtual model of your organization and being able to see how changes in logistics, products, packaging, and policies impact your organization can lead to cost savings and faster innovation.

3. Partnerships and Voluntary Memberships—The separate chapter on this issue illustrates its importance. Voluntary memberships are a great way to discover market practices among industry peers as well as market adjacencies. These memberships also provide powerful development experiences for emerging leaders and individuals who are being provided cross-functional job rotations to provide them insight into company-wide operations.

4. Talent Development—Rethink your talent development practices by making it a rite of passage for all emerging leaders to participate in sustainability committees, task forces, and external memberships. First-hand experience dealing with sustainability challenges and problem-solving is invaluable. It will also ensure that your project activities have a steady supply of talent that is eager to create success and is likely to provide a range of new ideas. Concurrently, your executives and senior leaders must be partnered with developing leaders as mentors, and also show

the commitment of the organization and the importance of the tasks.

5. Dialogue—Invest time in asking questions and listening to different perspectives. What are you hearing from suppliers? From partners? From voluntary memberships? From customers? Focus on building a portfolio of feedback from people with different backgrounds and perspectives. Improve your listening and reflection skills, summarize the observations, and socialize new knowledge in the organization. Low-maturity markets are characterized by rapid changes in information, the emergence of disruptive technologies in adjacent markets, and the emergence of new value propositions. The earlier you can detect a completive threat or opportunity, the faster you can respond.

Watch for Longer-Term Trends

All of the categories listed above provide boundaries within which you manage your disclosures, report on your compliance and tell your story to stakeholders. The complexity of that reporting and the volume of regulations can distract from the core goal of creating competitive solutions that make a difference in the marketplace. It is necessary at times to take a step back and look at how each area of information flows and how it relates to adjacencies. New heuristics are patterns or trends that we detect that can give us insights into future possibilities.

Trends may not always be precise, but they narrow the range of possible actions and help establish a sense of urgency. Although reading every available report on climate change and sustainable development may add context, it does not directly lead to improved business outcomes. If we use the IPCC reports as an illustration, a business leader needs to understand the core findings to the degree that it suggests a business transition is both necessary and urgent. If we consider some of the policy boundary conditions referenced in Chapter 1, we need to avoid jumping to conclusions based on single country, single market, or single politician changes. The concept of Integrated Thinking encourages a dialogue where different perspectives can be socialized over time with the end goal of discovering value creation in all its forms.

If you read all of the scientific reports on climate change as an example, it's easy to get consumed by the data and the various scenarios. The first IPCC report was published in part in 1990, with a supplement published in 1992. It established the importance of the climate change and suggested that it was more likely than not that human activities were the cause of much of the global warming observed. However, it also stated that additional research was needed. Although the assessment report was a landmark publication, it still did not accelerate changes in the business community, except with those who had the foresight to see the emerging trends supporting more sustainable brands. Early experimentation by a range of companies provided them the opportunity to build capability and market share over time. More substantial business engagement as well as public policy and compliance standards emerged over the next several decades. If we look back, it is possible to see the trend by comparing the key findings in the reports over time. The trend emerges as a useful illustration. Figure 11.6 summarizes key findings from 1990 through 2023.

Reports 1-2	Reports 5-6
Climate changes will be gradual	Changes may be abrupt and severe.
Climate change likely caused by human activity.	Climate change definitely caused by human activity.
Problems are manageable with existing technology	Costs of alternative technologies are cheaper than expected
Mitigation is expensive	Mitigation is cheaper than damages
Mitigation is possibly damaging to the economy	Decarbonization may be beneficial to the economy
Motivations are primarily non-market oriented (equity, preservation of nature) and hard to price	Solutions and definitions are maturing. Motivations are for economic growth at unprecedented scale

Figure 11.6 Comparison of IPCC reports.

Other relevant trends include changes to population dynamics and economic growth. For example, the global population in 1950 was approximately 2.5 billion people. Today, it is 8+ billion, and it is expected to increase to close to 10 billion by 2050. Economic development, as measured by gross domestic product (GDP) increased from approximately 10 trillion USD in 1950 to approximately 110 trillion today and is expected to increase to about 237 trillion by 2050. In parallel, carbon dioxide levels were about 270 parts per million (PPM) in pre-industrial times, which increased to about 315 by 1950 and are over 420 ppm today. As businesses look forward, it is reasonable to ask how high the level of greenhouse gases will go, what will be the implications and what will be the policy and regulatory response. Each of those billions of new people will consume products and services, and an increase of 100+ trillion USD in global GDP by 2050 is a lot of production and consumption. That will require a lot of energy, water, and other resources, and potentially generate a lot of waste. The trend seems clear as is the urgency for new business innovation.

Assume You Must Create and Evolve Your Data Model

Data models tend to anchor certain sets of facts supported by the reliability and validity of both established databases, larger datasets, and process standards as the source of truth upon which the company disclosures can be based. The data models are also sources of long-term standardization which lends itself to automation.

- *Look at Sector Adjacencies as Sources of Innovation*—Industry sectors often confront similar innovation challenges such as packaging optimization or the formulations for plastic containers or parts. As such, there is often concentrated capital and resource allocation that accelerates innovation. Identify the market leader practices not only in your sector but also in market and sector adjacencies struggling with similar challenges. Innovation often happens first in sectors with slightly different tolerances for price and performance, but that may be noteworthy as the beginning of a transferrable innovation as performance characteristics evolve.

- *Gain Insights from the Drafting Process of New Guidelines and Regulations*—Thought leaders often emerge in volunteer organizations, task forces, and committees that have a specific mandate and focus. The drafting process for both public policy and major guideline organizations is now very transparent which allows many sustainability specialists to participate by listening to updates via webinars, asking questions, or responding to draft guidelines. Simply by listening and determining who has the most to say or who is the key person drafting the idea or the policy summaries provides insight into people you should follow. Track those thought leaders as they communicate at conferences or as their parent companies invest in new sustainability practices.

- *Gain Insights from Multiple Practitioner Interpretations*— Consulting, accounting, and advisory firms all have established practices for sustainability, reporting, disclosures, or sustainability assessments of many kinds. In the 1990s and early 2000s, the early adopters in the consulting space were often too early with their service models and needed to scale back, but they have all expanded since the Paris Agreement in 2015. Each consulting organization will publish insights or run conferences where they share their opinions or co-publish research reposts with like-minded clients looking for the brand recognitions that comes with being seen as a best-practice company. These publications are often very operational and help with near-term implementation strategies, costing, or roadblocks.

Remain Aware of Boundaries of Uncertainty

Boundaries of uncertainty are those things that are under discussion, such as new international treaties or major trading block policies or guidelines changes that prove controversial. As a dialogue expands, the guidelines or policy positions may be watered down to increase support, or the timelines elongated to reduce industry costs. Since the science drivers of climate change don't change, it is usually true that the compromises are temporary, such as delays in scope 3 emissions reporting, but they will eventually become the norm.

Another boundary of uncertainty is voluntary regulations and reporting. This happens in many countries as a first step, such as new reporting rules in India, or the initial phases of carbon markets in Europe. The pattern of voluntary compliance has been what is voluntary today becomes required tomorrow. The Task Force on Climate-related Financial Disclosures (TCFD) is one of the best examples of an exploratory and voluntary program started in 2017, and which has become part of many required disclosure regimes by 2024. The TCFD was originally chartered to address some of the reporting limitations in the recently passed Paris Agreement (2015). Members of the task force were charged with the following mandate. "The Financial Stability Board (FSB) created the TCFD to develop recommendations on the types of information that companies should disclose to support investors, lenders, and insurance underwriters in appropriately assessing and pricing a specific set of risks—risks related to climate change."[14]

The TCFD was industry response to the need for climate-related disclosures and was run by industry executives and generally proactive in nature. Although the TCFD recommendations[15] were introduced as voluntary disclosures, they have been incorporated into national or regional policy for categories of companies in over hundred jurisdictions such as Brazil, the United Kingdom, Switzerland, New Zealand, Singapore, and countries of the EU.

Avoid the Clouds of Misinformation

Misinformation is content masquerading as fact or insight that creates a cloud of uncertainty where none should exist. Too often misleading headlines, purposeful misstatements, exaggerations, or excess lobbying gives us a false impression of market directionality. As discussed at the beginning of this book, every organization needs to establish knowledge of enduring value and the heuristics that are likely to help its scenario planning and decision-making. The practice of scenario planning, multi-source reliability testing, and third-party validation opinions should help sort through what is important and what is not. Ongoing dialogues can also help provide multiple perspectives that enhance decision-making.

Summary

The general principles of future-proofing your organization are as follows:

1. Transparency—Assume you must be transparent and prepare for transparency by discussing your communication plans at the end of every major planning or performance reporting meeting.
2. Data Collection—Begin collecting data on all scope 1–3 emissions and all business relationships. Data collection becomes a discipline and must also be subject to audits and third-party opinions to ensure accuracy and transparency.
3. Training—
   - Train your vendors on common data-collection techniques and your sustainability expectations. Although there is a direct cost to this training, it is well worth the investment to ensure alignment and find those vendors that align well with your goals and those that do not.
   - Train everyone in your organization on the foundation issues of sustainability. It is easier to innovate from a perspective of knowledge than ignorance. Each functional area must also engage in action learning exercises specific to their business line, geography of function. For example, salespeople need to be able to assess their prospective and existing customers for suitability on new sustainable products and services. Doing so, allows them to have an intelligent conversation about business challenges.

4. Disrupt and Adapt—Leaders must look at disruption as a core condition and rethink how to approach everything from product design to supply chain management to financial repotting. It is highly likely that business processes and incentives will become misaligned if market disruptions are continuous.

5. Sustainable Business Intelligence—This must be a regular part of leadership meeting discussions. There is a lot going on in every market and the ongoing process of socializing information leads to insights, better critical thinning, and innovation. For example, when socializing innovations, identify multi-value characteristics such as the validation of use for any of the six capital formation categories, the reliability (repeatability) of the innovation, the differentiation that the innovation can deliver to your business, new customer or non-customer opportunities, and reduced costs improved performance, particularly if those attributes affect carbon footprints, emissions, or other resource usage.

6. Transitions—Organizations must develop explicit transition plans to move from legacy products dependence to newer sustainable product lines. Because the market may change more rapidly than expected, there must be explicit scenario planning to account for both upside opportunities and downside risks.

7. Scenario Planning—Most public policy declarations related to sustainability have a timeline that is predictable. Although there are always potential changes, it is wise to spend the time considering the possible business issues. Will this affect my current or planned products and services? Will this add costs? Can those be mitigated? Will the new issues be global or market specific? Is there new competitive opportunity? Track the future-focused timelines and conduct scenario panning based on several possible futures.

Future-Proofing Reflection Checklist

Future-Proofing		
Is it more or less true that your organization ...		**Ranking**
1	Receives updates regarding major scientific milestones as they relate to the SDG or major interpretive models such as tipping points of planetary boundaries?	1 2 3 4 5 6 7 8 9 10
2	Tracks the keystone players involved in sustainability policy at major institutions and primary markets?	1 2 3 4 5 6 7 8 9 10
3	Maintains a mechanism for tracking both thought and practice leaders in knowledge domains determined to be critical to your organizational strategy?	1 2 3 4 5 6 7 8 9 10
4	Observes capital markets for fund flows and start-up companies working on innovations that directly or indirectly affect your products, services, customers, and markets?	2 2 3 4 5 6 7 8 9 10
5	Trains your vendors and partners on data collection and routinely seeks their perspective on customer and market trends?	3 2 3 4 5 6 7 8 9 10
6	Regularly socializes your business intelligence with key leaders and teams across your organization?	1 2 3 4 5 6 7 8 9 10
7	Routinely observes and discusses innovation in market adjacencies for potential application to your business?	1 2 3 4 5 6 7 8 9 10
8	Conducts team-based reviews of important information designed specifically to gain insights from multiple perspectives.	1 2 3 4 5 6 7 8 9 10
9	Maintains a process for identifying misinformation that may relate to key customers and markets, as well as company products and brands?	1 2 3 4 5 6 7 8 9 10

Future-Proofing	
Is it more or less true that your organization ...	**Ranking**
10	Remains aware of uncertainties by tracking and discussing the activities of major intergovernmental and government councils and research institutes?	1 2 3 4 5 6 7 8 9 10
Total Score	

Scoring:

- Score less than 50—A low score implies both a lack of focus and potential business risk. Anticipating market changes is key to having the time to plan, test, and adapt your strategies.

- Score less than 80—Future-proofing your organization is hard to do, and the information can seem overwhelming. However, developing core practices that become routine ensures that you are not surprised by new innovations or changes in market sentiment. Continue the process of refining your practices.

- Score greater than 80—A higher score suggests that you are on the right track. The real test is in the impact your business intelligence has on actual business decisions. Are you comfortable with your leadership position and at least a fast follower on most challenges? The challenge is not to be right all the time, but to have sufficient time and capability to make informed decisions.

APPENDIX 1: SIXTY-SIX TERMS WORTH KNOWING

Term	Definition
Additionality	Carbon credit projects work off a baseline. What happens without any intervention? Additionality describes the carbon sequestration from the project above that baseline and is the basis of the credit. The challenge is to decide what would have occurred without credit incentives and to establish the term of the benefits that are suggested. As such, the credit scenario is an educated guess based on best practices and is predictive in nature.
Article 6 (Paris Agreement)	Article 6 is one of the most important components of the Paris Agreement. It lays out mechanisms for managing greenhouse gas emissions and creates the idea of Internationally Transferred Mitigation Outcomes (ITMOs) so countries can offset emissions by using internationally achieved reductions. It also establishes the Paris Agreement Crediting Mechanism (PACM), Authorized Emission Reductions (AER), and Mitigation Contribution Units (MCUs). Anyone working on carbon markets or NDCs should spend some time reviewing sections 6.2, 6.4, and 6.8, at a minimum.
Benefit Corporation	A type of corporate allowable under U.S. law that specifically calls for the goal of achieving a public good and positive social and environmental impact in its mission and articles of incorporation. It is currently allowable in more than 30 U.S. states, and the key characteristics of the Benefit Corporation framework are used voluntarily by a variety of international organizations.

(Continued)

Appendix 1

Term	Definition
Biodiversity Credits	The Kunming-Montreal Global Biodiversity Framework, created in 2022, set goals and described funding gaps related to the biodiversity crisis. However, there is no formal mechanism like carbon credits. Biodiversity credits have been created and used by certain foundations and NGOs to help establish a market to help close the gap in biodiversity and ecosystem funding. There is little regulation of this space, and these credits remain largely experimental.
Blue Washing	Blue washing is a variation on the greenwashing idea of presenting misleading information about sustainability practices. This generally refers to claims about human rights practices.
Cap and Trade	The "cap" refers to a maximum limit on emissions, generally set for each company on a year-to-year basis. Slowly reducing the annual caps is a way to keep companies in line with larger commitments to reduce emissions. If your company is below its cap, it gets credits for the difference that it can "trade" to corporate buyers who are over their cap.
Carbon Border Adjustment Mechanism (CBAM)	The CBAM is a mechanism developed by the European Union (EU) to address the issue of carbon leakage, which comes from underreported or unreported emissions that happen during a product production process when the supply chain happens in multiple countries, largely outside of the EU. "As from October 1, 2023, Regulation 2023/956 introduced the EU's Carbon Border Adjustment Mechanism (CBAM) with the objective to reduce carbon emissions, put a fair price on the carbon emitted during the production of carbon intensive goods imported into the EU and encourage a cleaner industrial production through a methodology for calculating embedded emissions according to the Paris Agreement and the EU Fit for 55 package[a]."
Carbon Credit	Carbon credits come in many forms, but the idea is to provide an allowance for the production of 1 ton of carbon. A company purchases a credit from a voluntary market or from a government exchange and uses those credits as part of its emissions management plan. The credits are then used to reduce its total emissions, either below their allowed limits or toward a neutral or net benefit position. Companies can also create credits from their operations and sell them, which offers a reward for companies that invest in technologies or products that are more carbon neutral.

(Continued)

Term	Definition
Carbon Marketplace	There are both mandatory carbon marketplaces like the European Union Trading Emissions program and voluntary markets. The mandatory markets are often created to help hard-to-decarbonize industries and are variations of a cap (limit) and trade (credit) scheme. The voluntary markets are an attempt to create a way for companies to manage their emissions and to create revenues in markets around the world where investments in low emissions or sequestration strategies receive financial incentives to continue such efforts. The markets are characterized by standards (such as 1 ton of emissions per credit), projects (the acreage size of a sequestration offer), and verification practices (third-party verification) to improve transparency and the validity of carbon credits.
Carbon Neutral	This is a generally used term and is similar to Net Zero. The idea is to balance out a company's emissions with various mitigation strategies such as carbon sequestration or carbon credits, so the carbon emissions accounting is essentially zero or neutral.
Carbon Offsets	These are variations of the carbon credit. When one company purchases the carbon credit, it is used to "offset" 1 ton of emissions produced from its operations.
Causal Loop Modeling	A process of creating a visual model showing how business variables are interconnected. The relationships are generally labeled with a variable name, a behavior descriptor, a directional link, and a link for interconnectedness. This is a typical tool for mapping key business activities, how each activity supports or flows from another part of the process, converts activity into a new process, or reinforces certain activities. It also helps identify potential barriers and possible points of process failure.
Circular Economy	A circular economy model is one that seeks to reduce or eliminate the waste or impact of any product or service. The goal is to design products that reuse, recycle, or remanufacture and design things so they can be disassembled for reuse, so the total impact on resource extraction or virgin resources is minimized or eliminated.

(*Continued*)

Appendix 1

Term	Definition
Circular Product Assessment	This is a product assessment that considers how a product can be broken into component parts for repair, reuse, recycling, or repurpose. Understanding disassembly becomes part of the product design, so alternatives can be considered for all stages from material selection to assembly techniques and end-of-life activities. It is meant to optimize the product design for minimal environmental impact in the entire life cycle. The importance of the assessment is the lessons learned that can be embedded in later product development efforts.
Clean Capitalism	The term "clean capitalism" is most associated with the organization Corporate Knights and its founder Toby Heaps. The core concept is to fully understand the social, economic, and environmental costs in any product and reflect that in pricing, so all buyers know the full impact of their decision. As such, it emphasizes transparency and information in all product design and marketing.
Climate Smart Agricultural Practices	This generally applies to an evolving group of farming practices that try to improve the carbon sequestration of most crops and also targets the emissions from popular farm products like dairy.
Conscious Capitalism	The term "conscious capitalism" is generally credited to John Mackey, the co-founder of Whole Foods Market, and business professor Raj Sisodia, who co-authored the book *Conscious Capitalism: Liberating the Heroic Spirit of Business* (2013). The idea is to pursue business opportunities with a greater emphasis on social responsibility, not only to consumers but also other key stakeholders and the environment.
CORSIA	The Carbon Offsetting and Reduction Scheme for International Aviation (CORSIA) is an attempt to create a global program for offsetting airline emissions. Aviation is recognized as a difficult-to-decarbonize industry and is further complicated because airlines travel frequently between national boundaries and in international space while producing emissions. CORSIA has its own set of Emissions Unit Eligibility Criteria and is subject to the International Civil Aviation Organization (ICAO), which is a United Nations specialized agency.

(Continued)

Term	Definition
Debt for Climate Swaps	Many developing countries carry significant government debt, and the transition to a more sustainable economy requires significant investments. Organizations such as the Green Climate Fund and the International Institute for Environment and Development are encouraging debt-for-climate swaps, where some debts are reduced in exchange for the freed-up funds being used in climate action, environmental restoration, biodiversity protection, or other conservation programs.
Decoupled Growth	Decoupled growth is the idea that we should try to detach business growth from emissions and environmental impact. Generally, there is a strong correlation between the growth in emissions and waste with increases in revenue and product sales. As long as a company is dependent on fossil fuels, there is a limit to this idea. The same is true with waste or water usage. Although there can be relative declines in resource use, there need to be absolute substitutions of alternative energy for emissions and a serious commitment to reuse, recycling, and remanufacturing to substantially cut resource consumption.
Doughnut Economics	Doughnut Economics is generally credited to economist Kate Raworth, who authored the book *Doughnut Economics: Seven Ways to Think Like a 21st-Century Economist*. The concept involves three key areas, including a social foundation, the safe and just space for humanity, and an ecological ceiling. The idea is to balance the needs of people with the natural limits our planet can provide. *Doughnut Economics* focuses a lot on the idea of "create to regenerate" practices that limit resource degradation.
Dual Materiality	The idea is to create a new framework that describes the impact of sustainability issues on a company's operations as well as the impact the company's operations have on the environment and society. This is often called an inside-out and outside-in perspective.

(*Continued*)

Term	Definition
Environmental Product Declaration (EPD)	The EPD is intended as a standard declaration that provides environmental and impact information on a given product. It is required by law in the European Union and in certain U.S. states, including California, Colorado, Oregon, and Washington, although only for certain product types. Its use is growing in other countries, but you need to check on specific product and industry requirements. It is generally built around a life-cycle assessment methodology with the intention of expanding transparency. EPDs require a third-party verification before use and last several years before they need to be redeveloped and verified. Some industry EPDs are linked to ISO standards, but many are not.
ESG Audit	This is generally a checklist that follows one or more major disclosure frameworks. This can be created internally by your sustainability team with the idea of looking for documentation for all the plans, programs, and processes. Audits can also be done by third-party organizations on a more formal basis as a way to create a gap assessment or benchmark that can be shared with the organization.
ESG Ratings	ESIG ratings and scores are created by third-party organizations that provide an independent perspective on a company's risk management or performance with respect to the three primary sustainability pillars of environment, social, and governance. Most ratings then break those three pillars down into subcategories that may number several dozen and further refine these into topical areas and industry-specific subcategories. Examples of companies that provide ratings or scores include Sustainalytics, Bloomberg, MSCI, and Dow Jones.
Ethical Brands	A brand is often described as the promises your company makes to various stakeholders. What does it represent? An ethical brand refers to the guiding ethical principles that describe how a company acts.
Friendshoring	A variation on the idea of offshoring the manufacturing of various goods, but it takes into account newer competitive issues between countries. Friendshoring is the moving of offshoring partnerships from high-tariff or politically unstable relationships to partner countries where there may be a free trade agreement or where the distribution of relationships may be beneficial by reducing dependencies, eliminating global supply chain disruptions, or bringing manufacturing closer to the home market.

(Continued)

Appendix 1

Term	Definition
Future Scanning	This technique is a scenario planning tool where a group helps summarize several broad categories of information that are critical to the business. This would include the macroeconomic environment as well as anticipated technology development. Sustainability adds the policy and regulatory dimension for regional markets as well as insights into global policy competition in major markets. In addition, the evolving nature of governance, environmental, and biodiversity challenges is considered.
Global Stock Take	This is part of the Paris Agreement passed in 2015 and is intended as a way to summarize progress.
Green Bleaching	Green bleaching is the process of overemphasizing some characteristics of a product in an attempt to mask or avoid a focus on other characteristics that may be less positive. It is an attempt to manipulate opinion by distorting the relative merits of several attributes in relation to each other or to global standards.
Green Capitalism	Green capitalism is a generic term used in many forms, such as the Green New Deal in the United States, to explain how capitalism can be used to solve all problems of sustainability and climate change. The core idea is to shift the economy to "green" industries and jobs so the benefits of capitalism can be employed to create jobs and economic growth in newer industries like renewable energy.
Green Gaslighting	Gaslighting refers to the practice of making repeated, misleading statements in a deliberate effort to change public opinion, misrepresent facts, or to cause doubt or concerns. It is often described as a propaganda tool.
Greenhushing	Greenhushing differs from greenwashing in that the latter is about misleading information, and the former is about underreporting, withholding, or failing to disclose known information that may be environmentally negative.

(Continued)

Term	Definition
Green Tariffs	An electricity purchase program that allows the purchaser, generally a large industrial buyer, to get 100 percent of their electricity from renewable alternatives such as wind and solar. Green tariffs in the United States market are optional programs in regulated markets, and the power may be provided directly by a utility-owned source or through a utility contract with one or more third-party providers.
Greenwashing	Greenwashing has become the most common term used to describe misleading or false statements about the impact of sustainability practices. It is a variation on the idea of "whitewashing," except it is the color green to indicate an environmental quality to the statement. This may occur in product advertising, labeling, or general communications and is increasingly regulated in developed markets.
Global Warming Potential	Global Warming Potential, also referred to as GWP, is a metric generally applied in either a short-term 20-year timescale or a long-term 100-year timescale. It offers a standard way of looking at the impact of greenhouse gases as well as their tendency to remain in the atmosphere or break down over time. Methane, for example, has a Global Warming Potential that is 84 times greater than carbon dioxide on a 20-year timescale, but a Global Warming Potential that is 28 times greater than carbon dioxide when viewed on a 100-year timescale. The difference is due to the impact of oxidation in the upper atmosphere.
Impact Washing	Impact washing may be considered a variation on greenwashing, but the emphasis is on sustainability impact, as opposed to more generic statements about value creation or green attributes. As impact becomes more relevant in discussions of dual materiality, misstatements about the impact a company has, how it might be measured, and how it varies from standards, have become more common. One typical way of impact washing is to change the baseline date or baseline definition while claiming the apparent improvements or reductions are fact.

(Continued)

Term	Definition
Inclusive Capitalism	Inclusive capitalism is referenced by many, but perhaps the biggest push for a capitalist society that engages more of the world's poor and underserved was offered by C. K. Prahalad with his book, *The Fortune at the Bottom of the Pyramid: Eradicating Poverty through Profits* (2004). He addresses the issue that the billions of people in the world who are poor are also potential customers and that serving them also offers the possibility of job creation and profits.
Integrated Reporting	The goal with integrated reporting is to offer investors one report that consolidates, standardizes, and simplifies reporting, so companies can easily be compared on ESG compliance and performance.
Integrated Thinking	Integrated Thinking is the natural follow-on from integrated reporting. Where the goal in reporting is a simple and easy-to-read report with standardized features, Integrated Thinking is about the process and mental models used to synthesize information and gain insights, so it makes more informed decisions.
Internal Carbon Pricing	This is an internally generated pricing guideline developed by a company for use in scenario and financial planning. The idea is to develop a pricing model for use in opportunity assessments, based on regional market regulations and actual carbon pricing or pricing trends, and in risk analysis where emissions allocations or policy rules such as Zero Emission Vehicle regulations are in place.
Life-Cycle Assessment	This is a birth through death assessment with a specific view toward sustainability principles. The key is to identify the biggest impact at each stage from sourcing to logistics to production, packaging, shipping, selling, customer usage, and disposal. The value of the assessment is to allow reduction and mitigation strategies to be implemented while the product is still in the design phase.

(Continued)

Term	Definition
Mass Balance	Mass balance has become an increasingly popular practice in the plastics and chemical industries as they seek a more sustainable alternative to plastics, hard-to-degrade chemicals, or other petroleum-based products. The concept is to create new formulations that combine recycled and renewable materials with virgin petroleum-based materials. Although there is a more technical meaning to the term in chemistry, the practice in sustainability refers to tracking the inputs of raw materials during a transition to an eco-friendlier mix and allows for recording the net amount of each material used throughout the product development process. This contributes to both the goal and the auditable accounting processes now required under certain policy frameworks.
Multi-capital Value Creation	The idea is to frame a broader spectrum of value creation available to most organizations to include financial capital, human capital, social and relationship capital, manufactured capital, intellectual capital, and natural capital.
Nationally Determined Contributions (NDCs)	Paris Agreement Article 4 states, "Each Party shall prepare, communicate and maintain successive nationally determined contributions that it intends to achieve. Parties shall pursue domestic mitigation measures, with the aim of achieving the objectives of such contributions." These are reported in the NDCs to the United Nations and summarized in the global stock take.
Nature-based Solutions	Nature-based solutions are strategies for solving sustainability challenges by managing, protecting, or restoring natural areas. This may include soil conservation, forest restoration, green built environments, rainwater harvesting, or land conservation projects.
Net Benefit Strategy	The idea of a net benefit strategy reflects the challenge that most companies have a legacy business that has a carbon footprint, consumes resources, and produces waste. The offsets are actions taken to do something positive to reduce or "offset" those factors, even if the core product or service remains unsustainable. The overall business is then thought of as a new positive business.
Net Positive Leadership	This is the term used by former Unilever executive Paul Polman and his co-author Andrew Winston in their recent book, *Net Positive: How Courageous Companies Thrive by Giving More Than They Take* (2021). The authors argue that the road to a sustainable future means pursuing business development in areas that create a positive impact. The book details the lessons of Polman's tenure at Unilever and the lessons learned.

(Continued)

Term	Definition
Net Zero	This is a popular and widely used term that companies use to reference their goal of reaching carbon neutrality or exceeding neutrality and being positive in terms of the accounting of emissions (+) versus any credits or reduction allowances (-). Net Zero is also framed as a company pledge to be achieved by a certain date to put the company in compliance with international agreements. Achieving Net Zero is almost always done with offsetting carbon credits.
North Star Statement	The North Star Statement is an aspirational statement of a company's direction. Specific to sustainability, it often describes the impact a company wishes to have on society as well as how it wants to behave as a good corporate citizen or a steward of the planet, as it works to achieve its goals.
Offset Strategy	Offset are a common practice as a company takes stock of its legacy business emissions and waste stream. In the initial years of a transition strategy, the goal is to gather data on emissions and waste streams, plan a transition, and then do things like purchase carbon credits to "offset" the negative impact that the company has on the environment or biodiversity. It is a first stage in recognizing the level of harm that a company may be doing as a part of routine practices and then putting in place both reduction and mitigation strategies that are acceptable with the sustainability community or allowed under related public policy.
Off-site Power Purchase Agreement (PPA)	This represents a long-term agreement between a purchaser and a supplier. The agreement tends to specify the price, the length of the agreement, and any specialized terms. These are often used by project developers and large industrial buyers interested in long-term supplies of green energy for new efforts such as factories or data centers. These agreements are often created prior to the energy supply coming online as part of any financing with a bank or investing group. The agreement reduces the risk for the lender, ensures stable financing at lower rates, allows for a predictable rate of return for the energy company, and permits the buyer to plan long-term for net-zero energy use.
Real Zero	This is an alternative to net zero or offsets by establishing that a company's emissions from all activities, scope 1–3, are at zero without the use of offsets of credits.

(Continued)

Term	Definition
REDD+	The United Nations Climate Change website defines REDD+ as follows: "Countries established the 'REDD+' framework to protect forests as part of the Paris Agreement. 'REDD' stands for 'Reducing emissions from deforestation and forest degradation in developing countries. The '+' stands for additional forest-related activities that protect the climate, namely sustainable management of forests and the conservation and enhancement of forest carbon stocks. Under the framework with these REDD+ activities, developing countries can receive results-based payments for emission reductions when they reduce deforestation[b]."
Regenerative Agriculture	Regenerative agriculture is a variation on the idea of a circular economy where the inputs and outputs of a farm are balanced, so that additional water or fertilizer is minimized and actions are taken to preserve the soil quality, water cycle, biodiversity, the soil's carbon sequestration, and its productive capacity.
Regenerative Economics	The idea of regenerative economics starts with the concept that the earth, our shared environment, has value, and all goods and services are ultimately derived from it. As such, any asset derived from the earth should be thought of as something to preserve wherever possible. The goal is to move away from the serial exploitation of resources that starts with resource extraction and ends with waste by thinking of assets as reusable.
Renewable Energy Credits (RECs)	These are legal instruments in the United States that are largely governed by individual state laws. They assign a legal right (credit) when one megawatt of electricity is generated and delivered to the grid from a renewable energy source. According to the Center for Resource Solutions in California, "The 'environmental attributes' recognized by a particular state may include any combination of the following: the renewable energy source, the geographic location of the facility, the avoidance of emissions and/or local pollution associated with the generation of renewable power, the facility's contributions to workforce development, as well as many other environmental, economic, and social benefits."

(Continued)

Term	Definition
Science-based Targets	The Science-based Targets initiative (SBTi) was started in 2015 as a collaboration between the Worldwide Fund for Nature, the UN Global Compact, the World Resources Institute, and CDP. It sets standards and criteria and offers tools and guidance so companies can use similar techniques for measuring things like greenhouse gas emissions in alignment with international agreements to be net zero by 2050. The SBTi accepts submissions of data from companies and then validates the information as being consistent with their standards.
Shared Value Creation	The term "shared value creation" is credited to Mark Kramer and Michael Porter based on their *Harvard Business Review* article from 2011. In that article, they suggested that the view that companies have created social and environmental challenges in pursuit of profits did not need to be the corporate framework. They suggest that corporate culture could be modified to accept social and environmental challenges in parallel with the existing company mission and that productive capacity could be redirected to address those challenges—thus creating shared value.
Stakeholder Capitalism	The term "stakeholder capitalism" has been used by many people. Klaus Schwab, the founder of the World Economic Forum, is credited as an early advocate, and Professor Edward Freeman is often cited for developing a more rigorous analysis with the publication of his book, *Strategic Management: A Stakeholder Approach*, published in 1984. It essentially says that the purpose of a corporation is to serve multiple sets of stakeholders, including customers, suppliers, communities (including the environment), employees, and shareholders. The amount of emphasis on each is not defined and subject to some interpretation, although the general theory argues for self-regulation by the corporation in terms of broader corporate social responsibility and the use of ethical and moral standards in the management of a modern corporation.
Steady State Economy	Developed by noted economist Herman Daly, who argued that continued economic growth was itself unsustainable because it consumes too many finite resources. He argued for a steady state economy where qualitative improvements were valued above quantitative growth.

(*Continued*)

Term	Definition
Transition Finance	The Glasgow Financial Alliance for Net Zero (GFANZ) was established in 2021 at COP26 in partnership with the UNFCCC Race to Zero campaign. The goal is to expand the number of financial institutions with specific net-zero transition plans and help them accelerate financial commitments to viable decarbonization strategies.
Two Degree Centigrade Scenario	Scenario planning is a key part of the TCFD recommendations, which suggest the use of a 2°C scenario in planning. Various databases are emerging that are considered benchmarks for reference. The TCFD recommendations in particular cite the following as meeting appropriate criteria: IEA 2DS, IEA 450, Deep Decarbonization Pathways Project, and International Renewable Energy Agency.
Value Chain Mapping	This technique, with variations called value stream mapping, is used to visualize all the steps in a product process. Sometimes this technique is subdivided into a beginning, middle, and end, or downstream, midstream, and upstream. It helps illustrate how subprocesses are categorized, with different parties or groups identified for each subprocess. Each step is outlined and categorized, as are waste areas. Traditionally, this technique did not extend outside the legal frameworks of a company to include raw materials or components, but requirements for scope 1, 2, and 3 emissions data have expanded the use of the technique to full product value chains.
Woke Washing	This is a term that has come into vogue among culture warriors where a company tries to manipulate public opinion by representing its brand as supportive of certain progressive values. As with many such terms, there is little standard applied to the work woke' and its meaning can vary depending on the situation. The importance is the intent to misrepresent a certain set of values.
ZEV Credit	Zero emission vehicle credits are specific to the automotive industry and specify an allocation mix of traditional vehicles and electric vehicles that companies must meet or exceed by certain dates. There are programs in the United States (16 states) and Canada with ZEV incentive programs that vary in design in Europe and China, among others.

[a] Carbon Border Adjustment Mechanism (CBAM), European Commission website, October 17, 2023, https://trade.ec.europa.eu/access-to-markets/en/news/carbon-border-adjustment-mechanism-cbam, accessed September 6, 2024.

[b] What is REDD+?, United Nations Climate Change website, Topics, https://unfccc.int/topics/land-use/workstreams/redd/what-is-redd, accessed September 3, 2024.

APPENDIX 2: ELEVEN DATABASES WORTH USING

You cannot mandate productivity. A great tool improves the way you think. —ATTRIBUTED TO STEVE JOBS, FOUNDER OF APPLE AND PIXAR[1]

There are many sources of information that can be important depending on your role. If you are a climate scientist, for example, the United States National Oceanographic and Atmospheric Administration (NOAA), National Center for Environmental Information (NCEI) and the U.S. National Aeronautics and Space Administration (NASA Earth Data) both maintain datasets on temperature, weather, geophysical data, and forecasts. The European Space Agency (ESA) maintains a similar long-term dataset. There are also specialized datasets if you are interested in subtopics and need to examine the underlying datasets for complex predictive models.

- CRU TS (Climate Research Unit Time Series) that covers monthly data from the year 1901 until the present on temperature, precipitation, and cloud cover.
- Berkeley Earth Surface Temperature Dataset includes information from approximately 1750 until the present time with both land and ocean data, mostly on a monthly basis.
- Global Precipitation Climatology Project (GPCP) provides data from 1979 until the present based on physical precipitation gauges as well as satellite data.

- Hadley Centre Sea Ice and Sea Surface Temperature (HadISST) offers monthly data on sea ice and ocean temperature from 1870 until the present.

Although each of these is a rich set of information, they are not relevant to most business leaders. The following 10 databases contain information relevant to companies on issues such as compliance, planning, or training purposes.

EDGAR—The Emissions Database for Global Atmospheric Emissions

Established by the European Commission this website offers basic data on country-by-country emissions for CO2 and other GHG greenhouse gases. This is relevant for understanding the direction of Nationally Determined Contributions (NDCs) and actual data on greenhouse gas emissions. Most large companies comply align their compliance programs with major intergovernmental agreements so comparative data is relevant for long-term planning, for understanding the direction of future public policy and for compliance with Science-Based Targets and the GHG Protocol.

https://edgar.jrc.ec.europa.eu

Climate Trace

Climate Trace is a data set developed by coalition of more than 100 partners and is designed to provide comprehensive emissions tracking. Developed in 2019, it is based on annual emissions data from 2015 onwards with monthly data from 2021 onwards. It includes information on over 660,000,000 emitting assets on three Green House Gases and 8 other non-GHG pollutants. As of 2024, the data set is built using machine learning to analyze data from more than 300 satellites, 11,000 sensors, and various other reporting sources from 72,000 state and local regions and ten industrial sectors.

https://climatetrace.org

ERM Global Regulations Radar

ERM or Environmental Resources Management is a sustainability consulting and services company founded in London in 1971. Its website offers a page that summarizes many of the latest sustainability as well as environmental health and safety regulations from around the world. Although this is a private source of information, it does serve as a quick resource to understand the current state of government regulations.

https://www.erm.com/insights/the-global-regulations-radar/

Our World in Data

Self-described Mission: *What do we need to know to make the world a better place?* To make progress against the pressing problems the world faces, we need to be informed by the best research and data. Our World in Data makes this knowledge accessible and understandable, to empower those working to build a better world.[2]

This website offers both data and visualizations for the data that underpins many of the sustainability goals related to human health, human development, gendered equity and economic development. They also provide the data sources for their insights if you need direct access to the original materials.

https://ourworldindata.org/

Science-Based Targets

SBTi offers an emission target validation process where qualified organizations can submit their targets using the SBTi application process. Targets can include near term, net zero and FLAG (Forrest, Land and Agriculture) targets. SBTi targets focus on corporate entities of all sizes but does not include non-profits, public sector organizations, educational institutions or local governments. Companies that submit data targets will receive feedback on their submission and suggestions for adjustment. If the final targets are approved, they will be added to the SBTi dashboard of indicators.

Procedures for target validation: https://sciencebasedtargets .org/resources/files/Procedure-for-validation-of-SBTi-targets .pdf

SBTi criteria assessment indicators: https://sciencebasedtargets.org/resources/files/SBTi-Criteria-Assessment-Indicators .pdf

SBTi target dashboard: https://sciencebasedtargets.org/target -dashboard

Emissions Collection and Validation

Reporting on greenhouse gas emissions has become a common practice and organizational standard report templates is the first step in organizing your data collection practices. The United Nations Environmental Program (UNEP) offers a GHG reporting template that is a useful starting point for any organization trying to get started on emissions reporting.

https://unepccc.org/wp-content/uploads/2021/05/self-assessment-template-ghg-reporting-for-businesses.docx

GHG Emissions Inventory Template:

https://ghgprotocol.org/sites/default/files/2022-12/GHG -Protocol-Reporting-Template.docx

Sustainable Investing Research Reports and Training

The Principles for Responsible Investing website includes information on the PRI six core principles and provides the opportunity for you to sign up as a member and pledge your support. They also publish annual reports and research reports that summarize market insights.

https://www.unpri.org

The Principles for Responsible Investing Academy is the training arm of PRI that offers a range of online and in-person programs such as Understanding ESG and Advanced RI Analysis. The stated mission of the PRI Academy is, "Our mission is to bridge the critical ESG skills gap that hinders the advancement of responsible investment best practice. We equip industry professionals with an understanding of sustainable investment and ESG issues that is so vital to their professional development and to the ultimate success of their organization."[3]

https://priacademy.org

World Bank Open Knowledge Repository of Reporting Frameworks

The World Bank is a good source of a variety of information and maintain a series of open knowledge systems that are useful. Their financial data is often more extensive that other sources and major visualization datasets like "Our World in Data" often use them as source material.

https://openknowledge.worldbank.org/home

World Bank—Reproducible Research Repository

The World bank generates huge amounts of research on both development economics and broader sustainability measures. This database organizes packages of research that may include summary reports, the underlying data and code, and some of the analytics. There are three primary collections: Journal Articles, World Bank Reports, and Policy Research Working Papers.

https://reproducibility.worldbank.org/index.php/home

ESG Guidance Database for Listed Companies

The Sustainable Stock Exchange Initiative (SSE) currently tracks ~122 stock exchanges and collects data regarding each exchange's ESG disclosure requirements. They publish metrics, tools, reports and provide technical assistance.

https://sseinitiative.org/esg-guidance-database

United Nations Biodiversity Lab

The lab provides spatial data and analytic tools to help countries monitor conservation and sustainable development. Activities. The goal is to improve the consistency of monitoring and make more data available for analysis, insights and high-quality decision making.[4]

https://unbiodiversitylab.org/en/

APPENDIX 3: EIGHT REFLECTION EXERCISES TO REFINE YOUR THINKING

Problem-solving leaders have one thing in common: a faith that there's always a better way. GERALD M. WEINBERG[1]

Problem-solving is a thinking exercise that can be done alone but is best done in groups. Groups add the value of multiple perspectives but require some effort for critical thinking to enable insights. Who makes the insight is less important than it happens and can be recognized as an insight. Making that effort requires engagement with colleagues, good listening, and a commitment to the learning process.

This chapter is dedicated to short reflection stories or cases. The intention is to provide real-world illustrations of the challenges facing businesses as we create a more sustainable future. The stories are designed so they do not point to only one simple solution. Instead, they suggest that a sustainable future requires leaders who can think critically about the value creation trade-offs that often exist in order to have maximum impact.

Suggested approach:

1. Read each story or short case.
2. Engage with others who have also read the case. Peer-to-peer dialogue is a powerful learning tool, and multiple perspectives greatly enhance the learning experience.

3. Conduct additional research on the topic if needed, since all of the cases and stories reflect real-world examples.
4. Reflect on the questions that follow.

Is There Competitive Advantage in Creating a Hydrogen Economy?

The idea of a hydrogen-based economy has been with us for a long time. Individuals such as John O'Malley Bockris[2] described the idea in the 1970s. The concept is simple: substitute hydrogen for fossil fuels—particularly methane (natural gas). It does not have the problem of intermittent performance like solar power and is uniquely suited for difficult-to-decarbonize industries like steel and aluminum smelting, glass production, fertilizers, and chemicals. Although there are differences between methane and hydrogen as fuels, we have a lot of experience with gas systems for both industry and residential applications. A number of commentators have speculated that the oil majors have the capital, skill, and infrastructure knowledge to transition to a hydrogen economy at scale.

How large is the market for investment? The International Energy Agency (IEA) estimates that the world consumed about 12 billion tons of oil-equivalent energy in 2021.[3] Hydrogen can be created from many fossil fuels since they also contain hydrogen, or it can be split from water with the application of an electrical current. If solar energy is used to split water (H_2O), then the only resulting by-product of the gas-creation process is oxygen. Stored hydrogen can also be used as the battery for a combined-use energy grid when solar arrays are not working. When hydrogen is burned as fuel, some of the hydrogen recombines with oxygen in the combustion process, so water is re-created as one by-product. There are no polluting components of hydrogen combustion.

Pros

• Hydrogen is thought to be the most plentiful element in the universe. More than 70 percent of the world is covered by oceans, and water is a unique source of hydrogen. As a practical matter, we cannot exhaust the supply of hydrogen.

- The separation of water is a simple process that involves applying an electrical current, which splits the water into hydrogen and oxygen.
- We already have low-cost ways to generate the electricity needed to split hydrogen from water with solar, hydro, or wind power. A water-to-hydrogen system could also use non-peak time power availability to reduce the costs of generating the fuel.
- The world has more than a century of experience working with flammable gases like natural gas. There are infrastructure, transport systems, ecosystems, and the technical know-how to make it work.
- Hydrogen burns at a higher temperature than methane, so it provides advantages to industries needing a high processing temperature.
- Hydrogen has approximately 2.5 times the energy density of methane.
- A hydrogen-solar economy can exist anywhere, since it is a manu-factured capability and not based on extraction and location, other than access to water and a source of low-cost electricity.
- Large oil majors and upstream gas companies theoretically have the know-how to do the transition work.

Cons

- The gas is lighter than hydrogen, appearing first on the periodic table. As such, it may be more prone to leaks than methane or natural gas.
- Hydrogen will burn with both higher and lower amounts of air (flammability limits), so the flame is more difficult to regulate.
- Hydrogen can burn at a higher temperature than methane, so equipment must be designed to handle the higher range of temperatures.

- Because hydrogen can burn at a higher temperature than methane, hydrogen gas may be more dangerous in some applications if proper precautions are not observed.
- It can be more difficult to transport than methane, although there are several solutions for transporting hydrogen as ammonia.
- Large-scale transport use for shipping or aircraft would require redesign of engines and point-to-point refueling facilities that currently do not exist.
- The idea that oil majors could scale such a solution may be accurate at a theoretical level but seems unlikely. IBM, AT&T, Wang Laboratories, and Digital Equipment had the money, leadership, skills, and potential motivation to lead the personal computer revolution in 1983. Some disappeared, others fell from leadership positions, and none defined the new market. Is it possible [...] yes [...] but the history of business disruption and market transitions suggests that legacy companies rarely lead the way or make the transition.

Challenges and competing interests

- National Oil Companies, not the oil majors, control most of the world's oil reserves, and some countries like Saudi Arabia have a cost of production that is 90 percent below today's oil prices. If we successfully reduce demand for oil and natural gas by substituting hydrogen, will alternative energy face stiff competition from even lower-cost fossil fuels? Would that slow progress or starve the industry of capital?
- Most economies based on extraction industries have a very poor record of economic diversification. As such, they will likely become losers in this transition and serve as major barriers to change at intergovernmental bodies like the World Bank and the United Nations.
- Changing world energy markets from localized extraction economies to a distributed manufactured capability suggest big changes

to competitive advantages around the world. Social and ecosystem disruptions are powerful forces that will drive compromise solutions driven less by market efficiencies or technology and more by political demands.

- Brown, gray, or other colored hydrogen products (dirty hydrogen) may dominate the market because of supply factors and national subsidies. Australia has lots of coal and lignite, Canada a lot of tar sands, the Saudi a lot of oil. Canada has poured over 600 million dollars into a tar sand to hydrogen project. Will the political pressures to sustain jobs and avoid the stranding of fossil fuel assets prove too difficult to avoid?
- Large-scale market changes follow much later. Large shipping companies are under general pressure to reduce emissions, but the sad fact is that international shipping (and airline) emissions do not fall under any country's NDC reporting.
- Although companies like Toyota have championed hydrogen fuel cells for cars, the market has already made a significant investment in electric vehicles and charging networks. Switching again may prove difficult.
- Economic transitions are longer than the political terms of office-holders. Even the best public policies are subject to change as unexpected costs shift the political winds and reelection potential of supporters.

Case reflection questions:

- Is a large-scale economic transition to hydrogen desirable? Is it possible?
- Would hydrogen fuel cell power be a better short-term alternative than a battery electric vehicle?
- Is hydrogen an economy-wide solution or a very specific industry niche solution for services like trucking, rail transport, or global shipping?

- Is hydrogen power a better long-term choice at a global scale, as compared to any alternative?
- Could we achieve a hydrogen economy transition in the time required to make a difference with climate change?

Additional references:

- How Do We Build a Global Hydrogen Economy, International Energy Forum, IEF website, 28 January 2022, https://www.ief .org/news/how-do-we-build-a-global-hydrogen-economy.
- Creating the New Hydrogen Economy Is a Massive Undertaking, The Economist website, 9 October 2021, https://www.economist .com/briefing/2021/10/09/creating-the-new-hydrogen-economy -is-a-massive-undertaking.
- Hydrogen, International Renewable Energy Agency, IRENA website, 2024, https://www.irena.org/Energy-Transition/Technology /Hydrogen.

Is Biomass a Carbon-Neutral Fuel?

The concept of biomass as a carbon-neutral fuel rests on the following idea: if you grow a tree, it sequesters carbon. If you burn a tree, it releases carbon. But if you then regrow a tree, the carbon released by the first tree is reabsorbed. If you continue the cycle of sequestration, release, and re-sequestration, you balance out the inputs and outputs. Theoretically, you achieve carbon neutrality.

The EU Renewable Energy Directive (RED) of 2009 classified biomass as renewable energy, so it is essentially the same as solar or wind energy as an alternative energy source. In the United Kingdom, Drax Group has converted its large coal-fired power plant in Yorkshire to run on biomass made from wood pellets. The power plant project has claimed more than £7bn in clean energy subsidies since work on the conversion began in 2012. Drax claims on its website, "By using sustainable biomass to generate electricity the CO_2 emissions at the North Yorkshire site have dropped by 99%."[4]

However, a variety of sources such as the UK's Institute of Economic Affairs (IEA) are casting doubt on biomass claims of carbon neutrality.[5] The Drax power plant produced 11.5 tons of CO_2 emissions in 2023, equivalent to almost 3 percent of all UK emissions that year. The research company Ember reported that Drax was the single largest source of emissions in the UK based on data from the UK Emissions Trading Scheme Registry and company annual reports.[6] Yet the company claims, "By using sustainable biomass to generate electricity the CO_2 emissions at the North Yorkshire site have dropped by 99%." Drax claims it is "carbon neutral," because the trees felled for wood pellets absorb as much carbon dioxide while they grow as they emit when burned.[7]

In this example, it must be remembered that the wood pellets used by Drax come primarily from forests in Canada and the United States. Burning trees creates more carbon dioxide per megawatt of energy than fossil fuels, including coal, when the harvesting, processing, and transportation are accounted for along with the direct emissions from power generation.[8] The picture is further complicated by the carbon accounting rules. Combustion emissions from burning wood pellets are allowed to be counted as "zero" under international carbon accounting principles and EU and UK law, on the basis that any deforestation should be counted at the forest level where the trees were grown and cut down.

The purpose of this case is not to cast doubt on the intentions of everyone involved. The challenges of global warming are intense, and governments are routinely creating incentives for industry to accelerate actions considered to have a positive impact.

Case reflection questions:

- Would biomass be part of the UK's long-term energy planning if the carbon accounting practices and financial incentives were different?

- Is this the most effective form of incentive to reach net-zero goals?
- After you start on a path of long-term investments and incentives, can you change course?

Additional references:

- Richard Gwilliam, BECCS at Drax Can Accelerate the UK's Decarbonisation by Delivering Carbon Removals, 21 June 2024, https://www.drax.com/opinion/beccs-at-drax-can-accelerate-the-uks-decarbonisation-by-delivering-carbon-removals/, accessed 30 September 2024.
- Christopher Snowdon, Trees for Burning: The Biomass Controversy, IEA website, 18 January 2024, https://iea.org.uk/publications/trees-for-burning-the-biomass-controversy/#, accessed 18 September 2024.
- Frankie Mayo, The Largest Emitters in the UK: Annual Review, 9 August 2024, Ember website, https://ember-climate.org/insights/in-brief/the-largest-emitters-in-the-uk-annual-review/, accessed 20 September 2024.
- Richard Gwilliam, BECCS at Drax Can Accelerate the UK's Decarbonisation by Delivering Carbon Removals, 21 June 2024, https://www.drax.com/opinion/beccs-at-drax-can-accelerate-the-uks-decarbonisation-by-delivering-carbon-removals/, accessed 30 September 2024.

Can You Build a Sustainable Toy Company with Products Made from Plastic?

The Lego Group was founded in 1932 and has been manufacturing its iconic interlocking plastic toys since 1949. The company first made the blocks from cellulose acetate but switched to an acrylonitrile-butadiene-styrene (ABS) formula in 1963. ABS is a petroleum-based product known for its durability. The qualities that make ABS good for toys make it very bad for recycling, and its chemical bonds resist natural degradation in landfills. Most of the Lego blocks ever made that have been thrown in the garbage remain somewhere and likely will remain for many decades or even centuries to come.

The issue of plastic waste and plastic marine pollution became more pronounced in the early 2000s, coincident with a greater scientific awareness of sustainability issues. Major producers of plastic products began considering alternatives that would still meet consumer demand without sacrificing the properties that make plastics the material of choice. In its 2015 Sustainability Report, the management of Lego Group made the following statement: "Our ambition is a carbon neutral operation and to work with our supply chain to achieve the same. Our goal is to balance our consumption of energy with renewable energy by 2020. We also want to achieve net-zero waste and by 2030 use sustainable materials in all core Lego products and packaging."[9]

Lego made a significant commitment in 2015 to invest over 150 million USD in the development of a Sustainable Materials Center to tackle the problem of finding a more sustainable alternative to ABS. Lego Group reported 2023 revenue of DKK 65.9 billion (~9.7 billion USD), up 2 percent, and reported they increased spending on environmental initiatives by 60 percent over 2022. A variety of news media have reported on Lego Group's pursuit of plastic alternatives. The *New York Times* reported in 2018 that Lego has developed and tested over 200 alternatives.[10]

Despite those efforts testing bio-based plastics and products made from sugar cane, they are yet to find a satisfactory alternative. Their most recent approach is called "mass balance." According to Lego Group,

Mass balance is a way to increase the amount of renewable input in the raw materials we buy. Our suppliers mix virgin fossil sources with certified renewable sources (like used cooking oil or plant oil) to produce the material for LEGO products. This approach helps us to start the transition to using more and more

renewable raw materials, but it's not the end goal. Our ambition is that by 2032, our products will be made from materials that are renewable or recycled. But right now, there aren't enough quality recycled and renewable raw materials available. We will continue to join forces and work with industry to develop solutions and do our part to drive demand.[11]

Case reflection questions:

- Is Lego Group doing a good job meeting its obligations as a sustainable business?
- What are the pros and cons of their approach?
- Is their behavior consistent with being an ethical brand?
- Is this a best-practice company?

Additional References:

- Working Towards Sustainable LEGO® Bricks and Elements, Sustainability, Lego Group Sustainability webpage, https://www .lego.com/en-us/sustainability/sustainable-materials?locale=en-us.

How Should We Rebuild a Power Grid After a Forest Fire?

During the period from 2000 to 2016, wildfires in California caused a reported $700 million in damages to the California electricity grid, primarily in the form of damage to transmission lines, distribution centers, and transmission pathways.[12] More recent fires have been larger, burned hotter, and destroyed more forests. According to the US Forest Service, "Extreme wildfires tore through California, burning more than 4.2 million acres from 2020 through 2021."[13] The fires have an impact on air quality, wildlife, and water quality and threaten homes, businesses, and jobs.

The California power grid has a variety of vulnerabilities, from regulatory challenges to climate change and a lack of investment. Changes in sea levels will affect coastal power plants; aging infrastructure in some communities increases the chance of failure; and urbanization in fire-prone areas all contribute to the problem. Increases in renewable energy are coming online, but smart grids, backup systems, and improved transmission systems have all lagged.

Challenge:

After a series of recent wildfires, you are named to a working group considering replacements for the power grid. One set of decisions involves replacing damaged transformers. The transformers are a key part of the distribution grid since they allow electricity to travel over long distances and are crucial to providing safe and usable electricity. You have a choice between two types of replacements. Both product choices are filled with an oily chemical necessary to resist the extreme temperatures and pressures during electricity transmission.

- One product uses synthetic and toxic chemicals that are very hard to recycle and that pose health threats to humans and wildlife if damaged, spilled, or disposed of improperly. If burned in a wildfire, they can release cancer-causing toxins into the air and water. These products are, however, the most efficient with less power lost over long distances.
- The alternative product uses a biodegradable, vegetable-based oil that can be easily disposed of and has no known risks to humans or wildlife. It is more environmentally friendly at face value and does not cause damage if burned. However, it reduces electrical transmission efficiency by 15 percent.

Context:

- California's power generation is approximately 50 percent natural gas, 32.5 percent renewable (primarily wind and solar), 15 percent hydroelectric, and 2.5 percent nuclear (approximate totals from

Wikipedia, as of 2018). California's power needs are up to 30 percent higher, so it must import additional power from neighboring power grids.

- The California Public Utilities Commission had made assumptions regarding alternative energy usage that have proven overly optimistic. Recent droughts and low water in hydroelectric dams have greatly reduced power in some years.
- Poor planning can have a power plant offline for maintenance just when power demand has surged (*NY Times*, 4 September 2020).
- Increases in weather events across the US western states mean there is less power to be imported into California.
- An aging power grid, which includes many elements built in the 1960s and 1970s limits the flexibility of moving surplus power from one area to another.

Case reflection questions:

- What is the right transformer choice for a sustainable business?
- What are the principles upon which you made your choice?
- What are the potential barriers to making the right choice?
- Are there changes in circumstances or content that will affect how you decide?

Additional references:

- Ivan Penn, Poor Planning Left California Short of Electricity in a Heat Wave, *New York Times*, 20 August 2020: https://www
.nytimes.com/2020/08/20/business/energy-environment/california-blackout-electric-grid.html
- Andy Uhler, California Blackouts Trigger Debate About Electric Grid Resilience, Marketplace, 28 August 2020: https://www
.marketplace.org/2020/08/28/california-blackouts-electric-grid
-renewable-energy-heat-wave-utilities/

- Assessing the Impact of Wildfires on the California Electricity Grid, California's Fourth Climate Change Assessment, California Energy Commission website, August 2018, https://www.energy .ca.gov/sites/default/files/2019-11/Energy_CCCA4-CEC-2018 -002_ADA.pdf.
- Hilary Clarke, Extreme Wildfires Take a Toll on California Wildlife, US Forrest Service, USDA website, 6 March 2024, https://www.fs.usda.gov/about-agency/features/extreme-wildfires -take-toll-california-wildlife, accessed 30 September 2024.

Do We Value the Forests That Don't Grow on Land?

Kelp forests are a form of fast-growing brown algae. If you've ever walked a California beach after a storm, you would see the long strands of kelp at the tidal lines. Some species have hollow bulbs called air bladders that keep the kelp floating vertically like a tree as it sways in the ocean currents. The two main varieties are giant kelp and bull kelp, with some varieties growing to 200 feet in length. Because of their unique ability to make string root-like attachments to rocks or reefs, they can grow in intertidal areas where most other marine plants can't survive. They form incredibly productive habitats that serve as a home to all types of marine species and are often a nursery to small fish and crustaceans. Kelp forests grow all along the western coast of the United States from Alaska down to Baja California.

Kelp forests have been under stress for many decades from pollution, storm runoff, and sedimentation near urban areas, and they require cooler waters to thrive. Unfortunately, Northern California's undersea kelp forests have been decimated by purple sea urchins that eat the kelp. The urchins are native to the area, but a combination of warming waters and diseases killed the urchin's natural predator, the sunflower sea star, which would typically keep the urchin population in check. The result is an overpopulation of the kelp-eating urchins that have significantly reduced the kelp forests since 2014. Recent research by the US National Science Foundation offers a bleak assessment. "Satellite imagery shows that the area covered by kelp forests off the coast of Northern California has dropped by more than 95%, with just a few small, isolated patches of the bull kelp remaining. Species-rich kelp forests have been replaced by 'urchin barrens,' where purple sea urchins cover a seafloor devoid of kelp and other algae."[14]

Part of the challenge is that the loss of the kelp forests is not visible to most people. What people will also miss is the value of marine kelp forests in sequestering carbon. A kelp plant may grow up to 61 centimeters per day, and when it dies, most of the plant moves to the ocean floor and is reabsorbed. Fast growth suggests the plants are highly efficient at photosynthesis and the natural absorption of carbon. According to Earth.org, "Research has shown that kelp, a facet of blue carbon, is able to capture and sequester carbon at a faster rate than land forests."[15]

Case reflection questions:

- Is this a problem for California businesses?
- If I am a California business with a good water and waste management program that meets all of California's environmental and ESG standards, is this still my problem?
- Decide who owns the problem and who can create solutions. What is the role of business in general or your California business?

Additional references:

- Shanshan Doong, Northern California's Undersea Kelp Forests Decimated by Purple Sea Urchins, NBC News website, 1 December 2019, https://www.nbcnews.com/news/us-news/northern-california-s-undersea-kelp-forests-decimated-purple-sea-urchins-n1067906.
- Collapse of Northern California Kelp Forests Will Be Hard to Reverse, National Science Foundation website, 17 March 2021, https://new.nsf.gov/news/collapse-northern-california-kelp-forests-will-be.

- Laurie Smith, Zombie Urchins Are Destroying Kelp Forests. Can't We Just Eat Them? *New York Times*, 17 November 2012, https://www.nytimes.com/2021/10/04/dining/california-sea-urchin-kelp-coastline.html.

Will Planting More Trees Stop the Planet from Warming?

Is it possible to plant billions of trees to reduce the primary impact of excess greenhouse gases on climate warming? The importance of planting trees and maintaining natural ecosystems was a major point of emphasis in the Intergovernmental Panel on Climate Change special report in 2018. Independent studies suggested that we need to plant one trillion trees to help mitigate climate change. One of the most cited references is a 2019 *Science* journal report on global tree restoration. That report estimated the world has enough space on arable land to "support an additional 0.9 billion hectares of continuous forest. This would represent a greater than 25% increase in forested area, including more than 200 gigatons of additional carbon at maturity. Such a change has the potential to store an equivalent of 25% of the current atmospheric carbon pool."[16]

This idea of massive tree planting gained considerable popularity when the World Economic Forum launched its 1t.org program[17] and a separate "Trillion Trees" organization, which was developed by the World Wildlife Fund (WWF), Birdlife International, and the Wildlife Conservation Society (WCS).[18] Planting trees also became one of the most important mitigation strategies in Nationally Determined Contributions (NDCs) as countries began submitting their updates in 2020–2021. New updates are due in 2025 that will expand planning in detail through 2035.

The WWF tracks the number of NDCs that reference Nature-based Solutions (NbS) as part of their strategy to reduce emissions. "The number of NDCs that make explicit reference to NbS approaches has increased from 43 to 50 out of 55 Parties in their enhanced NDCs: 44 in the context of mitigation measures, 42 in the context of adaptation plans—with 36 of these in both mitigation and adaptation. This reflects a positive trend compared to previous submissions." In this instance, the term "enhanced NDCs" refers to country updates on mitigation strategies. The bottom line is that many countries see nature-based solutions such as tree planting, mangrove restoration, and similar solutions as key to meeting their net-zero targets.

One of the most ambitious country plans is the Saudi Arabian Green Initiative. This plan calls for the planting of 10 billion trees.[19] In practical terms, that involves planting almost 600 million trees by 2030 with the balance after that date. The longer-term plans require more restoration of degraded habitat and greater human intervention in the growing cycle.

Despite all of these plans and active carbon credit markets that seek to restore degraded habitat, there have been studies suggesting that "every year, about ten million hectares of land—an area roughly the size of South Korea—are deforested, mainly to clear land for commercial or subsistence agriculture."[20] The Global Forest Review (part of the World Resources Institute) states that, "The world has lost 488 million hectares (Mha) of tree cover since the turn of the century (2000), equivalent to about 12 percent of global tree cover in 2000."[21]

Case reflection questions:

- Reconsider the opening question: Is it possible to plant billions of trees to reduce the primary impact of excess greenhouse gases on climate warming?
- Are massive reforestation plans a good solution, or are they a "feel-good" plan that allows us to avoid making the harder choices to reduce actual emissions?
- Are global reforestation plans realistic on any scale with the human population set to expand by over 1 billion people by 2050?
- Is it possible to plan reforestation on this scale and maintain the planted trees through maturity?

- Is it good to add so much new forest cover to desert and arid areas like the Middle East, as under the Saudi Green Initiative?
- Should there be a shift in global policy toward net-zero programs that limit reforestation contributions while mandating absolute reduction in greenhouse gases?

Additional references:

- Trillion Trees website, https://trilliontrees.org.
- Zach St. George, Can Planting a Trillion New Trees Save the World? *New York Times*, 13 July 2022, https://www.nytimes.com /2022/07/13/magazine/planting-trees-climate-change.html.
- Robin Pomeroy, One Trillion Trees – World Economic Forum Launches a Plan to Help Nature and the Climate, 22 January 2020, https://www.weforum.org/agenda/2020/01/one-trillion-trees -world-economic-forum-launches-plan-to-help-nature-and-the -climate/.
- Saudi Arabia Unveils Roadmap to Reach Its 10 Billion Tree Target at MENA Climate Week, Saudi Press Agency website, https:// www.spa.gov.sa/en/4ee9ea2d6bl.
- SGI Target: 10 Billion Trees Across Saudi Arabia, Saudi and Middle East Green Initiatives, https://www.greeninitiatives.gov.sa /about-sgi/sgi-targets/greening-saudi/.

What Are the Lessons of a Big Oil Company's Decision to Go Sustainable?

BP, the former British Petroleum, has long been one of the world's largest oil and gas companies. In 2002, company chairman John Browne gave a speech at Stanford University in the United States in which he declared, "I believe the American people expect a company like BP [...] to offer answers and not excuses. Climate change is an issue which raises fundamental questions about the relationship between companies and society as a whole, and between one generation and the next."[22] This speech by an influential oil and gas executive was viewed as a turning point by many climate change advocates. Some suggested that the letters BP now stood for "beyond petroleum."

Over the next several decades, BP initiated investments in wind and solar energy and reduced its oil and gas exploration activities. Much of the early excitement about this change in strategy was lost when BP was involved in the Prudhoe Bay oil spill from a pipeline owned by BP in 2006. That was followed by the Deepwater Horizon oil spill in 2010. These two events cost the company tens of billions of dollars in damages, not counting other costs.

- BP was targeted by investor advocacy firm "Follow This" in 2020, where it proposed a climate action shareholder resolution to be voted on at the company's Annual General Meeting (AGM) in 2020. After some negotiation, BP and Follow This made a joint press release on March 27, 2020.

- The March 2020 joint press release included the following statement: "BP and shareholder group Follow This today announce that they have agreed to work together with a view to preparing a shareholder resolution for BP's Annual General Meeting in 2021. This would offer shareholders the opportunity to support BP's net-zero ambition and aims—including for scope 1, 2, and 3 emissions and for increasing the proportion of its investment that goes into non-oil and gas businesses—in support of the goals of the Paris Climate Agreement. Following BP's new ambition and this agreement, Follow This has now withdrawn the resolution submitted for BP's AGM in May 2020."[23]

- BP's stock has underperformed its competitive peers in recent years. According to reporting by Reuters (2024), "When unveiled in 2020, BP's strategy was the sector's most ambitious with a pledge to cut output by 40% while rapidly growing renewables by 2030. BP scaled back the target in February last year to a 25% reduction."[24]

- The new chairperson has indicated that the company has not changed its plans to achieve net-zero emissions by 2050, but needs to focus in the immediate term on profitability in its core businesses of oil and gas. According to reporting by Reuters, "The London-listed company is now targeting several new investments in the Middle East and the Gulf of Mexico to boost its oil and gas output, the sources said."[25]

Case reflection questions:

- Are executives at oil and gas companies in an impossible situation? The world still needs reliable supplies of oil and gas while we transition to energy alternatives. Are they wrong to continue such investments?
- Did the BP chairman have the right idea in 2002 but the wrong timing?
- Do the competing interests of shareholders wanting better returns and investor advocacy groups wanting faster and more sustainable transitions make it impossible for any leader to lead a successful transition to a more sustainable business?
- Is the current chairperson simply dealing with reality? You can't fund a transition without profits from legacy businesses, and you can't keep your job without support from shareholders?
- Are these business challenges a recipe for derailment regardless of the strategy a CEO may choose?

Additional references:

- Follow This Withdraws Climate Resolution for 2020 AGM, Press Release, BP website, 27 March 2020, https://www.bp.com/en/global/corporate/news-and-insights/press-releases/bp-and-follow-this-agree-to-work-towards-climate-resolution-for-bps-2021-agm.html.

- Scott Carpenter, After Abandoned 'Beyond Petroleum' Re-brand, BP's New Renewables Push Has Teeth, Forbes website, 4 August 2020, https://www.forbes.com/sites/scottcarpenter/2020/08/04/bps-new-renewables-push-redolent-of-abandoned-beyond-petro-leum-rebrand/.
- Ron Bousso, Exclusive: BP Abandons Goal to Cut Oil Output, Resets Strategy, https://www.reuters.com/business/energy/bp-drops-oil-output-target-strategy-reset-sources-say-2024-10-07/.

Are Carbon Markets Good or Bad for the Environment?

The *Economist Magazine* ran an article in 2002 called "The Invisible Green Hand"[26] commenting on the importance of market forces in helping the environmental movement. The success story article they referenced was the U.S. Clean Air Act of 1990 that regulated emissions of sulfur dioxide. The act not only required steep cuts in emissions but also allowed companies that exceeded their required cuts to sell the extra to other companies. This became the model for all of the other carbon commodity markets to follow.

Milestones in carbon markets:

- 1997: The Kyoto Protocol establishes the first internationally rec-ognized carbon market mechanism.
- 2005: the European Union Emissions Trading System (EU ETS) was created and became the world's largest carbon allocation and reduction mechanism.
- 2006: the U.S. state of California created its carbon cap-and-trade scheme.
- 2015: REDD+ (reducing emissions from deforestation and forest degradation in developing countries) is formalized in Article 5 of the Paris Agreement.
- The World Bank reported that "carbon pricing revenues reached a record $104 billion," according to its annual 2024 report. "There are

now 75 carbon pricing instruments in operation worldwide. Over half of the collected revenue was used to fund climate and nature-related programs." "24% of global emissions are now covered."[27]

- Many governments have provided funding for large-scale carbon capture and storage projects (CCS) intended to sequester emissions rather than eliminate them at the source.

Results

- Research on the mandatory California Cap and Trade System and the EU ETS suggests that both reduce emissions. These programs require the government to set company reduction targets, document actual company emissions, and allocate credits to sell.
- CCS projects are highly popular and are often undertaken by large energy companies with government support. However, these large-scale projects have a history of problems. According to reporting by Zero Carbon Analytics, "Between 1995 and 2018, over 260 CCS projects were undertaken. Of these, only 27 were ever completed. This result happened despite massive government support following the global financial crisis of 2008-2009. Governments across the world provided USD 8.5 billion in support to CCS projects, but only 30% of that funding was spent as projects failed to get off the ground."[28]
- Voluntary carbon credit markets rely on projects that can sequester carbon based on the idea of additionality. To achieve this, a baseline of carbon sequestration is established, generally on deforested land, then a project forecast is established based on documentation of the type of trees, soils, and sequestration potential.
    - Research published by the Yale School of the Environment indicates, "Although voluntary and offset markets have great potential, both have consistently failed to show that they lead to a net reduction in carbon emissions—what is known as additionality."[29]

- The *Guardian* newspaper and the Corporate Accountability organization conducted a study (2023) of the top 50 voluntary emissions offset projects, claiming that 78 percent had "one or more fundamental failing that undermines its promised emission cuts."[30]
- The organization, Corporate Knights, published a report arguing that, "Carbon offsets have a bad name for a good reason. Some of the biggest polluters exploit offsets purely to avoid making cuts to their emissions. And some of the biggest offset sellers rake in profits while failing to achieve equitable or even tangible climate benefits. With a fifth of the world's biggest companies already committed to United Nations net-zero targets, and virtually all relying on offsets to reach that goal, the growing climate accountability across the private sector is now driving growth of a carbon-offset industry that has its own climate accountability problems."[31]

Case reflections questions:

- Are capital markets the best way to manage emissions, or are they just a convenient excuse to allow emissions to continue?
- If there are problems with carbon credit markets, can they be improved? Are there alternatives worth exploring?
- If there are successes with carbon credit markets, can they be applied to other issues like plastic pollution, water usage, or waste production?
- How do you establish trust and transparency in a market with reputational challenges?

Additional references:

- How Cap and Trade Works, Environmental Defense Fund website, 22 January 2020, https://www.edf.org/climate/how-cap-and-trade-works.

- Nina Lakhani, Revealed: Top Carbon Offset Projects May Not Cut Planet-Heating Emissions, Guardian Newspaper website, 19 September 2023, https://www.theguardian.com/environment /2023/sep/19/do-carbon-credit-reduce-emissions-greenhouse -gases
- State and Trends of Carbon Pricing 2024, World Bank Group, Open Knowledge Repository, 21 May 2024, https://openknowl-edge.worldbank.org/entities/publication/b0d66765-299c-4fb8 -921f-61f6bb979087.
- Robert Mendelsohn, Robert Litan, and John Fleming, How to Repair the World's Broken Carbon Offset Markets, 18 November 2021, YaleEnvironment360 website, https://e360.yale.edu/features /how-to-repair-the-worlds-broken-carbon-offset-markets.
- Carbon cCapture and Storage: Where Are We at? Briefing, Zero Carbon Analytics website, 29 September 2022, https://zerocar-bon-analytics.org/archives/energy/carbon-capture-and-storage -where-are-we-at.
- Daimen Hardie, How to Fix the Broken Carbon-Offset system, Corporate Knights website, 27 June 2022, https://www.corpo-rateknights.com/climate-and-carbon/how-to-fix-the-broken -carbon-offset-system.

NOTES

Introduction

1. Jamie Dimon, Companies 'Have a Moral Obligation' to do more for Society, Business Insider, April 26, 2017, https://www.businessinsider.com/jpmorgan-ceo-on-business-and-being-socially-conscious-2017-4

2. Sofia Lotto Persio, Billionaire Jeff Bezos Takes Stage at COP26 to Pledge $2 Billion Towards Nature Conservation, *Forbes*, April 21, 2022, https://www.forbes.com/sites/sofialottopersio/2021/11/02/billionaire-jeff-bezos-takes-stage-at-cop26-to-pledge-2-billion-towards-nature-conservation/

3. Press Release, Apple Commits to be 100 Percent Carbon Neutral for Its Supply Chain and Products by 2030, Apple Inc., July 21, 2020, https://www.apple.com/newsroom/2020/07/apple-commits-to-be-100-percent-carbon-neutral-for-its-supply-chain-and-products-by-2030/

4. The Paris Agreement, United Nations Climate Change website, 2015, https://unfccc.int/process-and-meetings/the-paris-agreement, accessed August 4, 2024.

5. Transforming Our World: The 2030 Agenda for Sustainable Development, United Nations, 2015, https://sustainabledevelopment.un.org/post2015/transformingourworld/publication, accessed July 25, 2024.

6. Peter McAteer, *Sustainability Is the New Advantage: Leadership, Change, and the Future of Business*, Anthem Press, London, 2019.

7. Peter McAteer, *Pathways to Action: How Keystone Organizations Can Lead the Fight for Climate Change*, Anthem Press, London, 2022.

8. Damian Carrington, World's Top Climate Scientists Expect Global Heating to Blast Past 1.5C Target, *Guardian*, May 8, 2024, https://www.theguardian.com/environment/article/2024/may/08/world-scientists-climate-failure-survey-global-temperature/, accessed July 25, 2025.

9. Ibid.

10. John P. Kotter, *Leading Change*, Harvard Business School Press, Boston, September 1, 1996, page 4.

11. Explore Data on Population Growth, Our World in Data website, https://ourworldindata.org/population-growth?insight=the-world-population-has-increased-rapidly-over-the-last-few-centuries#key-insights, accessed August 6, 2024.

Chapter 1

1. Pulling Back from the Boundaries: An Interview with Johan Rockstrom, McKinsey and Company, Cyprus-CEO website, July 27, 2024, https://www.cyprus-ceo.com/62912/pulling-back-from-the-boundaries-an-interview-with-johan-rockstrom/, accessed August 19, 2024.

2. Zoe Kurland, Katie Hafner, and Elah Feder, The Woman Who Demonstrated the Greenhouse Effect, *Scientific American*, November 9, 2023, https://www.scientificamerican.com/article/the-woman-who-demonstrated-the-greenhouse-effect/, accessed August 23, 2024.

3. Ed Hawkins, John Tyndall: Founder of Climate Science? The Lab Book, April 18, 2018, https://www.climate-lab-book.ac.uk/2018/john-tyndall-founder-of-climate-science/, accessed August 28, 2024.

4. Biodiversity and Ecosystems Play an Essential Role for Climate Regulation, Nature's Role in Climate Change, Nature and Diversity, European Commission website, August 2009, https://climate.ec.europa.eu/document/download/f3af59f0-0b0a-4a0e-ac29-f10cc9b2e4d0_en?filename=nature_and_climate_change_en.pdf, accessed August 27, 2024.

5. Research Confirms Link Between Snow Crab Decline and Marine Heatwave, NOAA Fisheries website, October 19, 2023, https://www.fisheries.noaa.gov/feature-story/research-confirms-link-between-snow-crab-decline-and-marine-heatwave, accessed August 30, 2024.

6. Crab Abundance: Historic High to Record Low, NOAA Fisheries website, October 19, 2023, https://www.fisheries.noaa.gov/feature-story/research-confirms-link-between-snow-crab-decline-and-marine-heatwave, accessed August 30, 2024.

7. Kristen Shive, How Will Redwoods Fare Under Wildfires in a Changing Climate? Save The Redwoods League website, https://www.savetheredwoods.org/blog/how-will-redwoods-fare-under-wildfires-in-a-changing-climate/, accessed August 28, 2024.

8. Daniel Munch, U.S. Citrus Production – An Uphill Battle to Survive, American Farm Bureau Federation website, March 25, 2023, https://www.fb.org/market-intel/u-s-citrus-production-an-uphill-battle-to-survive, accessed October 14, 2024.

9. Ibid.

10. Drop in Florida Citrus Acreage, Citrus Industry, AgNet Media website, September 4, 2024, https://citrusindustry.net/2024/09/04/drop-florida-citrus-acreage/, accessed October 13, 2024.

11. Depository of Treaties, United Nations Treaty Collection website, https://treaties.un.org, accessed August 20, 2024.

12. The Untapped Power of Carbon Markets in Five Charts, Bloomberg NEF website, September 16, 2022, https://about.bnef.com/blog/the-untapped-power-of-carbon-markets-in-five-charts/, accessed August 30, 2024.

Notes

13. State and Trends of Carbon Pricing 2023, World Bank Open Knowledge Repository website, page 43, https://openknowledge.worldbank.org/bitstreams/bdd449bb-c298-4eb7-a794-c80bfe209f4a/download, License: Creative Commons Attribution CC BY 3.0 IGO, accessed September 2, 2024.

14. President Trump Announces Withdrawal From Paris Agreement, Columbia Law School, Columbia Climate School, Sabin Center for Climate Change Law, https://climate.law.columbia.edu/content/president-trump-announces-withdrawal-paris-agreement-0, accessed January 29, 2025.

15. UN Welcomes US Announcement to Rejoin Paris Agreement, United Nations Climate Change website, January 21, 2021, https://unfccc.int/news/un-welcomes-us-announcement-to-rejoin-paris-agreement, accessed January 29, 2025.

16. Putting America First in International Environmental Agreements, United States Government White House website, Executive Order of the President of the United States, January 20, 2025, https://www.whitehouse.gov/presidential-actions/2025/01/putting-america-first-in-international-environmental-agreements/, accessed January 29, 2025.

17. Mark Segal, Germany Pushes to Delay CSRD Sustainability Reporting Requirements for Smaller Businesses, ESG Today website, January 21, 2025, https://www.esgtoday.com/germany-pushes-to-delay-csrd-sustainability-reporting-requirements-for-smaller-businesses/, accessed January 29, 2025.

18. France Pushes for Major Delays and Revisions to CSRD and CSDDD Requirements, ESGVoices website, January 27, 2025, https://www.esgvoices.com/post/france-pushes-for-major-delays-and-revisions-to-csrd-and-csddd-requirements, accessed January 30, 2025.

19. The Future of European Competitiveness – A Competitive Strategy for Europe, European Commission website, September 9, 2024, https://commission.europa.eu/topics/eu-competitiveness/draghi-report_en, accessed January 30, 2025.

20. Zach Coleman and Marcia Brown, USDA Ordered to Scrub Climate Change from Websites, Politico website, January 31, 2025, https://www.politico.com/news/2025/01/31/usda-climate-change-websites-00201826, accessed February 2, 2025.

21. Jo Borras, $400 Million Electric Heavy Equipment Order from China is Biggest Ever (so far), Electrek website, November 30 2024, https://electrek.co/2024/11/30/400-million-electric-heavy-equipment-order-from-china-is-biggest-ever-so-far/, accessed February 1, 2025.

22. Climate Transition Plan – The Road to Real Zero, Fortescue website, September 2024, https://edge.sitecorecloud.io/fortescue17114-fortescueeb60-productionbbdb-8be5/media/project/fortescueportal/shared/documents/publications/environment-publications/climate-transition-plan.pdf, accessed January 30, 2025.

23. Caroline Crosdale, US, Banks Quit Agreements On Climate Change, Global Finance website, February 1, 2025, https://gfmag.com/economics-policy-regulation/net-zero-banking-alliance-paris-agreement-withdrawal/, accessed February 3, 2025.

24. Forever Chemicals, Called PFAS Show Up in Your Food, Clothes, and Home, Natural Resources Defense Council (NRDC) website, April 10, 2024, https://www.nrdc.org/stories/forever-chemicals-called-pfas-show-your-food-clothes-and-home, accessed September 3, 2024.

25. Containers Lost at Sea - 2024 Update, Reducing the Number of Containers Lost at Sea, World Shipping Council website, https://www.worldshipping.org/containers-lost-at-sea, accessed October 2, 2024.

26. Christine Larsen, Helen Wieffering, and Manuel Valdes, Time Capsules of Toxic Consumption: What Happens to the Shipping Containers Lost at Sea, Euro News website, October 3, 2024, https://www.euronews.com/green/2024/10/03/time-capsules-of-toxic -consumption-what-happens-to-the-shipping-containers-lost-at-sea, accessed October 4, 2024.

27. Potentially Polluting Wrecks, Project Tangora website, https://www.project-tangaroa .org, accessed October 2, 2024.

28. Hailey E. Hampson, Elizabeth Costello, Douglas I. Walker, Hongxu Wang, Brittney O. Baumert, Damaskini Valvi, Sarah Rock, Dean P. Jones, Michael I. Goran, Frank D. Gilliland, David V. Conti, Tanya, L. Alderete, Zhanghua Chen, Leda Chatzi, and Jesse A. Goodrich, Associations of Dietary Intake and Longitudinal Measures of Per- and Polyfluoroalkyl Substances (PFAS) in Predominantly Hispanic Young Adults: A Multicohort Study, *Environmental International*, Volume 185 (March 2024), https://www.sciencedirect.com /science/article/pii/S0160412024000400, accessed December 30, 2024.

29. Heather A. Leslie, Martin J. M. van Velzen, Sicco H. Brandsma, A. Dick Vethaak, Juan J. Garcia-Vallejo, and Marja H. Lamoree, Discovery and Quantification of Plastic Particle Pollution in Human Blood, *Environmental International*, Volume 163 (May 2022), https:// www.sciencedirect.com/science/article/pii/S0160412022001258.

Chapter 2

1. Henrik Henriksson: Rapidly Scaling a Green Steel Start-up, McKinsey Sustainability website, November 14, 2023, https://www.mckinsey.com/capabilities/sustainability/our -insights/henrik-henriksson-rapidly-scaling-a-green-steel-start-up, accessed August 28, 2024.

2. GDP Current USD, World Bank website, https://data.worldbank.org/indicator/NY.GDP .MKTP.CD, accessed August 17, 2024.

3. Marcus Lu, Visualizing the Future Global Economy by GDP in 2050, Visual Capitalist website, August 22, 2023, https://www.visualcapitalist.com/visualizing-the-future-global -economy-by-gdp-in-2050/, accessed September 3, 2024.

4. What is the Growth Share Matrix? BCG website, https://www.bcg.com/about/overview/ our-history/growth-share-matrix, accessed August 28, 2024.

5. Ian Wylie, Truth behind the 'Vainies, Brainies and Bainies' Labels, *Financial Times*, November 10, 2015, https://www.ft.com/content/ebffc9f8-718f-11e5-9b9e-690fdae72044 #axzz3rOmq1ink, accessed August 30, 2024.

6. Net Promoter Score System, Measuring Your Net Promoter Score, Bain and Company website, https://www.netpromotersystem.com/about/measuring-your-net-promoter -score/, accessed August 30, 2024.

7. Frederick W. Gluck, Stephen P. Kaufman, A. Steven Walleck, Ken McLeod, and John Stuckey, Thinking Strategically, McKinsey Quarterly, June 1, 2000, https://www.mckinsey .com/capabilities/strategy-and-corporate-finance/our-insights/thinking-strategically, accessed August 30, 2024.

8. Michael Porter, How Competitive Forces Shape Strategy, *Harvard Business Review*, March–April 1979, https://hbr.org/1979/03/how-competitive-forces-shape-strategy, accessed August 8, 2024.

9. Michael Porter, *Competitive Strategy: Techniques for Analyzing Industries and Competitors*, Free Press, New York, 1980.

10. Michael Porter, *The Competitive Advantage: Creating and Sustaining Superior Performance*, Free Press, New York, 1985.

11. Chancellor Unveils a New Era for Economic Growth, News Release, Government of the UK website, July 8, 2024, https://www.gov.uk/government/news/chancellor-unveils-a -new-era-for-economic-growth, accessed September 3, 2024.

12. S.1260 - United States Innovation and Competition Act of 2021, 117th Congress, Congress .gov, US Government website, https://www.congress.gov/bill/117th-congress/senate-bill /1260, accessed September 3, 2024.

13. H.R.4346 - CHIPS and Science Act, Legislation, 117th Congress, Congress.gov, US Government website, https://www.congress.gov/bill/117th-congress/house-bill/4346, accessed September 3, 2024.

14. H.R.3684 - Infrastructure Investment and Jobs Act, 117th Congress, Congress.gov, US Government website, https://www.congress.gov/bill/117th-congress/house-bill/3684, accessed September 3, 2024.

15. European Council Conclusions, April 17 and 18, 2024, European Council, Council of the European Union website, https://www.consilium.europa.eu/en/press/press-releases /2024/04/18/european-council-conclusions-17-and-18-april-2024/, accessed August 30, 2024.

16. F. Bickenbach, D. Dohse, R. J. Langhammer, and W-H. Liu, Foul Play? On the Scale and Scope of Industrial Subsidies in China, Kiel Policy Brief 173, Kiel Institute for the World Economy website, April 2024, https://www.ifw-kiel.de/publications/foul-play-on-the -scale-and-scope-of-industrial-subsidies-in-china-32738/, accessed September 8, 2024.

17. The Future of European Competitiveness: A Competitiveness Strategy for Europe, European Commission website, September 2024, page 2, https://commission.europa.eu/

topics/strengthening-european-competitiveness/eu-competitiveness-looking-ahead_en, accessed September 7, 2024.

18. Ibid., page 1.

19. Principles for Sustainable Insurance, United Nations Environmental Program website, https://www.unepfi.org/insurance/insurance/, accessed August 7, 2024.

20. Fashion Industry Charter for Climate Action, United Nations Climate Change website, https://unfccc.int/climate-action/sectoral-engagement-for-climate-action/fashion-charter, accessed August 13, 2024.

21. Empowering Sustainable Supply Chains, Supplier Ethical Data Exchange (SEDEX), https://www.sedex.com, accessed August 14, 2024.

22. Accelerating the Transition to a Net-zero Global Economy, Glasgow Financial Alliance for Net Zero website, https://www.gfanzero.com, accessed August 17, 2024.

23. Voice of the Consumer Survey 2024, Shrinking the Consumer Trust Deficit, PWC website, May 15, 2024, https://www.pwc.com/gx/en/issues/c-suite-insights/voice-of-the-consumer-survey.html, accessed September 3, 2024.

24. Leading in the Next Era of Corporate Sustainability, Unilever website, https://www.unilever.com/sustainability/, accessed September 3, 2024.

25. Unilever's Purpose-led Brands Outperform, Media Release, Unilever website, June 11, 2019, https://www.unilever.com/news/press-and-media/press-releases/2019/unilevers-purpose-led-brands-outperform/, accessed August 18, 2024.

26. Unmissably Superior Products that are Sustainable and Great Value, Unilever website, https://www.unilever.com/brands/home-care/clean-future/, accessed September 3, 2024.

27. Parley, For the Oceans, Parley website, https://parley.tv, accessed September 3, 2024.

28. How We Turn Plastic Bottles into Shoes: Our Partnership with Parley for the Oceans, Adidas website, March 2021, https://www.adidas.co.th/en/blog/639412-how-we-turn-plastic-bottles-into-shoes-our-partnership-with-parley-for-the-oceans, accessed September 3, 2024.

29. We Intercept. We Redesign, Adidas website, https://www.adidas.co.th/en/qr_originals_parley, accessed August 30, 2024.

30. Brian Caulfield, NVIDIA AI Summit Highlights Game-Changing Energy Efficiency and AI-Driven Innovation, October 8, 2024, https://blogs.nvidia.com/blog/nvidia-ai-summit-washington, accessed October 10, 2024.

31. Jensen Huang, Speaking at the Stanford Institute for Economic Policy Research, April 30, 2024, as recorded on YouTube, NVIDIA CEO Jensen Huang Leaves Everyone SPEECHLESS, https://www.youtube.com/watch?v=oNwoA5akBlg, accessed July 30, 2024.

32. Ibid.

33. China's Massive Subsidies for Green Technologies, News, Kiel Institute for the World Economy website, October 4, 2024, https://www.ifw-kiel.de/publications/news/chinas-massive-subsidies-for-green-technologies/, accessed November 5, 2024.

34. GCF at a Glance, Green Climate Fund website, https://www.greenclimate.fund, accessed August 14, 2024.

35. Progress Report on President Biden's Climate Finance Pledge, US Department of State website, December 2, 2023, https://www.state.gov/progress-report-on-president-bidens-climate-finance-pledge/, accessed August 12, 2024.

36. International Climate Finance, Climate Action, European Union website, https://climate.ec.europa.eu/eu-action/international-action-climate-change/international-climate-finance_en, accessed August 16, 2024.

37. Cost of Achieving the Pathways, The Cost of Achieving the SDGs, United Nation Conference on Trade and Development (UNCTAD) website, https://unctad.org/sdg-costing/about, accessed August 17, 2024.

38. International Private Investment Projects in Sustainable Development Goals Grows, Change in Number of Projects, 2021–2022 and 2015–2022, UNTAD website, https://unctad.org/publication/world-investment-report-2023, accessed September 2, 2024.

39. The Business Environment in Emerging Markets: A Landscape of Opportunities and Challenges, Global Council for the Promotion of International Trade, LinkedIn website, March 14, 2024, https://www.linkedin.com/pulse/business-environment-emerging-markets-landscape-opportunities-mke3c, accessed October 2024.

40. Burak Tansan, Nikolaus Lang, Michael Meyer, Aykan Gökbulut, Lisa Ivers, Rich Hutchinson, Sylvain Santamarta, Daniel Azevedo, and Ted Chan, The Sustainability Imperative in Emerging Markets, BCG website, March 14, 2023, https://www.bcg.com/publications/2023/the-importance-of-sustainability-in-business, accessed September 30, 2024.

Chapter 3

1. Natalie Mortimer, The Brands that will Thrive in the Coming Years are the Ones that have a Purpose beyond Profit says Richard Branson, The Drum website, February 26, 2024, https://www.thedrum.com/news/2014/02/26/brands-will-thrive-coming-years-are-ones-have-purpose-beyond-profit-says-richard, accessed August 19, 2024.

2. Adam Smith, The Wealth of Nations, originally published 1776 by W. Strahan and T. Cadell, London (current version published by CreateSpace Independent Publishing Platform, 2018).

3. GDP Current USD, World Bank website, https://data.worldbank.org/indicator/NY.GDP.MKTP.CD, accessed August 17, 2024.

4. Population, Total, World Bank website, https://data.worldbank.org/indicator/SP.POP.TOTL, accessed August 8, 2024.

5. Frederick Saltre and Corey Bradshaw, What is a 'Mass Extinction' and Are We in One Now? The Conversation, Australia, November 12, 2019.

6. Edelman Trust Barometer 2020 - Global Report, Edelman, 2020 (survey responses collected between October 19 and November 18, 2019), page 12.

7. Milton Friedman, The Social Responsibility of Business is to Increase its Profits, *The New York Times Magazine*, September 13, 1970, https://www.nytimes.com/1970/09/13/archives/a-friedman-doctrine-the-social-responsibility-of-business-is-to.html, accessed July 27, 2024.

8. Statement on Corporate Governance, Business Roundtable, New York, September 2997: Statement_on_Corporate_Governance_Business-Roundtable-1997.pdf, accessed July 27, 2024.

9. Statement on the Purpose of a Corporation, Our Commitment, Business Roundtable, August 19, 2019, WSJ_BRT_POC_Ad.pdf, accessed July 27, 2024.

10. Larry Fink, A Sense of Purpose, Letter to Shareholders of Blackrock, Inc., Harvard Law School Forum on Corporate Governance, Harvard Law School website, January 17, 2018, https://corpgov.law.harvard.edu/2018/01/17/a-sense-of-purpose/, accessed August 25, 2024.

11. Larry Fink, Purpose and Profit, Letter to Shareholders of Blackrock, Inc., Harvard Law School Forum on Corporate Governance, Harvard Law School website, January 23, 2019, https://corpgov.law.harvard.edu/2019/01/23/purpose-profit/, accessed August 25, 2024.

12. Gary Hamel, *What Matters Now*, Jossey Bass Publisher, San Francisco, 2012.

13. Michael Porter and Mark Kramer, Creating Shared Value, *Harvard Business Review*, January–February 2011.

14. Tim Cook, on X (formerly Twitter), post September 13, 2023, https://x.com/tim_cook/status/1701732427897491578, accessed July 27, 2024.

15. Paul Polman, Former Unilever CEO Paul Polman Says Aiming for Sustainability Isn't Good Enough—The Goal Is Much Higher, *Harvard Business Review*, November 19, 2021, https://hbr.org/2021/11/former-unilever-ceo-paul-polman-says-aiming-for-sustainability-isnt-good-enough-the-goal-is-much-higher, accessed July 27, 2024.

16. Net Zero Asset Managers Initiative, Net Zero Asset Managers Initiative website, https://www.netzeroassetmanagers.org, accessed August 20, 2024.

17. Climate Bonds Initiative website, https://www.climatebonds.net/market/data/, accessed August 10, 2024.

18. Chris Metinko, Crunchbase News, Crunchbase website, September 6, 2023, https://news.crunchbase.com/venture/biggest-rounds-august-2023-redwood-peregrine/, accessed August 15, 2024.

19. Danielo Guelfo, Nordic Climate Tech Startups to Watch in 2023, Netguru website, February 21, 2024, https://www.netguru.com/blog/nordic-greentechs, accessed August 12, 2024.

20. Corporate Culture, Vision, CATL website, https://www.catl.com/en/about/philosophy/, accessed August 15, 2024.

21. Our Principles of Governance, Vestas Wind Systems website, https://www.vestas.com/en/investor/corporate-governance/general-business-principles, accessed September 5, 2024.

22. Our 2025 Sustainability Vision is to Pioneer Regenerative Supply Chains, Brambles website, https://www.brambles.com/2025-sustainability-targets, accessed September 5, 2024.

23. C. K. Prahalad, Gary Hamel, The Core Competence of the Corporation, *Harvard Business Review*, May–June 1990, https://hbr.org/1990/05/the-core-competence-of-the-corporation.

24. What are the Fundamental Rules of Economics You Use to Make Money for Berkshire Hathaway? Berkshire Hathaway Annual Meeting (video), Warren Buffett Archive, 0.00 to 02:05, May 1, 1995, https://buffett.cnbc.com/video/1995/05/01/buffett-most-moats-arent-worth-a-damn.html, accessed August 6, 2024.

25. Our Mission, W.S. Badger Company website, https://www.badgerbalm.com/pages/who-we-are?srsltid=AfmBOor7P2PLQaoUN17lBR9NUP48yUVPRGaHK-7xKZ23TkR_GTm-Nf7c, accessed August 1, 2024.

26. Designing Sustainable North Stars, A Guide to Design Sustainable Products, Accenture, 2023 version 1.0, https://www.accenture.com/content/dam/accenture/final/capabilities/technology/technology-innovation/imagery/Designing-Sustainable-North-Stars-Accenture-Industrial-Design-v1-0.pdf, accessed August 1, 2024.

27. Nike Looks to their North Star, a Natural Step Case Study, June 8, 2015, https://thenaturalstep.org/?s=nike+case+study, accessed July 30, 2024.

28. C2C Certified® Circularity Standard Version 4.1, Cradle to Cradle Products Innovation Institute website, October 15, 2024, https://c2ccertified.org/the-standard/circularity-certification, accessed October 17, 2024.

29. ISO 14064-1:2018, ISO website, https://www.iso.org/standard/66453.html, accessed October 15, 2024.

30. What does Rainforest Alliance Certified Mean? Rainforest Alliance website, https://www.rainforest-alliance.org, accessed October 5, 2024.

31. What FSC Certification Means for Forests, FSC website, https://fsc.org/en/forest-managers, accessed October 15, 2024.

32. SA8000˚ Accreditation Program, Social Accountability International website, https://sa-intl.org/services/assurance/sa8000-accreditation/, accessed October 10, 2024.

33. Measuring a Company's Entire Social and Environmental Impact, B Corporation website, https://www.bcorporation.net/en-us/certification/, accessed October 12, 2024.

34. Sustainability Simplified, Ethy website, https://ethy.co.uk, accessed October 10, 2024.

35. Leaping Bunny Program, Leaping Bunny website, https://www.leapingbunny.org, accessed October 5, 2024.

Chapter 4

1. Einstein's Three Rules of Work, ELGL website, May 11, 2020, https://elgl.org/three-rules-of-work/, accessed August 20, 2024.

2. Jutta Bolt, Marcel Timmer, and Jan Luiten van Zanden, GDP Per Capita since 1920, OECD, 2014, page 68, https://read.oecd-ilibrary.org/economics/how-was-life/gdp-per-capita-since-1820_9789264214262-7-en#page1, accessed July 26, 2024.

3. Michail Moatsos, Global Extreme Poverty: Present and Past since 1820, OECD Library website, https://www.oecd-ilibrary.org/sites/3d96efc5-en/1/3/9/index.html?itemId=/content/publication/3d96efc5-en&_csp_=2c2e680562193998e9d20ed6a45a9242&itemIGO=oecd&itemContentType=book, accessed September 15, 2024.

4. Hannah Ritchie, Veronika Samborska, Natasha Ahuja, Esteban Ortiz-Ospina, and Max Roser, Global Education, Our World in Data website, 2023, https://ourworldindata.org/global-education, accessed September 13, 2024.

5. IPCC, 2023: Summary for Policymakers. In *Climate Change 2023: Synthesis Report. Contribution of Working Groups I, II and III to the Sixth Assessment Report of the Intergovernmental Panel on Climate Change* [Core Writing Team, H. Lee, and J. Romero (eds.)]. IPCC, Geneva, Switzerland, pages 1–34, https://doi.org/10.59327/IPCC/AR6-9789291691647.001

6. IPCC, 2023: Sections. In *Climate Change 2023: Synthesis Report. Contribution of Working Groups I, II and III to the Sixth Assessment Report of the Intergovernmental Panel on Climate Change* [Core Writing Team, H. Lee, and J. Romero (eds.)]. IPCC, Geneva, Switzerland, pages 35–115, https://doi.org/10.59327/IPCC/AR6-9789291691647

7. https://hdr.undp.org/about-hdro, accessed July 8, 2024.

8. https://unfccc.int, accessed July 8, 2024.

9. https://www.un.org/en/observances/biological-diversity-day/convention, accessed July 8, 2024.

10. https://sasb.ifrs.org, accessed July 8, 2024.

11. Zoe Kurland, Katie Hafner, and Elah Feder, The Woman Who Demonstrated the Greenhouse Effect, *Scientific America*, November 9, 2023, https://www.scientificamerican.com/article/the-woman-who-demonstrated-the-greenhouse-effect, accessed July 17, 2024.

12. The Royal Institution blog, Who Discovered the Greenhouse Effect? Originally published May 17, 2019, updated November 2022, https://www.rigb.org/explore-science/explore/blog/who-discovered-greenhouse-effect, accessed July 17, 2024.

13. Greenhouse Gas Protocol website, About Us, https://ghgprotocol.org/about-us, accessed July 17, 2024.

14. Where does the Heat Go? The Global Climate Observing System website, https://gcos.wmo.int/index.php/en/news/where-does-heat-go, accessed July 17, 2024.

15. NOAA Predicts above Normal Atlantic Hurricane Season, National Oceanic and Atmospheric Administration, NOAA website, https://www.noaa.gov/news-release/noaa-predicts-above-normal-2024-atlantic-hurricane-season, accessed July 18, 2024.

16. Snapshot of Global PV Markets 2023, International Energy Agency, April 2023, page 4, https://iea-pvps.org/wp-content/uploads/2023/04/IEA_PVPS_Snapshot_2023.pdf, accessed July 24, 2024.

17. Renewables 2023, Analysis and Forecasts to 2028, International Energy Agency, January 2024, https://www.iea.org/reports/renewables-2023#, accessed July 25, 2024.

18. Gregory Kiss, Hermen Jansen, Veronica Castaldo, and Lydia Orsi, *Procedia Engineering*, Volume 118 (2015), pages 326-355 (sourced through ResearchGate), https://www.researchgate.net/figure/Historical-trends-in-PV-efficiency-with-projections-to-2050-source-for-existing-data_fig_1_283172059, accessed July 26, 2024.

19. Charlie Cooper, New Brexit Cliff Edge Looms for UK Energy and Steel, Politico website, November 5, 2023, https://www.politico.eu/article/brexit-carbon-border-tax-eu-uk-energy-steel/, accessed September 17, 2024.

20. Katie Harris, Nigel Farage Erupts as 3,000 Jobs to be Axed in Hammer Blow for UK Steel Industry, Express website, January 19, 2024, https://www.express.co.uk/news/politics/1857585/nigel-farage-tata-port-talbot-net-zero, accessed September 20, 2024.

21. United Nations Conference on the Human Environment, Stockholm, Sweden, United Nations website, June 5–16, 1972, https://www.un.org/en/conferences/environment/stockholm1972, accessed July 18, 2024.

22. The Vienna Convention for the Protection of the Ozone Layer, United Nations Environmental Programme website, https://ozone.unep.org/treaties/vienna-convention, accessed July 18, 2024.

23. Montreal Protocol on Substances that Deplete the Ozone Layer, United Nations Environmental Programme website, https://ozone.unep.org/treaties/montreal-protocol, accessed July 18, 2024.

24. Amendment to the Montreal Protocol on Substances that Deplete the Ozone Layer, Kilgali, United Nations treaty Collection website, October 15, 2016, https://treaties.un.org/Pages/ViewDetails.aspx?src=IND&mtdsg_no=XXVII-2-f&chapter=27&clang=_en, accessed July 18, 2025.

25. Convention on Biological Diversity and its protocols, United Nations, 1992, https://www.un.org/ldcportal/content/convention-biological-diversity-and-its-protocols/, accessed July 25, 2024.

26. The Biodiversity Plan For Life on Earth, Convention on Biodiversity, Kunming-Montreal Global Biodiversity Framework, United Nations website, 2022, https://www.cbd.int/gbf, accessed July 25, 2024.

27. Kunming-Montreal Global Biodiversity Framework, United Nations Environmental Program, December 19, 2022, https://www.unep.org/resources/kunming-montreal-global-biodiversity-framework/, accessed July 25, 2024.

28. The Emissions Database for Global Atmospheric Emissions (EDGAR), European Commission website, https://edgar.jrc.ec.europa.eu/country_profile, accessed August 1, 2024.

29. Transforming Our World: The 2030 Agenda for Sustainable Development, United Nations website, https://sdgs.un.org/2030agenda, accessed July 18, 2024.

30. United Nations Global Compact, United Nations Global Compact website, https://unglobalcompact.org/participation, accessed July 26, 2024.

31. Universal Declaration of Human Rights, United Nations Website, 1948, https://www.un.org/en/about-us/universal-declaration-of-human-rights, accessed July 26, 2024.

32. International Labour Organization's Fundamental Principles and Rights at Work, ILO website, 1998,https://www.ilo.org/ilo-declaration-fundamental-principles-and-rights-work/, accessed July 26, 2024.

33. The Rio Declaration on Environment and Development, United Nations website, 1992, https://www.un.org/en/development/desa/population/migration/generalassembly/docs/globalcompact/A_CONF.151_26_Vol.I_Declaration.pdf, accessed July 26, 2024.

34. United Nations Convention against Corruption, United Nations Office of Drugs and Crime website, 2004, https://www.unodc.org/documents/brussels/UN_Convention_Against_Corruption.pdf, accessed July 26, 2024.

35. Guiding Principles on Human Rights, Office of the High Commission on Human Rights OHCHR website, 2011, https://www.ohchr.org/sites/default/files/documents/publications/guidingprinciplesbusinesshr_en.pdf, accessed August 17, 2024.

36. ESG Disclosure, Sustainable Stock Exchange initiative (SSE) website, https://sseinitiative.org/esg-disclosure, accessed September 17, 2024.

37. Ibid.

38. Exchanges with Guidance, Sustainable Stock Exchange initiative (SSE) website, https://sseinitiative.org/esg-guidance-database, accessed September 17, 2024.

39. Sustainability Policy, Bursa Malaysia Securities Berhad website, December 16, 2020, https://www.bursamalaysia.com/sites/5d809dcf39fba22790cad230/assets/606ed59939fba21d39f9a57a/Sustainability_Policy__clean__-_Amended_08042020.pdf, accessed September 25, 2024.

40. Sustainability Reporting, SGX website, https://www.sgx.com/sustainable-finance/sustainability-reporting, accessed September 29, 2024.

41. Understanding the Global Reporting Frameworks, International Finance Corporation, World Bank Group website, https://www.ifcbeyondthebalancesheet.org/understanding-global-reporting-frameworks, accessed September 20, 2024.

42. Giula Interesse, China Releases ESG Reporting Standards for Businesses, China Briefing website, June 20, 2024, https://www.china-briefing.com/news/china-releases-esg-reporting-standards-for-businesses, accessed October 1, 2024.

43. Sustainable Economy: Parliament Adopts New Reporting Rules for Multinationals, European Parliament website, Press Release, November 10, 2022, https://www.europarl.europa.eu/news/en/press-room/20221107IPR49611/sustainable-economy-parliament-adopts-new-reporting-rules-for-multinationals, accessed September 11, 2024.

44. Elena Philipova, How many Companies Outside the EU are Required to Report under Its Sustainability R? LSEG website, June 2, 2023, https://www.lseg.com/en/insights/risk-intelligence/how-many-non-eu-companies-are-required-to-report-under-eu-sustainability-rules, accessed August 30, 2024.

Notes

45. Simplified ESG Disclosure Guide (SEDG) for SMEs in Supply Chains, Capital Markets Malaysia website, October 2023, https://sedg.capitalmarketsmalaysia.com/, accessed October 9, 2024.

46. Human Rights and Labor Practices Guide, Capital Markets Malaysia website, May 2024, https://sedg.capitalmarketsmalaysia.com/wp-content/uploads/2024/05/SEDG-Human -Rights-and-Labour-Practices-Guide.pdf, accessed October 15, 2024.

47. The ESG Grant Scheme, Deloitte Malta, Deloitte website, September 7, 2023, https://www .deloitte.com/mt/en/services/tax/perspectives/gi3/esg-grant-scheme.html, accessed October 7, 2024.

48. GDP (current US$), World Bank National Accounts Data, and OECD National Accounts Data Files, World Bank Group website, https://data.worldbank.org/indicator/NY.GDP .MKTP.CD, accessed September 15, 2024.

49. National Sustainability Reporting Framework, Securities Commission Malaysia website, 2024, https://www.sc.com.my/api/documentms/download.ashx?id=e98c3900-7b35-4cf5 -a07d-fd17acf8734e, accessed September 20, 2024.

50. Malaysia Driving for a Green Economy, Reuters website, February 8, 2024, https://www .reuters.com/plus/malaysia-driving-for-a-green-economy, accessed September 25, 2024.

51. Our Approach, Sustainability, Transfertech website, https://www.transfertech.co.th/ sustainability, accessed September 30, 2024.

52. The European Green Deal, European Commission website, December 2019, https://ec .europa.eu/stories/european-green-deal, accessed August 3, 2024.

53. The Sustainable Finance Disclosures Regulation (SFDR), Implementing and Delegated Acts—SFDR, European Commission website, https://finance.ec.europa.eu/regulation -and-supervision/financial-services-legislation/implementing-and-delegated-acts/ sustainable-finance-disclosures-regulation_en, accessed August 3, 2024.

54. Corporate Sustainability Reporting Directive (CSRD), European Commission website, 2023, https://finance.ec.europa.eu/capital-markets-union-and-financial-markets/com- pany-reporting-and-auditing/company-reporting/corporate-sustainability-reporting _en, accessed August 4, 2024.

55. Directive 2014/95 EU, October 22, 2014, Official Journal of the European Union, https:// eur-lex.europa.eu/legal-content/EN/TXT/PDF/?uri=CELEX:32014L0095, accessed August 4, 2024.

56. Questions and Answers: Corporate Sustainability Reporting Directive Proposal, European Commission website, April 21, 2021, https://ec.europa.eu/commission/press- corner/detail/en/qanda_21_1806, accessed August 4, 2024.

57. EU Taxonomy for Sustainable Activities, EU Commission website, 2023, https://finance .ec.europa.eu/sustainable-finance/tools-and-standards/eu-taxonomy-sustainable-activi- ties_en, accessed August 4, 2024.

58. Corporate Sustainability due Diligence, European Commission website, July 25, 2024, https://commission.europa.eu/business-economy-euro/doing-business-eu/sustainability

-due-diligence-responsible-business/corporate-sustainability-due-diligence_en, accessed August 7, 2024.

59. Lanxiang Xu, Towards Green Innovation by China's Industrial Policy: Evidence From made in China 2025, *Frontiers of Environmental Science*, Volume 10 (July 22, 2022), https://www.frontiersin.org/journals/environmental-science/articles/10.3389/fenvs .2022.924250/full, accessed August 4, 2024.

60. China National ETS, International Carbon Action partnership website, 2021, https:// icapcarbonaction.com/en/ets/china-national-ets, accessed August 4, 2024.

61. China's Guidelines for Establishing the Green Financial System, Green Finance Platform website, 2016, https://www.greenfinanceplatform.org/policies-and-regulations/chinas -guidelines-establishing-green-financial-system, accessed August 4, 2024.

62. Green Compliance in China—How to Prepare for Environmental Regulations, China Briefing, Dezan Shira and Associates, June 20, 2022, https://www.china-briefing.com/ news/chinas-environmental-regulations-compliance-for-foreign-companies/, accessed August 4, 2024.

63. Code of Corporate Governance for Listed Companies (English version), European Corporate Governance Institute, 2019, https://www.ecgi.global/sites/default/files/codes /documents/code_of_cg_china_eng.pdf, accessed August 4, 2024.

64. Measures for the Administration of Information by Listed Companies (2021 revision), China Securities Regulatory Commission, March 18, 2021, https://www.lawinfochina .com/display.aspx?id=35,144&lib=law&EncodingName=big5, accessed August 4, 2021.

65. Sarah Carroll, California Adopts New Legislation on Climate Reporting, Grant Thornton website, October 23, 2023, https://www.grantthornton.global/en/insights/articles/ california-adopts-new-legislation-on-climate-reporting/, accessed August 7, 2024.

66. The Enhancement and Standardization of Climate-Related Disclosures for Investors, United states Securities and Exchange Commission website, April 26, 2024, https://www .sec.gov/rules-regulations/2024/03/s7-10–22, accessed August 7, 2024.

67. All OECD Guidelines, Due Diligence, OECD website, https://www.oecdguidelines.nl/ oecd-guidelines/due-diligence, accessed August 14, 2024.

68. Business Sustainability Reports, Securities and Exchange Board of India website, August 13, 2012, https://www.sebi.gov.in/legal/circulars/aug-2012/business-responsibility -reports_23245.html

69. Business Responsibility & Sustainability Reporting Format, Annexure 1, Securities and Exchange Board of India website, https://www.sebi.gov.in/sebi_data/commondocs/may -2021/Business.PDF, accessed August 30, 2024.

70. National Guidelines for Responsible Business Conduct, Indian Institute for Corporate Affairs website, https://iica.nic.in/sob_ngrb.aspx, accessed October 10, 2024.

71. Task Force on Climate-related Financial Disclosures, Task Force on Climate-related Financial Disclosures website, 2024, https://www.fsb-tcfd.org, accessed October 15, 2024.

72. Directive (EU) 2022/2464 of the European Parliament and of the Council, European Union website, December 14, 2022, https://eur-lex.europa.eu/legal-content/EN/TXT/?uri=CELEX:32022L2464, accessed September 27, 2024.

73. Ibid., section 1.

74. SEC Adopts Rules to Enhance and Standardize Climate-Related Disclosures for Investors, Press Release, US Securities and Exchange Commission website, March 6, 2024, https://www.sec.gov/newsroom/press-releases/2024-31, accessed September 17, 2024.

75. Our Story, About EcoVadis, EcoVadis website, https://ecovadis.com/about-us/, accessed September 22, 2024.

76. EcoVadis CSR Rating Methodology: Scoring Principles, EcoVadis website, https://resources.ecovadis.com/ecovadis-solution-materials/csr-rating-methodology-scoring-principles#, accessed September 23, 2024.

77. What Are Science-based Targets? Science Based Targets website, https://sciencebasedtargets.org/how-it-works, accessed September 30, 2024.

78. Ian Tiseo, Distribution of Carbon Market Size Worldwide in 2023, Statista website, May 8, 2024, https://www.statista.com/statistics/1399813/carbon-market-size-share-by-market-worldwide/#statisticContainer, accessed August 18, 2024.

79. Commission Implementing Regulation (EU) 2018/2067, EUR-Lex website, December 19, 2028, https://eur-lex.europa.eu/legal-content/EN/TXT/, accessed September 5, 2024.

80. Understanding International Standard on Sustainability Assurance 5000, International Auditing and Assurance Standards Board (IAASB) website, https://www.iaasb.org/focus-areas/understanding-international-standard-sustainability-assurance-5000, accessed October 14, 2024.

81. UN General Assembly Resolution 43/53 of December 6, 1988, https://unfccc.int/resource/docs/1989/un/eng/a44484.pdf, accessed July 3, 2024.

82. Human Development Reports, UNDP website, https://hdr.undp.org/data-center/human-development-index#/indicies/HDI, accessed July 2, 2024.

83. https://hdr.undp.org, accessed July 6, 2024.

84. https://www.mdgmonitor.org/millennium-development-goals/, accessed July 10, 2024.

85. https://sdgs.un.org/goals, accessed July 4, 2024.

86. Hemant Ahlawat, Peter Spiller, and Tim Koller, Managing Carbon: A New Role for the CFO, McKinsey and Company website, October 10, 2024, https://www.mckinsey.com/capabilities/strategy-and-corporate-finance/our-insights/managing-carbon-a-new-role-for-the-cfo, accessed October 17, 2024.

Chapter 5

1. Potter Stewart, Jacobellis v. Ohio, 378 U.S. 184, Justia website, 1964, https://supreme.justia.com/cases/federal/us/378/184/, accessed August 20, 2024.

2.   Carol Adams, Abdullah Alhamood, Xinwu He, Jie Tian, Le Wang, and Yi Wang, The Double Materiality Concept: Application and Issues, Global Reporting Initiative website, https://www.globalreporting.org, accessed October 23, 2024.

3.   Herman Daly Interview Summary, Blue Planet Prize, June 18, 2014, https://www.af-info.or .jp/better_future/html/vol_V/2014/Prof_Daly/2014a_Daly1.html, accessed August 6, 2024.

4.   The Calvert Principles for Responsible Investment, About Calvert, Calvert Research and Management website, https://www.calvert.com/media/public/34498.pdf, accessed August 21, 2024.

5.   The Pursuit of Happiness with Jeffrey Rosen, John F. Kennedy Library Presentation, March 13, 2024, YouTube Video 07:28 - 07:48, https://www.youtube.com/watch?v =bDkOLs55G2U, accessed October 2, 2024.

6.   Claire Andre and Manuel Velasquez, What is Ethics? University of Santa Clara (UCU), Markula Center for Applied Ethics, *Issues in Ethics*, Volume 1, Issue 1 (Fall 1987), UCU website, https://www.scu.edu/mcae/publications/iie/v1n1/whatis.html, accessed August 5, 2024.

7.   Peter McAteer, quotes from interview notes, Interviews with Virat Tandon and Amer Jaleel, July 26–29, 2022 and October 11, 2022, Mumbai, India, and via Zoom conferences.

8.   S. Subramanyeswar, *Brands to Stands, Every Brand Needs a Point of View*, Lintas India Pvt. Ltd., Mumbai, 2021.

9.   Ibid., page 13.

10.   Ibid., page 12.

11.   Blueprint for Corporate Sustainability Leadership, United Nations Global Compact website, 2010, https://d306pr3pise04h.cloudfront.net/docs/news_events%2F8.1 %2FBlueprint.pdf, accessed August 12, 2024.

12.   Ibid., page 217.

13.   The World's Most Ethical Companies Honoree List, Ethisphere, 2024, https://worldsm ostethicalcompanies.com/honorees/, accessed August 16, 2024.

14.   The World's Most Ethical Companies Overview, FAQ, Ethisphere, 2024, https://worldsm ostethicalcompanies.com/faq/, accessed August 16, 2024.

15.   Why Invest in Business Integrity? Ethisphere, 2024, https://worldsmostethicalcompanies .com, accessed August 16, 2024.

16.   Joe Lazer, How Bank of the West is Rewriting the Finserv Content Playbook with Sustainable Storytelling, 2024, https://contently.com/2021/04/20/bank-of-the-west-fin-serv-content-sustainability-storytelling/, accessed August 15, 2024.

17.   2024 Edelman Trust Barometer, Global Report, Daniel J. Edelman Holdings, Inc., page 53, https://www.edelman.com/trust/2024/trust-barometer, accessed August 5, 2024.

18.   Jensen Huang, Speaking at the Stanford Institute for Economic Policy Research, April 30, 2024, as recorded on YouTube, approximately 12:50 in video, NVIDIA CEO Jensen Huang Leaves Everyone SPEECHLESS, https://www.youtube.com/watch?v=oNwoA5akBlg, accessed July 30, 2024.

19. About, Mission, Carnegie Council for Ethics in International Affairs website, https://www .carnegiecouncil.org/about, accessed October 2, 2024.

20. Average Age of the EU Vehicle Fleet, by Country, European Automobile Manufacturers Association ACEA website, May 2, 2023, https://www.acea.auto/figure/average-age-of -eu-vehicle-fleet-by-country/, accessed September 8, 2024.

21. Nishant Parekh and Todd Campau, Average Age of Vehicles Hits New Record in 2024, S&P Mobility website, May 22, 2024, https://www.spglobal.com/mobility/en/research -analysis/average-age-vehicles-united-states-2024.html, accessed August 15, 2024.

22. Ibid.

Chapter 6

1. John Kennedy quotations, Address in the Assembly Hall at the Paulskirche in Frankfurt, Germany, John F. Kennedy Presidential Library, Boston, June 25, 1963, https://www .jfklibrary.org/learn/about-jfk/life-of-john-f-kennedy/john-f-kennedy-quotations, accessed August 24, 2024.

2. GDP Current USD, World Bank website, https://data.worldbank.org/indicator/NY.GDP .MKTP.CD, accessed August 17, 2024.

3. Marcus Lu, Visualizing the Future Global Economy by GDP in 2050, Visual Capitalist website, August 22, 2023, https://www.visualcapitalist.com/visualizing-the-future-global -economy-by-gdp-in-2050/, accessed August 19, 2024.

4. Communication on Progress, UN Global Compact website, January 2023 version, https:// unglobalcompact.org/participation/report/cop, accessed August 15, 2024.

5. EU Reaches Political Agreement on Groundbreaking New Rules for Corporate Sustainability Due Diligence Impacting US Companies, Cooley Alert, Cooley website, December 15, 2023, https://www.cooley.com/news/insight/2023/2023-12-15-eu-reaches -political-agreement-on-groundbreaking-new-rules-for-corporate-sustainability-due -diligence-impacting-us-companies, accessed August 20, 2024.

6. The Mass Balance Approach in Feedstock Substitution, Sustainability, BASF website, https://www.basf.com/global/en/who-we-are/sustainability/we-drive-sustainable -solutions/circular-economy/mass-balance-approach, accessed September 29, 2024.

7. World's most Polluted Countries & Regions, 2018–2023, IQAir website, https://www.iqair .com/world-most-polluted-countries, accessed September 17, 2024.

8. Shri Ashwini Kumar Choubey, Action Taken against Global Warming, Government of India, Ministry of Environment, Forest and Climate Change, Sansad website, July 21, 2022, https://sansad.in/getFile/annex/257/AU529.pdf, accessed September 17, 2024.

9. Pralhad Joshi, Renewable Energy to Power India's Economic Growth, The Economic Times website, September 14, 2024, https://economictimes.indiatimes.com/indus- try/renewables/renewable-energy-to-power-indias-economic-growth/articleshow /113355570.cms, accessed September 17, 2024.

Notes

10. Trade in 2024 will set another Record if Chinese Demand Continues, Trade, Coal Mid-Year Update – July 2024, IEA website, https://www.iea.org/reports/coal-mid-year-update-july-2024/trade, accessed September 15, 2024.

11. Sonu Vivek, Adani Group Shares Drop after Hindenburg's Fresh Allegations, India Today Business Desk, India Today website, https://www.indiatoday.in/business/story/adani-group-shares-drop-after-hindenburg-fresh-allegations-2599025-2024-09-13#, accessed 15 September 2024.

12. Nidhi Verma, Adani Begins Commercial Output of Wafers, Ingots for Solar Power, Reuters website, April 7, 2024, https://www.reuters.com/business/energy/adani-begins-commercial-output-wafers-ingots-solar-power-2024-04-07/, accessed September 14, 2024.

13. John Parnell, India's Adani Wins World's Largest Solar Tender, Green Tech Media website, June 10, 2024, https://www.greentechmedia.com/articles/read/adani-awarded-worlds-largest-solar-tender-win, accessed September 13, 2024.

14. Diksha Madhok, A Coal Billionaire is Building the World's Biggest Clean Energy Plant and It's Five Times the Size of Paris, CNN Business website, https://edition.cnn.com/2024/03/19/business/india-adani-green-energy-plant-climate-intl-hnk/index.html, accessed September 10, 2024.

15. Oil Reserves by Country, Oil Reserves (barrels) in 2016, Worldometer website, https://www.worldometers.info/oil/oil-reserves-by-country/, accessed September 3, 2024.

16. Yasmena Almulla and Vivian Nereim, Kuwait Is Awash in Oil Money. But It Can't Keep the Power On, *New York Times*, September 8, 2024, https://www.nytimes.com/2024/09/08/world/middleeast/kuwait-power-cuts-climate.html, accessed September 3, 2024.

17. How We're Reducing Our Environmental Impact, Levi's® first-ever circular 501® jeans, Levi's website, January 2022, https://www.levi.com/US/en_US/blog/article/501-renewcell?srsltid=AfmBOooqaIMV8dAIsXCFWzoOlmXuFpd6a2VaQORgc3dkbAS2vUiYntXn, accessed September 1, 2024.

18. Dasha Afanasieva, ESG Poster Child Unilever Waters Down Green Pledges, Bloomberg website, April 19, 2024, https://www.bloomberg.com/news/features/2024-04-19/esg-unilever-scales-back-sustainability-goals, accessed September 1, 2024.

19. What is the ZEV Mandate? EVA England website, https://www.evaengland.org.uk/our-work/zev-mandate/, accessed September 7, 2024.

20. Jack Williams, Car Makers are not on Track to Meet the Terms of the Government's Controversial ZEV Mandate this Year, the SMMT has Told MPs, CarDealer website, May 16, 2024, https://cardealermagazine.co.uk/publish/car-makers-set-to-fall-short-of-22-ev-target-set-out-in-zev-mandate-smmt/301913, accessed September 3, 2024.

21. June 2024 New Car Registrations, SMMT website, July 4, 2024, https://media.smmt.co.uk/june-2024-new-car-registrations/, accessed August 30, 2024.

22. Nearly Half of UK Homes Unsuitable for Electric Cars, Press release, Lloyds Banking Group website, December 20, 2022, https://www.lloydsbankinggroup.com/media/press-releases/2022/lloyds-bank/nearly-half-of-uk-homes-unsuitable-for-electric-cars.html, accessed August 30, 2024.

23. Crocs, Inc. to Acquire Casual Footwear Brand HEYDUDE, Press release, Crocs website, December 23, 2021, https://investors.crocs.com/news-and-events/press-releases/press-release-details/2021/Crocs-Inc.-to-Acquire-Casual-Footwear-Brand-HEYDUDE/default.aspx, accessed September 3, 2024.

24. Corporate Responsibility & Sustainability, Crocs website, 2023, https://investors.crocs.com/Responsibility/our-approach/default.aspx, accessed August 30, 2024.

25. Maria Rachel, Colgate Says it Might Miss 2025 Packaging Recyclability Target, Packaging Dive website, May 3, 2024, https://www.packagingdive.com/news/colgate-palmolive-sustainability-report-packaging-targets-recyclable-toothpaste/715031/, accessed September 5, 2024.

26. Brad Smith, Our 2024 Environmental Sustainability Report, Microsoft on the Issues, Microsoft website, May 15, 2024, https://blogs.microsoft.com/on-the-issues/2024/05/15/microsoft-environmental-sustainability-report-2024/, accessed September 3, 2024.

27. Andrew Freedman, Amid Record Disaster Losses, Swiss Re Issues Warning, AXIOS website, March 27, 2024, https://www.axios.com/2024/03/27/record-natural-disaster-losses-warning, accessed August 22, 2024.

28. IKEA Says 100% of Its Cotton Now Comes from More Sustainable Sources, Sustainable Brands website, November 2, 2015, https://sustainablebrands.com/read/supply-chain/ikea-says00-of-its-cotton-now-comes-from-more-sustainable-sources, accessed September 3, 2024.

29. Our Sustainability Focus Areas, IKEA website, https://www.ikea.com/global/en/our-business/sustainability, accessed August 30, 2024.

30. This is Vestas, Vesta Company website, https://www.vestas.com/en, accessed August 23, 2024.

31. Ford Recognized for Water Stewardship Commitment, Ford website, https://corporate.ford.com/articles/sustainability/water-stewardship-commitment.html, accessed September 3, 2024.

32. The A List 2023, CDP website, https://www.cdp.net/en/companies/companies-scores, accessed September 3, 2024.

33. Interview with Ayana Elizabeth Johnson, Science Friday podcast, September 18, 2024, audio 03:50-04:15, https://www.wnycstudios.org/podcasts/science-friday/articles/to-confront-climate-change-imagine-getting-it-right, accessed September 30, 2024.

34. Ibid., audio 05:00–05:20.

35. John C. Maxwell, Failing Forward: Turning Mistakes into Stepping Stones for Success, Harper Collins, New York, 2000.

Chapter 7

1. Unpacking the Mysteries of Productivity, Forward Thinking, McKinsey Institute website, July 2, 2024, https://www.mckinsey.com/mgi/forward-thinking, accessed August 20, 2024.

2. Nicole Lepre, Spencer Burget and Noah Gabriel, U.S. Investment in Electric Vehicle Manufacturing (2023), Atlas Public Policy website, January 12, 2023, https://atlaspolicy.com/wp-content/uploads/2023/05/U.S.-Investments-in-Electric-Vehicle -Manufacturing-2023.pdf, accessed August 17, 2024.

3. Ibid.

4. Trends in the Electric Vehicle Industry, Global EV Outlook 2024, International Energy Agency (IEA) website, 2024, https://www.iea.org/reports/global-ev-outlook-2024/ trends-in-the-electric-vehicle-industry, accessed August 17, 2024.

5. Andrew Loh, Rob Grosvenor, Aakash Arora, Brian Collie, Aykan Gökbulut, Nathan Niese, and Lauren Taylor, Can OEMs Catch the Next Wave of EV Adopters? Boston Consulting Group, March 20, 2024, https://www.bcg.com/publications/2024/can-oems-catch-the -next-wave-of-ev-adopters, accessed August 18, 2024.

6. Nathan Niese, Edward Anculle, Aakash Arora, Aykan Gökbulut, Aditya Khandelia, Eric Li (李科), and Tycho Möncks, A Tale of Two Tomorrows in EV Sales, Boston Consulting Group, September 14, 2023, https://www.bcg.com/publications/2023/exploring-diver-gent-futures-of-ev-sales, accessed August 17, 2024.

7. Ian Thibodeau, Ford's Plan: 40 New Electric Vehicles in 4 Years, *The Detroit News*, January 14, 2018, https://www.detroitnews.com/story/business/autos/detroit-auto-show/2018/01 /14/ford-detroit-auto-show/109472328/, accessed August 28, 2024.

8. Ford Accelerating Transformation: Forming Distinct Auto Units to Scale EVs, Strengthen Operations, Unlock Value, Ford Newsroom, Ford website, https://media.ford.com/ content/fordmedia/fna/us/en/news/2022/03/02/ford-accelerating-transformation.html, accessed August 24, 2024.

9. Chris Isidore, Ford just Reported a Massive Loss on Every Electric Vehicle it Sold, CNN website, April 25, 2024, https://edition.cnn.com/2024/04/24/business/ford-earnings-ev -losses/index.html, accessed September 1, 2024.

10. Ibid.

11. Ford+ Delivers Solid 2023, Provides Outlook for Healthy '24; Company Declares Regular, Supplemental Stock Dividends, Press release, Ford website, February 6, 2024, https:// media.ford.com/content/dam/fordmedia/North%20America/US/2024/02/06/Ford %202023%20Earnings.pdf, accessed October 15, 2024.

12. Mathilde Carlier, Global Market Value of Carmakers as of March 14, 2024, by Market Cap, Statista website, March 12, 2024, https://www.statista.com/statistics/1130533/global -market-value-of-carmakers-by-market-cap/, accessed August 15, 2024.

13. Jennifer L. Schenker, Tesla's Profit Sees a 5-Year Low but Carbon Credit Sales Hit Record High, CarbonCredits.com website, https://carboncredits.com/teslas-profit-margin-hits-a -5-year-low-but-carbon-credit-revenue-hit-record-high-q2/, accessed August 30, 2024.

14. A Kyoto Protocol to the United Nations Framework Convention on Climate Change, Article 17, United Nations Treaty Collection website, December 11, 1997, https://treaties .un.org/Pages/ViewDetails.aspx, accessed August 28, 2024.

15. China's EV Makers Got $231 Billion Aid Over 15 Years, Study Says, Bloomberg News, Bloomberg website, June 21, 2024, https://www.bloomberg.com/news/articles/2024-06-21/china-s-ev-makers-got-231-billion-in-aid-over-last-15-years?embedded-checkout=true, accessed August 17, 2024.

16. Philip Blenkinsop, EU to Investigate 'Flood' of Chinese Electric Cars, Weigh Tariffs, Reuters website, September 13, 2023, https://www.reuters.com/world/europe/eu-launches-anti-subsidy-investigation-into-chinese-electric-vehicles-2023-09-13/, accessed August 18, 2024.

17. FACT SHEET: President Biden Takes Action to Protect American Workers and Businesses from China's Unfair Trade Practices, The White House website, May 14, 2024, https://www.whitehouse.gov/briefing-room/statements-releases/2024/05/14/fact-sheet-president-biden-takes-action-to-protect-american-workers-and-businesses-from-chinas-unfair-trade-practices, accessed August 18, 2024.

18. PowerBuoy, PBT website, 2024, https://oceanpowertechnologies.com/industries/science-and-research/, accessed October 24, 2024.

19. We Harness Ocean Energy to Make the World more Sustainable, Carnegie Clean Energy website, 2024, https://www.carnegiece.com, accessed October 24, 2024.

20. Everett M. Rogers, *The Diffusion of Innovations*, Simon and Shuster, New York, 1962, pages 279–285.

21. Tesla Motors Reports Fourth Quarter and Full Year 2010 Results, Globe Newswire website, February 15, 2011, https://ir.tesla.com/press-release/tesla-motors-reports-fourth-quarter-and-full-year-2010-results, accessed October 15, 2024.

22. Johnna Crider, Tesla's 10-Year Challenge: 2009 vs. 2019, December 12, 2019, https://cleantechnica.com/2019/12/12/teslas-10-year-challenge-2009-vs-2019/, accessed October 12, 2024.

23. Tesla Announces Official Battery Tech for Tesla 2025. No More Lithium, posted on AdamTech YouTube Page, video, at 3:36 mark, https://www.youtube.com/watch?v=bYT-nIWkePe8, accessed August 17, 2024.

24. CATL Launches Condensed Battery with an Energy Density of up to 500 Wh/kg, Enables Electrification of Passenger Aircrafts, CATL website, April 19, 2023, https://www.catl.com/en/news/6015.html, accessed August 17, 2024.

25. Neil E. Boudette and Keith Bradsher, Ford Will Build a U.S. Battery Plant with Technology From CATL, *New York Times*, February 13, 2023, https://www.nytimes.com/2023/02/13/business/energy-environment/ford-catl-electric-vehicle-battery.html, accessed August 10, 2024.

26. Michael Wayland, Ford to Scale Back Plans for $3.5 Billion Michigan Battery Plant as EV Demand Disappoints, Labor Costs Rise, Autos, CNBC website, November 21, 2023, https://www.cnbc.com/2023/11/21/ford-scales-back-ev-battery-plant-in-michigan.html, accessed August 10, 2024.

27. W. Edwards Deming, *Out of Crisis*, The MIT Press, Cambridge, MA, 1982.

28. Maasaki Imai, *Kaizen: The Key to Japan's Competitive Success*, McGraw-Hill Education, New York, 1986.

29. Michael Hammer and James Champy, *Reengineering the Corporation: A Manifesto for Business Revolution*, Harper Business, New York, 1993.

30. Clayton Christensen, *The Innovator's Dilemma*, Harvard Business School Press, Boston, 1997.

31. Hasso Plattner Institute of Design (d.school), Stanford Engineering, Stanford University, https://engineering.stanford.edu/get-involved/support-engineering/funding-initiatives/hasso-plattner-institute-design-dschool, accessed August 20, 2024.

32. Ford CEO Jim Farley's Fascinating 'Take' On Taking On Chinese Car Companies, Everything Electric Show, Fully Charged podcast, October 21, 2024, YouTube video 24:40, https://youtu.be/PGx7AyD9okg, accessed October 23, 2024.

33. Nitish Pahwa, Why Toyota Spent Years Treating Electric Cars Like the Enemy, Slate website, January 19, 2023, https://slate.com/business/2023/01/toyota-electric-vehicles -slow-why-hybrid-prius-bz4x-rav4.html, accessed August 10, 2024.

34. China Auto Company Customer July Complaints – Top 10 Models (translated from Chinese), July 2023, https://www.12365auto.com/ranking/, accessed August 20, 2024.

35. Shirin Ghaffary and MacKensie Hawkins, Altman Infrastructure Plan Aims to Spend Tens of Billion in US, Bloomberg website, September 4, 2024, https://www.bloomberg.com/news/articles/2024-09-03/altman-infrastructure-plan-aims-to-spend-tens-of-billions-in -us?embedded-checkout=true, accessed September 19, 2024.

36. Cade Metz and Tripp Mickle, Behind OpenAI's Audacious Plan to Make A.I. Flow Like Electricity, NY Times website, September 25, 2024, https://www.nytimes.com/2024/09 /25/business/openai-plan-electricity.html, accessed September 26, 2024.

37. Bank of the West Launches the 1% for the Planet Account, PR Newswire website, July 20, 2020, https://www.prnewswire.com/news-releases/bank-of-the-west-launches-the-1-for -the-planet-account-301095760.html, accessed September 15, 2024.

38. Ruby Hinchliffe, Mastercard and Doconomy bring Carbon Tracking to Bank of the West and Nordea, Fintech Futures website, December 12, 2019, https://www.fintechfutures .com/2019/12/mastercard-and-doconomy-bring-carbon-tracking-to-bank-of-the-west -and-nordea/, accessed August 30, 2024.

39. Bamboo — Nature's Eco-friendly Packaging Solution, Dell website, https://www.dell.com /learn/bm/en/bmcorp1/corp-comm/bamboo-packaging, accessed September 20, 2024.

40. Carbon Minds Partners with BASF to Provide Consistent Chemical Carbon Footprint Data in Alignment with BASF Standard Methodology, Carbon Minds website, September 6, 2022, https://www.carbon-minds.com/2022/09/06/carbon-minds-partners-with-basf -to-provide-consistent-chemical-carbon-footprint-data-in-alignment-with-basf-standard -methodology/, accessed September 3, 2024.

41. Ian Tiseo, Distribution of Carbon Market Size Worldwide in 2023, Statista website, May 8, 2024, https://www.statista.com/statistics/1399813/carbon-market-size-share-by-market -worldwide/#statisticContainer, accessed August 18, 2024.

42. Guy Usher and Steven Burrows, Emissions Allowance Financing – Structuring, Legal and Regulatory Considerations, Fieldfisher website, November 14, 2023, https://www .fieldfisher.com/en/insights/emissions-allowance-financing-structuring-legal-and -regulatory-considerations, accessed September 3, 2024.

43. Amy Edmondson, *Right Kind of Wrong: The Science of Failing Well*, Simon Acumen, New York, September 2023, page 290.

44. Reena Jana, Nike Quietly Goes Green, Bloomberg website, June 12, 2009, https://www.bloomb- erg.com/news/articles/2009-06-11/nike-quietly-goes-green, accessed October 7, 2024.

45. Cameron Ward, Amazon Shopper Finds Tower of Nine Boxes Outside Door Containing Items that would have Half-filled One Box, Deadline website, January 24, 2020, https:// www.deadlinenews.co.uk/2020/01/24/amazon-shopper-finds-tower-of-nine-boxes-out- side-door-containing-items-that-would-have-half-filled-one-box/, accessed October 9, 2024.

46. Reality Check: Do We Use 8.5 Billion Straws a Year in the UK? BBC website, April 19, 2028, https://www.bbc.com/news/science-environment-43825197, accessed October 9, 2024.

47. The Recycling Partnership Welcomes McDonald's Corporation to the Polypropylene Recycling Coalition and Awards Its 100th Recycling Facility Grant, The Recycling Partnership website, May 16, 2024, https://recyclingpartnership.org/the-recycling -partnership-welcomes-mcdonalds-corporation-to-the-polypropylene-recycling -coalition-and-awards-its-100th-recycling-facility-grant/, accessed October 9, 2024.

48. Paul W. Ferris, Philips Lighting Company: The Earth Light, Darden School of Business Case, September 23, 2023, https://store.hbr.org/product/philips-lighting-company-the -earth-light/, accessed October 10, 2024.

49. Robert Metzke, How Can We Drive Circular Economy to Scale? Phillips website, April 29, 2021, https://www.philips.com/a-w/about/news/archive/blogs/innovation-matters/2021 /20210429-how-can-we-drive-circular-economy-to-scale.html, accessed October 9, 2024.

50. Sustainable Innovation through EcoDesign, Philips website, https://www.philips.com /a-w/about/environmental-social-governance/environmental/ecodesign.html, accessed October 15, 2024.

Chapter 8

1. Steve Jobs Offered Rare Insights during '60 Minutes' Interview, CBS News website, October 6, 2011, https://www.cbsnews.com/sanfrancisco/news/steve-jobs-offered-rare -insights-during-60-minutes-interview/, accessed August 27, 2024.

2. The SDSN Mobilizes the World's Knowledge Community for Science-based Solutions for Sustainable Development, Sustainable Development Solutions Network website, https:// www.unsdsn.org/about/, accessed September 30, 2024.

3. Kimberly Weisul, How Lowe's Is Using Supplier Education to Tackle Scope 3 Emissions, Trellis website, May 13, 2024, https://trellis.net/article/how-lowes-is-using-supplier-edu- cation-to-tackle-scope-3-emissions/, accessed October 2, 2024.

4. Supplier Registration, Lowe's website, https://www.lowes.com/l/about/suppliers, accessed October 3, 2024.

5. Powering a New World, Raven website, https://ravensr.com/about/#main-about, accessed September 30, 2024.

6. Raven SR, Chevron and Hyzon Motors Collaborate to Produce Hydrogen from Green Waste in Northern California, PR Newswire, January 9, 2023, https://www.prnewswire.com/news-releases/raven-sr-chevron-and-hyzon-motors-collaborate-to-produce-hydrogen-from-green-waste-in-northern-california-301716237.html, accessed September 15, 2024.

7. A Partner-of-choice to the most Outstanding Global Investors, and a Partner-in-arms with all Constituents Fighting for Conservation, Office of Investments, The Nature Conservancy website, https://www.nature.org/en-us/about-us/who-we-are/how-we-work/finance-investing/office-of-investments, accessed October 3, 2024.

8. Timing Is Everything for Arkansas Farms, The Nature Conservancy website, November 16, 2020, https://www.nature.org/en-us/what-we-do/our-priorities/provide-food-and-water-sustainably/food-and-water-stories/arkansas-farmers-saving-water-resources/, accessed September 15, 2024.

9. Dow's Blueprint for Valuing Nature, Dow website, https://corporate.dow.com/en-us/purpose-in-action/2025-goals/blueprint/valuing-nature-blueprint.html, accessed April 14, 2025.

10. Walmart Inc. / Walmart Foundation, Companies Investing in Nature, The Nature Conservancy, September 26, 2024, https://www.nature.org/en-us/about-us/who-we-are/how-we-work/working-with-companies/companies-investing-in-nature1/walmart/, accessed September 30, 2024.

11. Companies Investing in Nature, Working With Companies, The Nature Conservancy website, https://www.nature.org/en-us/about-us/who-we-are/how-we-work/working-with-companies/companies-investing-in-nature1/, accessed September 21, 2024.

12. Progress towards Our Science-based Targets, Yum! Brands 2023 Global Citizenship and Sustainability Report, October 8, 2024, page 30, https://www.yum.com/wps/wcm/connect/yumbrands, accessed October 9, 2024.

13. Pizza Hut Puts Good on Its Menu with Investments in Sustainably Sourced Cheese with Dairy Farmers of America, Press release, Pizza Hut website, https://blog.pizzahut.com/pizza-hut-puts-good-on-its-menu-with-investments-in-sustainably-sourced-cheese-with-dairy-farmers-of-america, accessed October 8, 2024.

14. Enabling a Net-zero Chemicals Future, Global Impact Coalition website, https://globalimpactcoalition.com/about-us, accessed October 17, 2024.

15. Our Global Impact Topics, Global Impact Coalition website, https://globalimpactcoalition.com/our-projects, accessed October 17, 2024.

16. This New Collaboration will Move the Chemical Sector Closer to Net Zero. Here's How, World Economic Forum website, January 30, 2024, https://www.weforum.org/agenda/2024/01/chemicals-closer-to-decarbonization/, accessed October 16, 2024.

17. Creation of International Standard on Net Zero Gets Underway, ISO website, June 27, 2024, https://www.iso.org/contents/news/2024/06/netzero-standard-underway.html, accessed October 15, 2024.

18. Avago Technologies to Acquire Broadcom for $37 Billion, Financial News, Broadcom website, May 28, 2015, https://investors.broadcom.com/news-releases/news-release-details/avago-technologies-acquire-broadcom-37-billion, accessed October 5, 2024.

19. Acquisitions by Broadcom, Tracxn website, October 2024, https://tracxn.com/d/acquisitions/acquisitions-by-broadcom, accessed October 16, 2024.

20. Broadcom (AVGO) Total Return, FinanceCharts website, October 17, 2025, https://www.financecharts.com/stocks/AVGO/performance/total-return, accessed October 17, 2025.

Chapter 9

1. Frances X. Frei and Anne Morriss, Storytelling That Drives Bold Change, *Harvard Business Review*, November–December 2023, https://hbr.org/2023/11/storytelling-that-drives-bold-change? accessed August 27, 2024.

2. Who Cares Wins, 2004–2008, Issue Brief, IFC Advisory Services in Environmental and Social Sustainability, IFC World Bank Group website, https://documents1.worldbank.org/curated/en/444801491483640669/pdf/113850-BRI-IFC-Breif-whocares-PUBLIC.pdf, accessed September 3, 2024.

3. The Global Compact Leaders Summit 2004 – Final Report, 2004, UN Global Compact website, https://unglobalcompact.org/library/255, accessed September 3, 2024.

4. Arabesque Announces Appointment of Georg Kell as New Chairman, Business Wire, Arabesque Partners, July 7, 2017, https://www.businesswire.com/news/home/20170707005514/en/Arabesque-Announces-Appointment-Georg-Kell-New-Chairman, accessed August 30, 2024.

5. What Are the Principles for Responsible Investment? Principles for Responsible Investing website, https://www.unpri.org/about-us/what-are-the-principles-for-responsible-investment, accessed September 30, 2024.

6. PRI Academy, Principles for Responsible Investing website, https://priacademy.org, accessed August 30, 2024.

7. International IR Framework, Integrated Reporting, IFRS Foundation website, 2021, page 7, https://integratedreporting.ifrs.org/wp-content/uploads/2024/08/IntegratedReporting_Framework_061024.pdf, accessed October 2, 2024.

8. Ibid., page 56.

Chapter 10

1. Catherine S. Neal, Dennis Kozlowski Was Not a Thief, *Harvard Business Review*, January 8, 2014, https://hbr.org/2014/01/dennis-kozlowski-was-not-a-thief, accessed September 30, 2024.

2. Matt Stevens and Matthew Haag, Jeffrey Skilling, Former Enron Chief, Released After 12 Years in Prison, *New York Times*, February 22, 2019, https://www.nytimes.com/2019/02/22/business/enron-ceo-skilling-scandal.html, accessed October 2, 2024.

3. Nivedita Bhattacharjee, Satyam Founder Raju Sentenced to Seven Years in Jail in Fraud Case, Reuters website, April 9, 2025, https://www.reuters.com/article/world/satyam-founder-raju-sentenced-to-seven-years-in-jail-in-fraud-case-idUSKBN0N00CP/, accessed October 5, 2024.

4. Rob Wile, Elizabeth Holmes Sentenced to 11 Years in Prison after Conviction in Theranos Fraud Case, NBC News website, November 18, 2022, https://www.nbcnews.com/business/business-news/elizabeth-holmes-sentenced-theranos-trial-rcna57344, accessed October 17, 2024.

5. Eleanor Pringle, Meta Reportedly Fires Staffer on $400K a Year for Spending $25 Meal Credits on Toothpaste and Tea, Fortune website, https://fortune.com/2024/10/17/meta-staff-layoffs-meal-credits, accessed October 17, 2024.

6. Sanford M. Jacoby, Employee Attitude Testing at Sears, Roebuck and Company, 1938-1969, *The Business History Review*, Volume 60, Number 4 (Winter 1986), includes interview with V. Jon Bentz, Appendix R, https://doi.org/10.2307/3115660, accessed August 18, 2024.

7. Morgan McCall, Michael Lombardo, and Ann Morrison, *The Lessons of Experience, How Successful Executives Develop on the Job*, Simon and Schuster, New York, 1988.

8. Michel Watkins, *The First 90 Days*, Harvard Business Review Press, Boston, 2013.

9. Mark Segal, Deutsche Bank, DWS Offices Searched by Authorities on Greenwashing Claims, ESG Today website, May 31, 2022, https://www.esgtoday.com/deutsche-bank-dws-offices-searched-by-authorities-on-greenwashing-claims, accessed October 15, 2024.

10. Mark Segal, SEC Fines Deutsche Bank Subsidiary DWS $19 Million Following Greenwashing Investigation, ESG Today website, September 26, 2023, https://www.esgtoday.com/sec-fines-deutsche-bank-subsidiary-dws-19-million-following-greenwashing-investigation, accessed October 15, 2024.

11. Sustainable Finance Roadmap 2022–2024, European Securities and Markets Authority website, https://www.esma.europa.eu/sites/default/files/library/esma30-379-1051_sustainable_finance_roadmap.pdf, accessed October 15, 2024.

12. 2022 Climate Check: Business' Views on Climate Action Ahead of COP27, Deloitte website, October 2022, page 4, https://www.deloitte.com/content/dam/assets-shared/docs/gx-risk-deloitte-climate-pulse-report-2022.pdf, accessed October 15, 2024.

13. Deloitte 2024 CxO Sustainability Report, Signs of a Shift in Business Climate Action, Deloitte website, September 2024, https://www.deloitte.com/content/dam/assets-shared/docs/about/2024/deloitte-2024-cxo-sustainability-report.pdf, accessed October 15, 2024.

14. By Chris Mooney, Juliet Eilperin, Desmond Butler, John Muyskens, Anu Narayanswamy, and Naema Ahmed, Countries Climate Pledges Built on Flawed Data, Post Investigation

Finds, *The Washington Post Newspaper*, November 7, 2021, https://www.washingtonpost
.com/climate-environment/interactive/2021/greenhouse-gas-emissions-pledges-data/,
accessed August 10, 2024.

15. Nationally Determined Contributions (NDCs), The Paris Agreement and NDCs, United
    Nations Framework Convention on Climate Change website, https://unfccc.int/process
    -and-meetings/the-paris-agreement/nationally-determined-contributions-ndcs,
    accessed August 28, 2024.

16. Ibid.

17. Ibid.

18. Ibid.

19. Questions and Answers on Food Information to Consumers, Press Corner, European
    Commission website, December 11, 2014, https://ec.europa.eu/commission/presscorner
    /detail/en/MEMO_14_2561, accessed August 20, 2024.

20. Your Guide to Safer Personal Care Products, EWG's Kin Deep Database, EWG website,
    https://www.ewg.org/skindeep/, accessed August 20, 2024.

21. CFTC Charges Former CEO of Carbon Credit Project Developer with Fraud Involving
    Voluntary Carbon Credits, News Release Number 8994-24, United Stated Commodities
    Futures Trading Commission website, October 2, 2024, https://www.cftc.gov/PressRoom
    /PressReleases/8994-24, accessed October 3, 2024.

22. Ibid.

23. The Year Ahead, Global Disputes Forecast 2024, Baker McKenzie website, January 24,
    2024, https://www.bakermckenzie.com/-/media/files/insight/publications/2024/the
    -year-ahead-report-2024.pdf, accessed October 15, 2024.

24. How to Avoid Greenwashing When Offering or Promoting Sustainability-Related
    Products, Information Sheet 271, Australia Securities and Investments Commission web-
    site, June 2022, https://asic.gov.au/regulatory-resources/financial-services/how-to-avoid
    -greenwashing-when-offering-or-promoting-sustainability-related-products/#Questio
    nstoconsiderwhenofferingorpromoti, accessed August 20, 2024.

25. Heather Clancy, CSRD: How AstraZeneca, Netflix and Pandora are Preparing for Europe's
    New ESG Disclosure Rules, AstraZeneca Preps CSRD Dry Run, Trellis website, October
    3, 2024, https://trellis.net/article/csrd-prep-brings-corporate-sustainability-and-finance
    -teams-closer-together/, accessed October 8, 2024.

Chapter 11

1. M. Isabel Smith, Yutian Ke, Emily C. Geyman, Jocelyn N. Reahl, Madison M. Douglas,
   Emily A. Seelen, John S. Magyar, Kieran B. J. Dunne, Edda A. Mutter, and Woodward
   W. Fischer, Mercury Stocks in Discontinuous Permafrost and their Mobilization by River
   Migration in the Yukon River Basin, *Environmental Research Letters*, Volume 19, Number
   8 (August 2024), https://iopscience.iop.org/article/10.1088/1748-9326/ad536e, accessed
   August 24, 2024.

2. Grim Outlook for Antarctica's Thwaites Glacier, Field Activities, International Thwaites Glacier Collaboration website, September 20, 2024, https://thwaitesglacier.org/news/grim-outlook-antarcticas-thwaites-glacier, accessed September 21, 2024.

3. A Breakthrough in Inexpensive, Clean, Fast-charging Batteries, Science News website, July 3, 2024, https://www.sciencedaily.com/releases/2024/07/240703131808.htm#:~:text=Scientists%20have%20created%20an%20anode,grid%20storage%20closer%20than%20ever, accessed September 20, 2024.

4. Solar Energy Breakthrough could Reduce Need for Solar Farms, News and Events, University of Oxford website, August 9, 2024, https://www.ox.ac.uk/news/2024-08-09-solar-energy-breakthrough-could-reduce-need-solar-farms-0, accessed September 20, 2024.

5. EU Position in World Trade, Trade, European Union Website, 2022 data, https://policy.trade.ec.europa.eu/eu-trade-relationships-country-and-region/eu-position-world-trade_en, accessed August 30, 2024.

6. Gross Domestic Product (GDP) of European Union Member States in 2023, Economy and Politics, Economy, Statista website, https://www.statista.com/statistics/1373346/eu-gdp-member-states-2022/, accessed August 30, 2024.

7. History of the European Union 1990–99, Maastricht Treaty, European Union website, February 7, 1992, https://european-union.europa.eu/principles-countries-history/history-eu/1990-99_en, accessed August 31, 2024.

8. China to Issue 70 National Standards for Carbon Emission Calculations in 2024, ESG News website, August 8, 2024, https://esgnews.com/china-to-issue-70-national-standards-for-carbon-emission-calculations-in-2024/, accessed October 17, 2025.

9. The Sustainability Awards, Packaging Europe website, https://packagingeurope.com/sustainability-awards?navCode=262, accessed September 5, 2024.

10. Global Cooling Prize, Global Cooling Prize website, https://globalcoolingprize.org/about-the-global-cooling-prize/, accessed September 10, 2024.

11. The Earthshot Prize, The Earthshot Prize website, https://earthshotprize.org, accessed September 7, 2024.

12. Champions of the Earth, UN Environmental Program website, https://www.unep.org/championsofearth/, accessed September 10, 2024.

13. The Importance of Being a Failure, Medium website, October 29, 2020, https://medium.com/@DBSBank/the-importance-of-being-a-failure-bf503c5f7afa#, accessed September 20, 2024.

14. The Challenge We're Addressing, Task Force on Climate Related Financial Disclosures (TCFD) website, https://www.fsb-tcfd.org/about/, accessed September 3, 2024.

15. Recommendations of the Task Force on Climate Related Financial Disclosures, June 2017, https://assets.bbhub.io/company/sites/60/2021/10/FINAL-2017-TCFD-Report.pdf, accessed September 5, 2024.

Appendix 2: Eleven Databases Worth Using

1. Marcel Schwantes, It Took Steve Jobs 2 Sentences to Teach One of the Greatest Leadership Lessons You Will Ever Hear, Inc. website, October 19, 2022, https://www.inc.com/marcel-schwantes/it-took-steve-jobs-2-sentences-to-teach-one-of-greatest-leadership-lessons-you-will-ever-hear.html, accessed October 5, 2024.

2. Our Mission, Our World in Data website, https://ourworldindata.org, accessed September 3, 2024.

3. PRI Academy, Who We Are, PRI Academy website, https://priacademy.org/about/, accessed September 4, 2024.

4. Who We Are, UN Biodiversity Lab website, https://unbiodiversitylab.org/en/about/, accessed September 20, 2024.

Appendix 3: Eight Reflection Exercises to Refine Your Thinking

1. Gerald M. Weinberg, *Becoming a Technical Leader: An Organic Problem-Solving Approach*, Dorset House Publishing, New York, 1986, page 21.

2. John O'Malley Bockris, *Energy: The Solar-Hydrogen Alternative*, The Architectural Press, London, 1976.

3. World Energy Balances, International Energy Agency (IEA) website, https://www.iea.org/data-and-statistics/data-product/world-energy-balances, accessed August 13, 2024.

4. Richard Gwilliam, BECCS at Drax Can Accelerate the UK's Decarbonisation by Delivering Carbon Removals, June 21, 2024, https://www.drax.com/opinion/beccs-at-drax-can-accelerate-the-uks-decarbonisation-by-delivering-carbon-removals/, accessed September 30, 2024.

5. Christopher Snowdon, Trees for Burning: The Biomass Controversy, IEA website, January 18, 2024, https://iea.org.uk/publications/trees-for-burning-the-biomass-controversy/#, accessed September 18, 2024.

6. Frankie Mayo, The Largest Emitters in the UK: Annual Review, Ember website, August 9, 2024, https://ember-climate.org/insights/in-brief/the-largest-emitters-in-the-uk-annual-review/, accessed September 20, 2024.

7. Richard Gwilliam, BECCS at Drax Can Accelerate the UK's Decarbonisation by Delivering Carbon Removals, June 21, 2024, https://www.drax.com/opinion/beccs-at-drax-can-accelerate-the-uks-decarbonisation-by-delivering-carbon-removals/, accessed September 30, 2024.

8. J. D. Sterman, L. Siegel, and J. Rooney-Varga, Does Replacing Coal with Wood Lower CO_2 Emissions? Dynamic Lifecycle Analysis of Wood Bioenergy. *Environmental Research Letters*, Volume 13, Number 1 (2018), pages 015007.

9. Lego Group Responsibility Report 2015, A Strategic Responsibility Agenda, Lego Group Website, 2016, page 6, https://www.lego.com/cdn/cs/aboutus/assets/blt8630ef4d3066bc76/Responsibility-Report-2015.pdf, accessed August 30, 2024.

10. Stanley Reed, Lego Wants to Completely Remake Its Toy Bricks (Without Anyone Noticing), *New York Times*, August 31, 2018, https://www.nytimes.com/2018/08/31/business/energy-environment/lego-plastic-denmark-environment-toys.html, accessed August 28, 2024.

11. Working Towards Sustainable LEGO® Bricks and Element, Sustainability, Lego Group website, https://www.lego.com/en-us/sustainability/sustainable-materials?locale=en-us, accessed September 3, 2024.

12. Assessing the Impact of Wildfires on the California Electricity Grid, California's Fourth Climate Change Assessment, California Energy Commission website, August 2018, https://www.energy.ca.gov/sites/default/files/2019-11/Energy_CCCA4-CEC-2018-002_ADA.pdf, accessed September 30, 2024.

13. Hilary Clarke, Extreme Wildfires Take a Toll on California Wildlife, US Forrest Service, USDA website, March 6, 2024, https://www.fs.usda.gov/about-agency/features/extreme-wildfires-take-toll-california-wildlife, accessed September 30, 2024.

14. Collapse of Northern California Kelp Forests Will Be Hard to Reverse, National Science Foundation website, March 17, 2012, https://new.nsf.gov/news/collapse-northern-california-kelp-forests-will-be, accessed September 30, 2024.

15. Christiana Jansen, Utilizing Kelp Forests for Carbon Sequestration, Earth.org website, February 1, 2023, https://earth.org/kelp-forests-carbon-sequestration/, accessed September 29, 2024.

16. Jean-Francois Bastin, Yelena Finegold, Claude Garcia, Danilo Mollicone, Marcelo Rezende, Devin Routh, Constantin M. Zohner, and Thomas W. Crowther, The Global Tree Restoration Potential, *Science*, Volume 365, Issue 6448 (July 5, 2019), pages 76–79.

17. Robin Pomeroy, One Trillion Trees – World Economic Forum Launches a Plan to Help Nature and the Climate, January 22, 2020, https://www.weforum.org/agenda/2020/01/one-trillion-trees-world-economic-forum-launches-plan-to-help-nature-and-the-climate/, accessed September 30, 2024.

18. Forests are Our Greatest Hope, Trillion Trees website, https://trilliontrees.org, accessed September 30, 2024.

19. Saudi Arabia Unveils Roadmap to Reach Its 10 Billion Tree Target at MENA Climate Week, Saudi Press Agency website, October 9, 2023, https://www.spa.gov.sa/en/4ee9ea2d6bl, accessed September 30, 2024.

20. Nicolas Denis and Alastair Hamilton, Transition to Net Zero, Forestry, McKinsey Quarterly, August 1, 2022, https://www.mckinsey.com/capabilities/sustainability/our-insights/spotting-green-business-opportunities-in-a-surging-net-zero-world/transition-to-net-zero/forestry-and-other-land-use, accessed September 24, 2024.

21. How Much Tree Cover is Lost Globally Each Year? World Resource Institute, Global Forest Review website, https://research.wri.org/gfr/forest-extent-indicators/forest-loss#how-much-tree-cover-is-lost-globally-each-year, accessed October 4, 2024.

22. Darcy Frey, How Green Is BP? *New York Times Magazine*, December 8, 2002, page 99, https://www.nytimes.com/2002/12/08/magazine/how-green-is-bp.html, accessed October 15, 2024.

23. Follow This Withdraws Climate Resolution for 2020 AGM, Press Release, BP website, March 27, 2020, https://www.bp.com/en/global/corporate/news-and-insights/press-releases/bp-and-follow-this-agree-to-work-towards-climate-resolution-for-bps-2021-agm.html, accessed March 15, 2024.

24. Ron Bousso, Exclusive: BP Abandons Goal to Cut Oil Output, Resets Strategy, Reuters website, October 7, 2024, https://www.reuters.com/business/energy/bp-drops-oil-output-target-strategy-reset-sources-say-2024-10-07/, accessed October 15, 2024.

25. Ibid.

26. The Invisible Green Hand, Special Report, *The Economist*, July 6, 2002, https://www.economist.com/special-report/2002/07/06/the-invisible-green-hand, accessed October 15, 2024.

27. Global Carbon Pricing Revenues Top a Record $100 Billion, Press Release, World Bank Group, May 21, 2024, https://www.worldbank.org/en/news/press-release/2024/05/21/global-carbon-pricing-revenues-top-a-record-100-billion, accessed October 15, 2024.

28. Carbon Capture and Storage: Where Are We At? Briefing, Zero Carbon Analytics website, September 29, 2022, https://zerocarbon-analytics.org/archives/energy/carbon-capture-and-storage-where-are-we-at, accessed October 15, 2024.

29. Robert Mendelsohn, Robert Litan, and John Fleming, How to Repair the World's Broken Carbon Offset Markets, YaleEnvironment360 website, November 18, 2021, https://e360.yale.edu/features/how-to-repair-the-worlds-broken-carbon-offset-markets, accessed October 10, 2024.

30. Nina Lakhani, Revealed: Top Carbon Offset Projects May Not Cut Planet-heating Emissions, Guardian Newspaper website, September 19, 2023, https://www.theguardian.com/environment/2023/sep/19/do-carbon-credit-reduce-emissions-greenhouse-gases, accessed October 15, 2024.

31. Daimen Hardie, How to Fix the Broken Carbon-offset System, Corporate Knights website, June 27, 2022, https://www.corporateknights.com/climate-and-carbon/how-to-fix-the-broken-carbon-offset-system/, accessed October 15, 2024.

INDEX

Note: Page references in **bold** represents figures and tables.